24.95
LOB

D1593644

Unless Return

# COWTOWN LAWYERS

*John Mulvany's painting* The Preliminary Trial of a Horse Thief—Scene in a Western Justice's Court *was exhibited for the first time at the National Academy of Design in 1876. Courtesy Kansas State Historical Society.*

# COWTOWN LAWYERS

## Dodge City and Its Attorneys, 1876–1886

## C. Robert Haywood

UNIVERSITY OF OKLAHOMA PRESS: NORMAN AND LONDON

RECEIVED

FEB 27 1991

MSU - LIBRARY

By C. Robert Haywood

*Trails South: The Wagon-Road Economy in the Dodge City–Panhandle Region*
(Norman, 1986)
*Cowtown Lawyers: Dodge City and Its Attorneys, 1876–1886* (Norman, 1988)

KF
355
.D63
H39
1988

Library of Congress Cataloging-in-Publication Data

Haywood, C. Robert (Clarence Robert), 1921–
    Cowtown lawyers : Dodge City and its attorneys, 1876–1886 /
C. Robert Haywood.—1st edition.
        p.      cm.
    Bibliography: p.
    Includes index.
    ISBN 0-8061-2146-7 (alk. paper)
    1. Lawyers—Kansas—Dodge City—Biography.   2. Justice,
Administration of—Kansas—Dodge City—History.   I. Title.
KF355.D63H39   1988
340'.902'2—dc19                                                          88-10643
                                                                              CIP

The paper in this book meets the guidelines for permanence and durability of
the Committee on Production Guidelines for Book Longevity of the Council
on Library Resources, Inc.

Copyright © 1988 by the University of Oklahoma Press, Norman, Publishing
Division of the University. Manufactured in the U.S.A. First edition.

17767296                                                     3/21/91 RB

TO: **Sandra, Alan, Ray**

# Contents

# Illustrations

# Preface

UNDOUBTEDLY, MORE HAS BEEN written about Dodge City than any other town of comparable size in the United States. Most of the accounts that have any semblance of historical accuracy have retold the same story with the same limited cast of characters. The historical town has suffered even more at the hands of fiction writers. The image created by the early dime novels, the Grade A and B movies, and the *Wyatt Earp–Gunsmoke* variety of TV serials has replaced that of the original cattle town with an agreed-upon legend. Few mythical sites have more recognizable landmarks than Dodge City of the 1870s and 1880s: Boot Hill, Front Street, the Long Branch Saloon, the Dodge House, and Ham Bell's Elephant Barn Livery. But these familiar places bear little positive resemblance to the original sites. Very few historical structures remain, and those that do exist, such as Richard J. ("Jack") Hardesty's and John Mueller's homes, are not featured in the fictional Dodge City. Today, cowtown Dodge City belongs more to the creative imagination of fiction writers than to its own history. There probably is little hope of rescue at this late date, since Dodge City, the Cowboy Capital of the World, is too deeply imbedded in the national folklore to be presented as anything but the one-dimensional cardboard background for whatever story of violence or heroism is being unfolded.

What is true of the fiction is scarcely improved by formal histories that repeat the familiar accounts. Only a few studies with depth, such as Robert R. Dykstra's *The Cattle Towns,* have attempted to go beneath the surface conditions to discover the workingman's center of transportation populated by individuals other than cowboys, gunmen, prostitutes, saloonkeepers, and gamblers.

This study attempts to add one more character to the *dramatis personae:* the cowtown lawyer.[1]

Both Lawrence Friedman and Francis Heller, historians of American law, have lamented the dearth of legal history "on a microcosmic level." It is the intention here to fill one small space in that void and to answer questions Heller raised: "What kind of practice did resident attorneys have? What role did lawyers play in the city and country?" There is no attempt to analyze the law as a tool and product of societal and economic growth. If the reader is seeking an analysis of code pleading, the concept of fixture, or the doctrine of adverse possession in frontier law, this is not the book to consult. The concern here is with the professional, and, to a lesser degree, the private lives of the attorneys who actively practiced law in Dodge City between 1876 and 1886 and with drawing some general inferences about the judicial system's influence on the late frontier experience.[2]

From 1876 to 1886, Dodge City was in the second of its early transitions. Emerging from an economy and culture based on the slaughter of buffalo, Dodge had felt the effects of the Texas trail-herd trade and was maturing into a transportation center and regional market. The twenty-seven attorneys who were in active practice at some time during the period played an impressive role, for good or ill, in these developments. The town also affected the lives of the attorneys. I hope my description of the interaction of the two will help to restore a balanced picture of how and why Dodge developed as it did during the years in which the Santa Fe stockyards attracted Texas herds to western Kansas.

The Dodge City lawyers began, as did most frontier attorneys, by accepting conditions as they found them. During those first Texas-cattle seasons, they were willing participants in the flamboyant lifestyle of the Beautiful, Bibulous Babylon of the Frontier outside, and occasionally inside, the courtroom. As the town evolved from the male-dominated center of highly mobile cattlemen into a permanent home for business people, laborers, and their families, the earlier camaraderie and shared values of the local bar began to erode. Some of the unencumbered lawyers retained their enthusiasm for the old and lusty days; others saw the potential for a more settled and sober community suitable for family life and ordered prosperity. The law of any community comes to represent just about what a society considers convenient, proper, and profitable. Some of the attorneys became the leaders of the various reform movements—assuming roles that extended to politics, social, economic, and religious life. The earlier harmonious relationships were replaced by quarrels over individual values, public policy, and community conscience. As was true of other frontier communities, Dodge was never to return to the early unity of its struggling foundation years. Beginning as merely another element seeking reconciliation and accommodation to conditions as they found them, the lawyers and the courts of Dodge City became effective instruments of change. It was a pattern of progress to be found in all communities that survived brief careers as end-of-the-trail cattle towns.

Attorneys, more than other professionals, leave a clear, documented trail of their activities. It must be added that in Dodge City the paper trail has been attractive to fungus, is biodegradable, and, when the documents bear the signatures of such fascinating figures as Bat Masterson and Wyatt Earp, has become the object of pilfering. Dodge City records have suffered losses from all these hazards and from a certain carelessness in preservation from the beginning. The clearest records are not the official documents of trials or the personal files of attorneys, but the newspapers that have been preserved in the microfilm files of the Kansas State Historical Society. Dodge was blessed with journalists who were keen observers and active participants in all aspects of the town's life. Their reporting is not only informative but highly readable. Whenever possible in this narrative, the people of the day are allowed to speak, which means that journalists have much to say about law and lawyers. Although newspaper accounts are predominant, they have been checked against whatever legal documents and other sources are available.

A cautionary note related to the organization of this book: Many of the lawsuits brought to the district court and occasionally to lower courts were prosecuted and defended by several attorneys. Consequently, a case may be discussed under the biographical sketches of three or four attorneys. I have tried to layer these accounts in a manner that will minimize repetition of facts and de-

scription yet still provide full coverage of the case and the participants' roles in it.

A number of people have been helpful in this project, including Betty Braddock of the Kansas Heritage Center in Dodge City;
the staff at the Kansas State Historical Society, especially Terry
Harmon, Assistant State Archivist; Wilma Rife, Director of Mabee
Library, Washburn University; Roy Bird, Reference Librarian,
Washburn University Law School Library; and Herb Hyde, for his
editorial contributions. Special thanks go to Mary Rowland, Virginia Pruitt, and Linda Hughes of the Washburn University faculty,
who read individual chapters with a generous, if critical, eye. Joe
Snell of the Kansas State Historical Society and Raymond Spring of
the Washburn University Law School faculty gave helpful sugges-
tions after reading the "rough-finished draft." My wife, L. Marie
Haywood, and Anne Fund of the Washburn University History Department performed yeoman service in bringing the "rough unfinished drafts" to a readable document. A sincere word of appreciation goes to Washburn University for time release to pursue the
elusive cowtown lawyers.

*Topeka, Kansas*                                    C. ROBERT HAYWOOD

# COWTOWN LAWYERS

# 1. Dodge City: The Venue

"WELCOME TO DODGE CITY, the biggest, wildest, wickedest little city on the continent" was the exuberant greeting given out-of-town visitors to Dodge's Fourth of July celebration in 1883. For that day and time, it was a standard orator's opening and conformed to the image most outsiders believed to be the real thing. The town, located on the one-hundredth meridian in Kansas where the old Santa Fe Trail skirted the Arkansas River, had from its beginning attracted the attention of flamboyant and fanciful journalists and writers. The *Washington Post*, the *New York Times*, and the *Kansas City Evening Star* delighted in poking sophisticated fun at the town's "lewd women and rough men" who cavorted beyond the bounds of respectable society. With perverse pride, Dodge City's own newspapers republished such claims as a mark of distinction. When the *Washington Post* referred to Dodge as "a wicked little town," the "very embodiment of waywardness and wantonness" where there were "no hopeful signs of moral improvement," the *Dodge City Ford County Globe* faithfully reproduced the slander.[1]

It was an image some Dodge Citians cherished, and other Kansans were happy to help perpetuate it. The most scurrilous pieces came from presses in nearby towns that hoped to profit by favorable comparison. The *Hays Sentinel* declared:

Dodge is a fast town. . . . The employment of many citizens is gambling, her virtue is prostitution and her beverage is whiskey. She is a merry town, and the only visible means of support of a number of her citizens is jocularity. Here rowdiness has taken its most aggravated form. . . . Seventeen saloons furnish inspiration, and many people become inspired—not to say drunk. Every facility is afforded for the exercise of conviviality and no restriction is placed on licentiousness.

3

*Front Street in Dodge City at the height of the cattle-town era. Ob-
viously it was a quiet day with the court not in session. Courtesy Kansas State Historical Society.*

The rivals for new settlers saw positive advantages in keeping the
image alive as long as possible. In 1886 the editor of the *Wilburn
Argus,* in the same county as Dodge, compared his "moral town"
favorably to the county seat because of the "conspicuous absence . . . of the dram shop, gaming hall and their votaries." It was
an editor from the neighboring town of Kinsley who fastened the
title *Beautiful, Bibulous Babylon of the Frontier* on Dodge City.
Friend and foe alike joined in perpetuating Dodge's scarlet and wayward reputation; both believed it good for their own businesses.[2]
    The patriotic young orator on that red-, white-, and blue-
bedecked rostrum may have delivered his boast with tongue in
cheek, hoping for the titillating shock value of his remarks, but
many of his fellow townsmen cultivated and helped to spread the
image out of loyalty to a way of life they thought was profitable
to their community. With a frontier penchant for exaggerated self-
glorification, they encouraged the stereotype of a town populated
only by "hard cases"—cowboys, gunmen, gamblers, prostitutes,

and saloonkeepers—presumably in the hope that more of the same would be attracted to Front Street. Small wonder that reporters, dime novelists, and moralists picked up on the theme of sin and fun that appeared unrestrained.

Was it a true picture or a fabricated myth? Would a reputation of waywardness and excitement attract people other than drifters and adventurers? Would a minister seeking to spread salvation, or a merchant looking for liberal spenders, or a doctor searching for tattered clients, would they have been lured west by the stories of Dodge City's offerings? Would lawyers have been attracted by fact or fiction to what seemed an ideal place in which to practice their profession?

Whether the popular image was true or false, Dodge City was to be the venue for twenty-seven attorneys during the decade from 1876 to 1886. Dodge was the place where juries were drawn and trials were held; it was also the site of lawyers' nonlitigious business, their social life, and, eventually, their hope for advancement, security, and family. Dodge was, for varying lengths of time, their home. It also had all the elements from which they were to fashion their professions and livelihood. If they had no commitment to see the community change, attorneys at least had to understand the people, their moods, their prejudices, and their preferences in order to serve as effective counselors. What Dodge was, stripped of myth and legend, and what it would become were of singular importance to any attorney who hoped to make a living there. To understand the cowtown lawyer, it is as essential for today's historian to know Dodge's prior history and demography as it was for the frontier lawyer to know and understand his venue.

As the year 1876 began, Dodge City was in a state of transition, leaving behind what had been a lucrative trade catering to the "wild and wooly" buffalo hunters and moving to the accommodation of Texas cattlemen looking for a shipping terminus. The next decade was to see a remarkable change in the physical features of the town and in the character of its residents.

The railroad arrived in what was to be the "wicked little city" in early September 1872. The first marking of the townsite occurred when George M. Hoover converted the tailgate of his wagon into a bar on June 17, 1872, to the great delight of Fort Dodge soldiers,

railroad men, and thirsty (some insist bloodthirsty) buffalo hunters.
The town company was organized in the summer of 1872, immediately ran into bureaucratic red tape, and had its first lawsuit over
the validity of its elected officers. After the town had borrowed its
first judge, an ex officio probate judge from Ellis County, to hold
court and settle the matter, the deed for the townsite was legalized.
The town, however, was not officially incorporated until November 2, 1875. By then, its reputation as a violent Sodom and Gomor-
rah, based on the buffalo men's exploits, was well established.

The influx of hunters attracted by the market for hides and meat
and the delights of the crude bars, brothels, and gambling joints
operating in temporary quarters had created a new kind of boom
town. There is no accurate account of how many buffalo hunters
there were in and around Dodge City, but one fairly reliable esti-
mate put the figure at two thousand in all of western Kansas in
1872, and Dodge was the center for their operations. In the years
1872–74, Dodge merchants shipped 3,158,730 hides east on the
Atchison, Topeka and Santa Fe, and in 1873 they shipped more
than 1,500,000 pounds of buffalo meat. As late as 1878, some
40,000 hides were shipped out of Dodge City. There was little
need for lawyers while Dodge was the rendezvous for hide men
because they found more direct and personal means of settling disputes without third-party involvement and the law's delay. A consequence of unrestrained independence was frequent bloody confrontation and death on the streets as the hunters, who callously
pursued their trade, were allowed to express volatile tempers in
quick and violent ways. George Hoover, who started it all with his
jug of cheap whiskey, recalled fifteen killings that first year, but historians have put the number of killings from August 1872 to July
1873 at twenty-five to thirty. In part, this bloody record was a result of the absence of organized local government. Tradition has
placed several lawmen in Dodge during the buffalo days and the
merchants may have banded together to pay a hired gun to protect
their holdings, but there was no effective justice system. In the
words of Calvina Anthony, wife of one of Dodge's earliest merchants, who lived through the rough times: "The revolver being a
very strong factor in all departments of social life, differences and
disputes often ended in violence, as Boot Hill could testify, if it

could speak. Every few days we used to hear of some poor soul gone to his account from sudden death."[3]

The town's notoriety, honestly come by, carried over into the cattle-town days. Contrary to the popular image of Dodge City, the cattle trade brought an end to the worst period of violence, not because of the placid nature of cowboys, but because the municipal government was functioning and the legal system was in place. Although the Santa Fe had built a small stockyard in Dodge City in 1875, shipments from it before 1876 were so small they escaped official mention. The first year in which there was "any discernible volume of traffic" on the western cattle trail leading into Dodge City was 1876. By then the town had begun to take on the measure of order necessary to fulfill the requirements of a cattle-trade center. The machinery for law enforcement had been established, and there were years (1877 and 1882, for example) in which there would be no killings. During Dodge City's cattle days, 1876–86, an average of one and a half persons per year met violent death by gunshot. On the other hand, the administration of local government in Dodge fell into the lax hands of a group of men who were sympathetic to and personally involved with gambling halls, saloons, and brothels. Violence, especially of the lethal sort, was curbed, but Front Street remained open to vices declared illegal in the rest of Kansas. Eventually, when the town council levied fines for prostitution and gambling, the ordinances were understood and treated as revenue measures intended to fill depleted city coffers and not as proscriptions for ridding the town of an undesirable element. The income generated from sin helped to fuel the Dodge City economy.[4]

The town was, however, far more than a mere mecca for cowboys intent on whoring, drinking, and gambling. In fact, it was a railroad shipping and receiving center of exceptional energy and growing diversification. The three blocks of false-fronted stores on Front Street, the heart of the town, were firmly established and business was flourishing. While it was true that the Alhambra, Occident, Old House, Lone Star, Long Branch, Alamo, Saratoga, and Beatty and Kelley saloons, as well as Hoover's Wholesale Liquor Store, were trying to prevent any traveler from leaving Dodge still dry and thirsty, the big money was found in the legitimate trade of goods and supplies. The commercial firm of Charles Rath was at the peak of its development. Although he and his partner, Robert M. Wright, were still shipping buffalo hides out of Dodge, they also were building a freighting trade that was sending thousands of pounds of goods south into the Oklahoma and Texas panhandles. The *Dodge City Times* boasted that in 1881, Rath shipped 150,000 pounds of freight a week to Mobeetie, Texas, alone, where the partnership of Rath and Conrad handled from $100,000 worth of merchandise annually. P. G. Reynolds established a successful stage and mail line into Texas that same year, tying the Panhandle even closer to Dodge City. The names of prosperous merchants, such as Morris Collar, Thomas L. McCarty, Frederick C. Zimmermann, Herman J. Fringer, and Hamilton B. ("Ham") Bell, were to become legendary a hundred years later in the creative hands of Hollywood. Dodge City in 1876 was no longer exclusively "the daughter of the hide men" Mari Sandoz has described but was a commercial center catering to cattlemen and traders from the Texas and Oklahoma panhandles.[5] In the transition, Dodge lost none of its notoriety, none of its saloons, and few of the motley crew of sinners attracted by the earlier buffalo trade. But by 1876 it was clearly a town and not a stinking, brawling depot for dead hides and flesh. Its municipal government was functioning, and Dodge showed unmistakable signs of being a permanent address.

For the first two or three years of the town's new mission, there was no rapid growth in population except in the spring and early summer months when the cowboys with the trail herds reached the stockyards. The cowboys' high spirits were kept within lethal limits, but punishment for rowdyism and macho indiscretions was mild, the culprits being treated with humorous tolerance. An account of one "eventful day," described by the *Dodge City Times* on July 13, 1878, reported that "a gambling sport was chaired by a pugilistic concubine, . . . a gambler was spitooned on the head, . . . a drunken prostitute . . . broke loose, . . . and a seemingly rural youth" was fleeced by a con artist of his hard-earned $81. Thirsty Texans, once delivered of their herd, enjoyed the unrestrained and unsophisticated "high ol' times" that seemed to be Dodge's major concern. It was estimated that during "the season," some fifteen hundred cowboys and cattlemen were in town. Because of their presence, partners Wright and Wrath could count on a retail trade valued at $250,000 annually; the later partnership of Wright and Henry Beverley was even more profitable. The prosperity that came with the stockyards made old-time Dodge Citians inordinately grateful for the cattle trade. But even at its height the economic influence of being the end-of-trail market was exaggerated. Dodge was first and last a transportation center. Goods arriving on the Santa Fe docks were distributed by freighters to forts, ranches, and farms in an area larger than some eastern states. During Rath's profitable year of 1879 nearly five million pounds of goods were received in Dodge by the army quartermaster, four million pounds of which were hauled to forts and troops in Indian Territory and the Texas Panhandle. The *Ford County Globe* estimated that this netted $75,000 for the teamsters alone.[6]

Cowboys, cattlemen, and people who served their pleasures—gamblers, saloonkeepers, prostitutes, hotel servants—furnished the lawyers a steady stream of cases, but like the businessmen the lawyers found other clients when homesteaders began to arrive in and around Dodge. First the German immigrants settled the northeastern part of Ford County and, by the mid-1880s the rest of the county and the lands south of Dodge became the object of a land rush. The nature of Dodge City's population changed with the coming of permanent settlers. Women other than "soiled doves" took up residence and sponsored or supported such "civilizing influences" as schools, churches, literary societies, lodges, and decorous private parties and balls. Croquet courts were laid out on the buffalo grass of backyards, and a skating rink became a popular source of amusement. As the town and the surrounding territory took on the character of a settled family community, there was less tolerance of the crudities and high jinks of the old cattle town.

Dodge's fashions and morality were following its pocketbook, and cattle shipments were clearly only one of the town's advantages. In 1883 an editor observed:

The steady, slow progress in moral and material growth of Dodge is indicative of a prosperous and stable future. The degree of growth is slow, permanent, and substantial. It is needless to detail the minute progress of the town. The buildings at present are of the most substantial character. They are erected with a view to stability, endurance and comfort. . . .

With a safe and prosperous trade established, Dodge City is not on any "uncertain ground." It has required time to build for permanence and establish for the future, and the reward lies within the hands of those who have secured the permanency. There are millions in grass, and everyone is recognizing that fact. Those who contemplated the rich harvest from the soil are pursuing a course that will bring them sure and safe returns. The stock interests are growing fast. With these interests Dodge City will go forward.[7]

For a time, grass and soil—that is, ranchers and grangers—were seen as equal partners in future growth and prosperity. The army also continued to make its contribution, and freighting kept southwestern Kansas and the Oklahoma and Texas panhandles tied to Dodge City. In 1883 the Santa Fe docks received 30,576,575 pounds of freight for civilian use and 3,576,575 pounds for the army. Receipts for freight were to remain high throughout the mid-1880s. In May 1884 the Santa Fe unloaded 5,253,080 pounds of goods at the Dodge depot. The poorest month that year, February, saw 1,865,170 pounds deposited on the dock.[8]

The birth of small inland towns to the south (that is, those towns not served directly by a railroad) and granger's demands for new and varied goods put the cattle trade in a different perspective for merchants who had counted heavily on the cattlemen's trade. The eventual loss of the business generated by Texas trail herds was accepted with far more equanimity than the early history of the town would have suggested. On November 7, 1885, the *Dodge City Kansas Cowboy,* created exclusively to be the journalistic spokesman for the cattle industry, editorialized:

The days of the cowboy in his pristine glory at Dodge are almost numbered now, and varied interests are rapidly springing up, the quiet pursuits of agriculture and manufacturing will soon take the place of the once great cattle interests, and with them will come the better element already there, and the lawless will disappear before the higher civilization as has the Indian and buffalo, and Dodge City from a rough frontier town will soon emerge into an embryo city, virtuous and good, and discarding the vicious and lawless elements of society, and we believe she is even now undergoing that change.

The final displacement of the "vicious and lawless elements" occurred with the remnants of the original political power structure fighting a stubborn but losing rear-guard action. The battle lines were drawn on the issue of prohibition. The evils of public saloons and demon rum became the rallying symbols for those who hoped to see mature "an embryo city, virtuous and good." Since the "festive cowboy" was closely associated with the worst aspects of the symbols, the Texas cattle trade became a prime target for the reformers. From Bat Masterson's and Luke Short's unsuccessful venture during the Saloon War in 1883 until Dodge ceased to be a cattle town in 1886, the focal point of political conflict was the wet-dry issue.

Supporting the antiliquor reformers were the new settlers, especially those in the small towns and on homesteads. Between March 1, 1885, and March 1, 1886, six hundred to seven hundred families located on public lands within the Dodge City precinct that had been released for settlement, and the population of the city was estimated to have doubled between 1884 and 1885. The platting of Wilburn, Ford City, Wright, and Bellefont, coupled with growth in the already thriving communities of Windhorst and Spearville, forecast an even larger population in the rural areas of Ford County. The raw frontier character of Dodge City was swept away in the flood of homesteaders and settlers seeking a more stable and less exciting place to rear a family.[9]

The old image of wickedness became a liability that many of Dodge City's leaders hoped to erase. It was no longer popular to paint Dodge as a mecca of sin and fun. Although it was never at any time exclusively a cattle town, editorials and public speeches began to emphasize the diversity of its economy, its cultural advantages, and its family atmosphere. Dodge was no longer filled with prostitutes, gamblers, gunmen, and cowboys. The local propagandists insisted that it was the quiet, peaceful home of the butcher, the baker, and, if not the candlestick maker, the wagon maker, merchant, carpenter, railroad man, clerk, doctor, and other honest, God-fearing folk. And, of course, the lawyer.

For the rest of the world, it was a hard, unfamiliar image to buy.

Because of the romantic aura surrounding the cowboy, it has been difficult to this day for writers, both popular and professional, to remember that Dodge City from 1876 to 1886 was, above all else, a laborer's town. Hard work, more than hard drinking, characterized the lives of most of its men and women, and their backgrounds and occupations were quite diverse. The rough element tended to attract attention; other residents went unnoticed in their unspectacular but necessary work in building the community.

Estimates of Dodge City's population at the height of its cowtown days have varied widely. Robert M. Wright, who knew Dodge better than most writers of his day, estimated it at "about 1200" in 1877. The *Second Biennial Report of the Kansas State Board of Agriculture* placed the population of Dodge City at 996 and that of Dodge City Township at 1,854 in 1880. Wright's figure may have been high if only permanent residents were considered, but the figure is more accurate than the one usually accepted. A visitor impressed by Dodge's wild side reported in August, 1879: "The morals of the city are rapidly improving. There are only fourteen saloons, two dance halls, forty-seven cyprians in our metropolis of 700 inhabitants." Unfortunately, these figures were picked up as authoritative and frequently have been cited as indicative of the people and their occupational commitments in the 1870s. The saloon count was accurate, but the writer was better at counting buildings than people. [10]

Robert Dykstra, who has made a systematic analysis of the 1880 census, used a restricted area of the defined city limits. The problem of a count limited to the city boundaries is that it misses many individuals who thought of themselves as Dodge Citians. Individuals living in what today would be called the immediate suburbs were very important in determining what kind of town Dodge City was and the kind of business a lawyer could expect. Eliminating the suburbs would exclude such well-known townsfolk as A. J. Anthony, one-time mayor and one of twelve men who secured the town charter; merchants A. B. Webster, Morris Collar, and Frederick Zimmermann; Frederick Singer, the undersheriff; and Daniel M. Frost, the newspaper editor. [11] It would seem more reasonable and accurate to set a somewhat larger boundary than the city limits and to eliminate the temporary camps and the Fort Dodge soldiers. When this is done, the head count for "greater Dodge City" was 1,279 in 1880. The date, 1880, represents the height of cattle-town acceptance in Dodge and lies roughly halfway between the old buffalo town and the new mercantile center. The census taken that year gives a fair picture of the demographic, social, and economic structure of Dodge City as a cattle town and, consequently, the kind of clients and community climate to be served by attorneys. [12]

As determined by information in the 1880 census, of the 643 persons in the work force (more than half the total population), most were not gunslingers, gamblers, cowboys, or dance-hall girls. Nicholas B. ("Nick") Klaine, the optimistic do-gooder editor, reported that people came "here to live and get rich—if we can." It was an exaggeration. Most folks in Dodge were content just to make a living; their demands on the lawyers' time were minimal.[13]

The largest occupational group was that of laborer, with 120 individuals representing 18.7 percent of the work force. Servants accounted for another large segment of the population; 73 people, 11.4 percent, both men and women, were listed as servants or engaged in some type of work normally considered in the service classification, such as table waiter, chambermaid, porter, or cook. Adding servants and laborers to construction workers makes clear that most Dodge Citians earned a modest living by the sweat of their brows and their strong backs. Since domestic servants earned between $1.50 and $3.00 a week, laborers $1.25 to $1.75 a day, and a skilled carpenter $2.00 to $2.50 a day, most Dodge Citians were not getting rich.[14]

Of course, what made Dodge City a cowtown, or for that matter a town of any description, was the railroad. Without the shipping yards on the Atchison, Topeka and Santa Fe line, there would have been no reason for Texas trail herds to beat a path to that particular spot on the Arkansas River. The railroad was to remain the major force in the early history of Dodge, and the citizens of that day, if not later historians, realized that the town was first and last a transportation center. A brief scanning of the Dodge City newspapers makes the point clear; frequently, as much space was allotted to railroad news as was given cattle news, with special sections carrying such headings as "Railroad Dots" or "Railroad News." Just how influential the Santa Fe was in the life of the community is revealed in the settlement of the Dodge City Saloon War. The reform spirit that had sparked that clash and had divided the community was being eroded steadily by the procattle status quo faction when a single threat from one railroad official reversed the trend and ended the reign of the likes of Luke Short and Bat Masterson.[15]

One of every ten members of the labor force worked for the railroad. Narratives of early-day Dodge may casually include crotchety characters, such as conductors, firemen, and engineers, but a brakeman, machinist, boilermaker, or "boss of the railroad laborers" is never mentioned, even by formal historians. Yet the 1880 census lists these occupations along with railroad agents, section bosses, telegraphers, car repairers, and railroad clerks. Sixty-six men gave their occupations as jobs related directly to the railroad. Undoubtedly, others working for the Santa Fe reported their occupations simply as those of laborer or bookkeeper without indicating the railroad connection.

Railroading was important because it was a year-round job in contrast to the seasonal trade generated by the trail herds. Freight receipts remained high throughout the mid-1880s, and so did the level of Santa Fe employment. The winter months saw some reduction in shipping, but February 1881, the year's slowest month, saw nearly two million pounds of goods deposited on the Dodge City docks.[16]

The railroad stimulated other transportation industries, which led to the development of a lucrative wagon-road economy. In Nick Klaine's words, Dodge City's "center of gravitation was equal to that of a state." Its trade area extended deep into Indian Territory and the Texas Panhandle, and much of its prosperity depended upon supplying ranchers, forts, and settlements in that region. Freighting and related maintenance were important sources of employment. The wagonyards of Dodge served as a kind of informal employment agency where unskilled men and those new to the frontier could find a job. In the 1880 census, forty-nine men said they were freighters. When people engaged in transportation-related activities, such as those involving wheelwrights, wainwrights, and livery operators (twenty-seven individuals), are added to the number employed by the railroad, the total number of Dodge Citians involved in transportation represented 36.5 percent of the work force. Transportation, not cattle, was Dodge City's major industry. Litigation involving the railroad was a major item on the district-court docket, and suits involving transportation-related incidents occupied much of Dodge attorneys' time. The amount of legal work generated by the Atchison, Topeka and Santa Fe Railroad and the wagon-road economy was far larger than the ratio of employees to the total population would indicate, even when such employees represented more than a third of the work force.[17]

The census tabulation of craftsmen would seem normal for a town of twelve hundred serving a large trade area. One painter, four cobblers, a tinker, a cabinetmaker, one gunsmith, one tailor, and one saddler would not seem excessive for any town the size of Dodge City, regardless of whether it was associated with the cattle industry. Six physicians and five lawyers, however, might indicate a town with considerable action and trouble. A listing of merchants also yields a hint of the entrepreneurial uniqueness of Dodge. Seventeen individuals listed themselves as merchants, but of these only seven were reported as saloon operators, which hardly matches the known number (at least fourteen) of saloons. But even seven saloon proprietors, plus six bartenders, would suggest that an average rural community was not being surveyed.[18]

A surprisingly large number of women were in the work force, representing 10 percent of all persons employed. By far the largest single classification of female employees was that of servant, 58 percent. Few women were self-employed: a milliner, one restaurant owner, the sporting ladies (?), some of the nine laundresses, and the dressmakers. Three women are listed under "teacher" or "music teacher," but none of these was included in reports of public-school personnel. Most of the employed women were in their late teens or twenties, although nine were over forty. Sallie Frazier, the lone business proprietor, was sixty-six and one chambermaid listed her age as seventy. Few married women worked outside the home.

The forty-two individuals recorded in the census as either Negroes or mulattoes represented 3.3 percent of Dodge City's population, a larger figure than is usually recognized. As an ethnic group, blacks were relegated, economically as well as socially, to the lowest stratum of society; there was little upward mobility. Many were employed in the hotels and saloons, but the largest number (fourteen) were employed as domestic servants. None was self-employed. The position of cook apparently was the highest attainable. Five listed that as their occupation, and seemingly the pay was sufficient to maintain a family because four of the cooks were the only breadwinners in their households. Since domestic servants earned less than $3.00 a week and laborers about $1.25 a day ($35.00 by the month), life for most blacks was at the subsistence level. Although a number indicated they had been un-

employed sometime during that year, as a group blacks were less
frequently without a job than their white counterparts. If there was
little hope to rise above personal service, housework, or common
labor, at least the demand for their services was steady; forced
unemployment was rare. Only four housekeepers and two other
adults appeared to be unemployed at the time the census was
taken.

As a melting pot, Dodge City tended to follow the population pattern of other Kansas frontier communities. The number of foreign-
born was never as large in Kansas as in other frontier states:
slightly more than 11 percent of Kansans in 1880 had been born
outside the United States. In spite of Dodge City's employment
needs, the town attracted only a slightly higher percentage (13.2)
of foreign-born than the rest of the state. Nearly all of those listed
in the census as foreign-born came from Northern or Central Europe, with the largest number coming from Germanic and Austrian
states. Dodge was considerably more attractive than the rest of
Kansas to these two groups. As a whole, Kansas had 27.4 percent
of its foreign-born recorded as being from these regions, while
Dodge City had 37.2 percent. Only one Hungarian, one Pole, and
two Russians represented Eastern Europe. There were no Asians
reported, although there are notices in the newspapers of Chinese
laundrymen before 1880, and one of the attorneys was to bring in a
number of Chinese laundrymen within a few months. Only five
Dodge Citians were counted as born in Mexico. The census re-
affirms that Dodge City was a town of mostly Caucasion people
with Western European backgrounds.

The homogeneous nature of the population was heightened by
interstate migration; Kansas attracted residents from neighboring
states. Individuals born in the Midwest, particularly in Kansas and
Missouri, made up about half of Dodge City's population. Because
of the state's recent settlement (barely nineteen years from its admission to the Union), there were few adult Kansas-born residents. It was not unusual for a Dodge family of six to have only one
member, the youngest, born in the state. A significant number of
residents, sixty-nine, listed western-state birthplaces. Both the
cattle business and the freighting connection attracted an unusual
number of settlers from Texas, which was itself still attracting

settlement. The census of 1880 confirms the accepted picture of a cowtown population and makes the early western movies appear all the more accurate with their all-white casts, even though the census and the movies fail to depict accurately the multicultural character of the working cowboy.

Historians of the American West have noted frequently that the population on the frontier consisted of more men than women. The men were, furthermore, young and unmarried. This imbalance of age and gender is revealed in 1880 census statistics. Young males in their twenties and thirties constituted a third of Dodge City's population (430 individuals representing 33.6 percent of all Dodge Citians). When the 202 young women of the same age bracket are added, approximately 50 percent of the population falls in the 20–39 age group—considerably higher than the state total of 41.3 percent. The number of young married couples, in turn, accounts for the large number of children under fifteen years of age. Nearly equaling the 20–39 age group, children under fourteen accounted for 30.1 percent of the population. This large percentage of children explains the relatively lower percentage of persons in the work force and is consistent with a laboring-class community. The number of children also is indicative of a town beginning the transition into a more settled community (more "civilized" was the way the Dodge City reform element put it). The large number of children was typical of Kansas as a rural frontier state; in fact, the number was considerably lower in Dodge than in the state as a whole (30.2 percent compared to 41.4 percent).

The small nuclear family was the typical household unit, although there were a few extended families. The most frequent variations from the nuclear household were those that were all male, those headed by a woman, and those taking in boarders. The relatively large number of adults, mainly unmarried, living in hotels and private homes would be expected in a community with an imbalance of males and females (61.6 percent males and 38.3 percent females). Approximately 11 percent of all names on the census roll were marked as boarders. Seventy-nine individuals, all but three of whom were male, lived alone. All-male household units were, however, as large as seven.

There were indications of the more notorious population element. The census of 1880 was a particularly frank one. Laura Vaughn was recorded as both "servant and mistress"; for five other women, their relationship to the head of the household was listed as "concubine"; and Rufus Wells was put down as Ada Robinson's "paramour." In listing the seven young women, ranging in age from eighteen to twenty-five, as "sporting," the census takers were using a euphemism less pejorative than the usual "soiled dove," "scarlet lady," or "demimonde" but still quite specific. With only a bit of reading between the lines, the number of prostitutes disguised in the census records as "dressmakers," "boarders," and "servants" increased the total considerably. Nick Klaine, so prim and proper that most folks called him Deacon, thought there were around forty prostitutes plying their trade in 1878; the number most frequently cited at this time and later was forty-seven.

Tending bar and gambling were common enough and important enough to the Dodge City economy that they were reported as acceptable occupations. Although the major impression left by the census was that of a working community following legitimate trades and professions typical of a railroad center, the fact that Dodge City intended to feed, house, clothe, and entertain some 1,300 cowboys and 250 ranchers during the summer trail-herd season did make for a unique and volatile community.[19]

This, then, was the milieu in which the cowtown lawyer was to practice his profession. Dodge City was moving rapidly through economic and social change and had a highly mobile population that was young, ambitious, frequently volatile, and often thwarted by the nature of the frontier setting. Even if it were not the terminus of a trail-herd cattle trade, such a community would be a fertile field for litigation. Although most Dodge residents were hardworking, God-fearing folk who remained free of legal entanglements, there was always a rousting minority to fill the police court and require the services of an understanding attorney. The influx of stable homesteaders merely added to lawyers' caseloads with their need for proper legal forms, their confusion of land rights and obligations, their disputed claims, and their hasty and informal sales, leases, and rentals.

Dodge remained, even in 1886, a part of the cutting edge of the frontier, one of the last towns to see that edge blunted by settlement. Still, its people were rooted in the traditional English conviction of the efficacy of law and its process. As recent migrants from settled communities, they came with an appreciation of legal control. This same ingrained respect for "law and order" has been noted in other frontier settings. John Phillip Reid found a large measure of "law-mindedness of nineteenth-century Americans" reflected in the behavior of those who traveled the overland trails beyond the reach of established law officers and courts. On the trail, the travelers respected the "rights of property of owners much as if still back east in the midst of plenty." Such acknowledgment went beyond adherence to obvious self-interest or adaptive custom. "Rather it was the expression of an agrestic, community-centered world we have lost, a custom bottomed on the sovereign's law, learned by living in a coercive state, and instilled into the marrow of social behavior." Dodge Citians of the cattle town era were guided by values and practices learned in the established communities they had left. Settling quarrels and contentions with fists and guns, even the legendary romantic six-guns, was deplored increasingly as evidence of immaturity and backwardness. Permanence, family, economic growth—all required the orderly marshaling of business and private lives.[20]

The law was to be Dodge City's civilizing armor, the lawyers were to be the champions of these maturing expectations, and the courts were to be the disciplined arenas in which the struggle would be resolved, remembering always that the letter of the law was to be tempered by the spirit of fairness, extenuating circumstances, and compassion for those who deserved consideration. And any right-thinking Dodge Citian knew precisely who the deserving souls were.

Any lawyer who was to contribute to the accepted scenario of progress held by Dodge Citians—or, for that matter, survive with a roof over his head and food on the table—would need to know well his clients and his venue. The practicing attorney had to accept his particular situation: he was stuck with the people of Dodge City and with their moods, whims, and convictions. His first obligation was to know and understand the people of Dodge. Only then could he, the law, and the courts fulfill their essential function.

# 2. The Courts

THE STEREOTYPE of frontier or cattle-town justice as being "make shift as the towns that sprang up along the frontier's far edges" does not hold for the district court of the Ninth Judicial District in Dodge City, nor, for that matter, the municipal courts.[1] Part of the misinterpretation can be blamed on the traditional image that all cattle towns adhered to quick, raw justice of the Judge Roy Bean vintage. The contemporary press gave a note of authenticity to these fanciful accounts with its own lurid stories, printed at the time as jests and satire by journalists given to a flamboyant style of reporting. Unfortunately, these burlesques have been accepted as true eyewitness accounts. Dodge City's reputation owes much to both sources: contemporary exaggeration and later stereotype.

The stereotype has been enhanced by the assumption that the same lawless conditions present before the town became a cattle-trade center continued after the Texas trail herds arrived. At least three of the Kansas cattle towns had deserved violent reputations and shoddy or little law enforcement before they began their careers as centers of the cattle trade. Violence on the streets during Dodge City's first three years after settlement, if not condoned, was not prosecuted in any orderly or consistent manner simply because the justice system was not in place. None of the cattle towns, including Dodge, remained static for any length of time. They grew rapidly and changed their characteristics as economic and social changes occurred. In Dodge City, community attitudes toward law and order were altered substantially after the buffalo business declined, and the townspeople's standards continued to move toward the accepted national norms while Dodge developed as an important reception point for Texas cattle. The courts charged with management of crime moved to keep pace in the enforcement of new values and expectations. Although county status was secured in 1873, it was not until after Dodge received municipal status as a third-class city in the fall of 1875, that a full legal system was established that required even more significant changes in community attitudes and policies.

Obviously, by 1875 the United States court system and legal procedures in the settled parts of the country were mature and sophisticated. But courts are no better than the individuals who interpret the law and serve on bench and bar. Fair and impartial trials depend upon how carefully those administering justice abide by acceptable standards. Frequently, depictions of the conditions under which justice was attempted during the last quarter of the nineteenth century in the West stress the ignorance, if not the corruption, of the court officials. Such an unflattering image of those responsible for cattle-town justice is offered in a recent popular account:

> In the best of circumstances, with a conscientious jury and well-intentioned lawyers, a district judge still had his frustrations. Because many lawyers are abysmally ignorant of the law—only a relative few had been formally schooled in it before hanging out their shingles—a judge could expend a good deal of effort in prompting and guiding both prosecutor and defense. Nor was he himself necessarily versed in procedures and precedents. Though judges who presided over jury trials were expected to have some formal education in the law, those appointed to the Western bench often were men left over after others had picked off preferred judicial plums back East.[2]

The major actors in the Dodge City court dramas between 1876 and 1886 bear slight resemblance to the untutored amateurs administering the law represented by this description. The judges and lawyers were, in the main, competent and were generally sensitive to the requirements of preserving correct rules and form. If cases were decided much faster than they are today, the speed reflects more on the nature of the docket than on hasty and erratic procedures. Obviously, there have been changes in form and practice over the years, but the decorum and basic rules in important

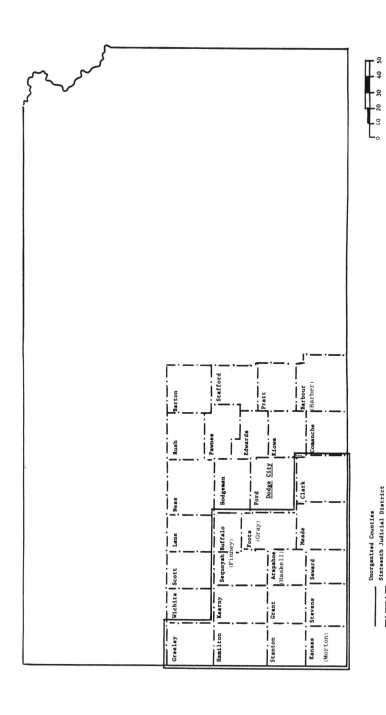

The Sixteenth Judicial District and the Unorganized Counties Attached to the Dodge City District Court

matters are not vastly different. Today's lawyers would not feel terribly uncomfortable in the Dodge City district court of the 1880s, nor would they find the language of the court profoundly changed.

When Kansas in 1909 adopted a new code of civil procedure, referred to as the Field Code, the changes in civil cases were substantial. Says one authority: "Free-wheeling in litigation was largely quashed. The importance of written pleadings was enhanced. There was now a premium on careful study, preparation and written documents. A ready tongue was still important, but its relative importance declined." The initial pleading under the Field Code was required to state "facts constituting a cause of action," and the facts were expected to become more specific and particularized. Under the new code, acceptance of facts rather than the pleaders' conclusions became crucial, frequently tested by a demurrer. The plaintiff had the burden of supplying evidence (facts) to justify a judgment in his favor if he expected the jury to accept the case as he presented it.[3]

To a much more limited degree, the same general judicial philosophy was to apply to the new criminal proceedings. More consistency and precision in both oral and written expression are required in criminal cases today than was the case in the older courts. There is little evidence, however, that in the serious cases in Dodge City's district court the judge tolerated excessive bombast or oratorical pyrotechnics. Oratorical flourishes were more popular in the nineteenth century in any public presentation, whether in court or before civic, religious, or educational audiences. Lawyers were expected to be great, even grand, speakers. Such generalizations, however, need to be understood in terms of degree rather than as absolutes.

The written briefs of Dodge City lawyers like Michael W. ("Mike") Sutton, Harry E. Gryden, and James T. Whitelaw were carefully drawn. When their appeals reached the Kansas Supreme Court, considered the most practiced and exemplary judicial body in the state, the justices there used the language and arguments of the Dodge City briefs in reporting their judgments. But even the written statements submitted to the Supreme Court would appear overdrawn and excessive by today's standards. In a civil suit defended by Mike Sutton, J. C. Strang, and Charles Walker, the crucial point was made with exaggerated embellishments:

How, then, can the law for the sale of school lands be enforced in an unorganized county, except by giving authority to the officers of the organized county to which it is attached, to enforce and carry out the provisions of this act? This act alone renders life and the pursuit of happiness secure in all the unorganized counties of the state. Without it, crime would run riot, and the murderer would no longer need to seek the shades of midnight to wreak his deadly vengeance, or secure his unhallowed gains. Not alone in the mountain fastnesses, nor in foreign climes, nor yet in the dense and crowded hordes of criminals that infest our cities, would he whom justice seeks be found; but in the beautiful plains of the western part of our noble state he might revel in the delights of a pleasant home, beautified perhaps by the money taken from his slain victim. Public policy alone would dictate, were it necessary, that this act be upheld.

The rest of the argument was more prosaic, relying on proper marshaling of logic and facts.[4]

Equally wide of the mark is the propular picture of quick, hasty, and certain convictions in which judges and juries ignored the niceties and safeguards of individual rights. In most instances, the trials were conducted with dignity and careful attention to proper procedure. Juries were no more hasty, emotional, or partial than they are today. They usually took less time to reach a verdict, but there were instances of prolonged jury deliberation; for example, the Atkinson-Warren case in 1886 found the jury confined in a room from March 24 until March 29. There are other instances of juries' moving at a snail's pace and lawyers' resorting to delaying tactics, which added to the judge's task. Yet there is little evidence to suggest that district judges badgered the lawyers to hurry cases or tolerated shortcuts, even though the district judge's work load was heavy, made doubly so by the distances he had to travel.[5]

If the trials proceeded without undue haste or pressure from the judges, convictions in the district courts of one hundred years ago were about the same as they are today. Even the notorious frontier "Hanging Judge of Arkansas," Isaac Parker, hanged only seventy-nine of the 13,490 he tried, with 4,046 (30 percent) being acquitted. In Indian Territory, 30 percent of the indictments at the trial led to nolle prosequi, judicial dismissal, or not-guilty verdicts. In

1984, Kansas found 30.4 percent of felony defendants and 28.8 percent of misdemeanor defendants not guilty. Apparently, County Attorney M. W. Sutton had a considerably higher ratio of convictions than the average prosecutor, but he never reached the 100 percent the press claimed for him. A random sample of three sessions (1878, 1879, 1881) of the district court in Dodge City as reported in newspapers placed convictions at 53.8 pecent, continuances at 19.2 percent, and nonconvictions at 27 percent.[6]

One procedure that has changed and that invalidates many comparisons is the current use of plea bargaining. The need to clear backlogged dockets did not have the priority it now has. There was, however, a kind of modified process in which charges and punishments were scaled down. In one instance a man named James Dempster, charged with first-degree murder, was "persuaded" to plead guilty, "owing to the circumstantial character of the evidence and sentence was made murder in the second degree." In several cases the defendant was tried first on an attempted-murder charge; when the jury failed to agree, the charge was reduced to assault and battery. Although neither process closely resembles 1980s plea-bargaining efficiency, the more awkward early process had the same effect. In those cases, neither haste nor crowded dockets motivated the court, but, rather, an attempt was made to "make the punishment fit the crime."[7]

Reducing the charge from assault with intent to kill to the lesser crime of assault and battery was a frequent adjustment in the lower courts. After tempers cooled or on direction of the judge, who could look at the circumstances more dispassionately, a justice of the peace could and often did try the case. One such instance received full coverage by the *Ford County Globe,* which treated a fracas in a neighboring town with the levity it deserved:

The case was opened by Judge Burns [acting county attorney], who surprised the opposite side by asking that the defendant be placed on trial for assault and battery, instead of assault with intent to kill. The defense objected, and a long argument ensued, in which each side exhibited great legal ability in expounding the law and smoking cheap five cent cigars, to the great disgust of the honorable court. At the close of the argument, court was adjourned for six hours, to take a rest and consider the matter.

*Carl Julius Adolph Hunnius made this sketch while he was in Dodge City on June 29, 1876. He wrote in his journal, "On top of the calaboose there is a new story, which I was informed is City Hall." Courtesy Kansas Collection, Spencer Research Library, University of Kansas.*

Although the reduction was hotly contested by the defense attorney, the justice of the peace decided to insist on the lesser charge.[8]

Undoubtedly, the surroundings in which a trial was held contributed to the degree of decorum in the procedure. When court was held in the cramped upper story of the old jail, where prisoner, prosecutor, judge, sheriff, witnesses, and spectators sat cheek by jowl, the room forced a more informal and lax atmosphere. Dodge City was blessed in 1876 with a new courthouse in which district-court trials were held. The building, of native stone and locally fired brick, had, according to the *Ford County Globe,* "the best courtrooms in western Kansas, good offices for county officers, and a splendid jail." The "splendid jail" in the basement, fashioned from limestone and known to those lodged there as the lime kiln, added to the sense of security and reduced the need for release on inadequate bail, a situation that earlier had led to many prisoners' escaping prosecution by fleeing the county once they were released. The new facility was a great improvement over the old wooden-plank jail south of the tracks on Front Street. Although the new jail was not totally escape proof, it was no longer possible for a prisoner to carve his way out with a penknife as one prisoner did in the old wooden structure. But the major physical improvement was in the courtroom, which was large enough to serve as a theater occasionally and was designed and furnished in traditional courtroom style. In this more commodious and formal setting, individuals charged with crimes and the parties to legal disputes could sense more easily the somber and judicious implications of the process. The legal actors—judges, lawyers, jury, and witnesses—were more

*Fort County courthouse, built in 1876 of native stone and Dodge City–fired brick, as it looked in 1886. According to the* Ford County Globe, *it had "the best courtrooms in western Kansas, good offices for county officers, and a splendid jail." The drawing is from* Hand-book of Ford County, Kansas, *published by C. S. Burch Publishing of Chicago in 1887. Courtesy Kansas State Historical Society.*

willing to observe the proprieties of court procedures, and court etiquette seemed more appropriate. On the local level, the district courtroom provided a setting for government in its most formal and mature development.[9]

The types of crime on the dockets in the 1880s somewhat resembled those of today, with a major difference related to automobile and traffic violations. Drunkenness, disorderly conduct, and petty larceny occupied much of the municipal courts' time. Dodge was also more aware of vagrants than most towns and usually punished them by ordering them out of town by sundown. For a time after the passage in August 1878 of a revenue-producing ordinance fining any "inmate or resident of any brothel, bawdy house or house of ill-fame" and an ordinance against gambling, the city did a brisk business in those categories.[10]

The district courts dealt with a large variety of civil and criminal cases as determined by state statute. The only ones not handled were the minor offenses—small claims, misdemeanors, and breakage of local ordinances—which were settled by the city courts and the justice of the peace. Horse-stealing and cattle-rustling cases appeared rather frequently, although not so often that they can be compared to auto thefts on today's dockets. Larceny, divorce, and assault outnumbered other suits; heinous crimes were far down the list. As a place of wild lawlessness, Dodge City's reputation was and is highly exaggerated. Although Dodge was no place for faint hearts and although it remained fairly wide open as long as Texas cattle came to the stockyards, its most lethal period had preceded the cowboy. After 1876 the criminal justice system, from the peace officers through the courts, did a commendable job in curbing violence.

Civil cases do not appear as similar to today's suits as do the criminal cases. The human emotions generating crimes in that era were not much different from those a hundred years later. Crimes resulting from passion, greed, covetousness, and uncontrolled tempers spawn similar criminal actions in any age, but since civil suits deal in material matters, the nature of the economic life and the state of the material development cause disputes to appear markedly different. Damages caused by livestock grazing on growing crops, the loss of "One Brown Canvas copper riveted over Coat," debts of five dollars for Osage-orange seeds, and attachments of "bay horses, harness, and buggies" speak of a far different time. Even in civil suits, however, many of the cases are quite familiar: damages caused by loss of goods, work uncompleted, divorce, and wages unpaid would not appear out of place in a contemporary court.[11]

The district court's docket was always heavy with civil cases, usually five or six times more civil matters than criminal suits. Although given careful treatment, civil disputes were not granted priority and rarely received extensive coverage in the press. Criminal trials were always disposed of first, and seldom were the cases held over for another session when the judge's schedule cut into Dodge City's court time. However, neither the lawyers nor the courts treated the civil cases lightly.

A fair sample of treatment accorded a minor suit whose paper trail is fairly complete is shown in the June 1878 action brought by Miles Mix against George M. Hoover. Mix, Bat Masterson's deputy sheriff, sued liquor wholesaler Hoover to recover damages caused by the loss of "a pump with pipe attached" valued at $25. The legal question centered on whether the pump was a part of "permanent fixtures" of a plot of land Mix had purchased. The two surviving pages of a longer brief presented by Harry Gryden for the plaintiff contain clear and concise questions and answers citing five legal sources and one case precedent. The surviving case file contains thirty-three documents, including those from justice of the peace court. Eleven witnesses were called and the record of minor fees (but not all the court costs) amounted to $27.90. The cost of recovering Mix's $25 loss was far larger than the pump's value, but personal satisfaction in gaining the victory cannot be measured. Justice and vindication were not reckoned in time and money. The amount of time spent on this case after it reached district court may have appeared excessive to an overburdened and travel-weary judge, but there appears to be no neglect or slighting of procedure.[12]

Both the Ninth and Sixteenth judicial districts required much travel by judges, who were obligated to hold court at least twice each year in each of the counties with a district court and, if the docket demanded, special sessions at other times. The Ninth District included eleven counties with district courts and "all that portion of the state lying south of the fourth standard parallel, and west of the counties of Hodgman, Ford, and Clark." The Sixteenth District included twenty-seven counties. Because of the Ford County district's western location, the unorganized counties in southwestern Kansas were attached to it for judicial purposes. In 1881 these counties included Clark, Meade, Seward, Stevens, Kansas, Stanton, Grant, Arapahoe, Foote, Sequoyah, Kearney, Hamilton, Greeley, and Buffalo. Only two district judges served the Dodge City lawyers: Samuel R. Peters of Newton from March 1, 1875, to December 12, 1882, while Dodge was in the Ninth District, and Jeremiah C. Strang of Larned from March 8, 1881, to January 1, 1890, while serving the Sixteenth District. Both men had considerable experience before coming to the district bench and both moved on to important political, legal, or judicial positions.[13]

In Dodge City, the travel required of the judgeship, which wore out many a frontier judge, was relieved by the easy access of the Atchison, Topeka and Santa Fe Railroad. Still, it was a grueling job. Just how onerous is illustrated in the description by the *Ford County Globe* of Judge Samuel R. Peters's work in the year 1877, when he was reported to have dispensed with 919 docketed cases and traveled 8,170 miles in performing his "herculean task." The record of the district court judges was a remarkable one, and the process and the procedures maintained were at least on a par with district courts in the more settled eastern states.[14]

The justice-of-the-peace courts, although they represented the lowest state unit, the township, were constitutional courts of much importance on the frontier. Each township could elect two justices of the peace for two-year terms, with the governor filling vacancies that might occur between elections. The powers of the court were impressive, including original jurisdiction in petty civil and criminal suits, holding preliminary examinations preparatory to handing cases to the grand jury or referring them to the district court, confining the insane, acting as coroner, collecting assessments made on the premium notes of the insured, and staying execution of judgments. The JP also could perform marriages and administer oaths. Matters of great importance came first to the attention of the JP. At inquests, he determined cause of death, the initial need to con-

*Samuel Ritter Peters, judge of the Ninth Judicial District from 1875 to 1882. Courtesy Kansas State Historical Society.*

sider a charge, and the appropriateness of jail or bail. In civil suits the JPs handled cases in which sizable amounts of money were in dispute. When the county commission refused to pay a warrant to H. P. Myton, he sought redress from Justice of the Peace R. G. Cook, who awarded him the full amount of $299.30 plus 7 percent interest from the date of issue. A number of similar cases were acted on by Cook and other JPs. Compensation was by fee; the rate was established by state statute. Police courts resembled JP courts and a JP could serve as police judge in the absence of that official. State statutes provided that "the police judge shall be a conservator of the peace, and shall have exclusive original jurisdiction to hear and determine all offenses against the ordinance of the city." As with the JPs, no legal training was required of police judges and they were compensated with fees based on the same schedule as that used for JPs.[15]

The local courts have suffered most from popular account, as well they should. The municipal and township courts generally mirrored the values and expectations of the community, and the judges serving them usually were respected by the electorate. The lower courts were charged, in the words of Anne M. Butler in her study of frontier prostitution, "with the responsibility for crime management." The JPs, even more than the town council, were expected to mold, adjust, and curb activities that were needed by the community but were disapproved by law or ordinance. In the management of crime, the cattle trade in Dodge required sharp distinction between destructive acts (murder, highway robbery, horse stealing) and attractive vices (drinking, gambling, and whoring). The destructive acts would drive away buyers and sellers carrying large sums of money; attractive vices would lure "the festive cowboy" to Front Street. The community understood that prostitution required regulation for the common good; its elimination could not be tolerated because of the adverse effect on the economy. Recognized as an unpleasant, sordid vice, the business generated by the prostitute more than offset the liabilities when the trade was properly curbed. An inmate of a house of prostitution and the house itself could be taxed more than other businesses, but the levies could not be so burdensome as to drive the women out of business. On the other hand, the intrusion of the prostitutes into the public life of the community had to be restrained. Disturbing the public peace by fighting in the street, malicious mischief, indecent exposure, and public swearing and cursing needed to feel some weight of community disapproval through the JP's fine. The same general rules applied to other forms of necessary vices: gambling, drinking, and boisterous rowdiness. Neither knowledge of jurisprudence nor pratical legal training was as essential to the magistrate of the lowest court as his knowledge of community mores and his sense of fair play. It was a demanding job, and not all who held it were deserving of the honor and meager fees.[16]

Although the record in Dodge City during the cattle-town era was superior to that of most frontier towns, the justice-of-the-peace and municipal courts occasionally fell into the hands of incompetents and at times the proceedings bordered on the farcical. The newspapers did much to perpetuate the ludicrous image, since what they reported as happening in court bore only a general resemblance to what actually occurred. Nick Klaine's description of "a day in the life of the Dodge City police court" has been widely distributed as the real thing. Stripped of his hyperbole, the story reports the court dealing with three cases: two of disturbing the peace, in which one of the defendants had to be restrained by a peace officer, and one for carrying a concealed weapon. Klaine converted these dull facts into readable copy:

"The Marshal will preserve strict order," said the Judge. "Any person caught throwing turnips, cigar stumps, beets, or old quids of tobacco at this Court will be immediately arranged before this bar of Justice." Then Joe [policeman J. W. Mason] looked savagely at the mob in attendance, hitched his ivory handle a little to the left and adjusted his moustache. "Trot out the wicked and unfortunate, and let the cotillion commence," said his Honor.

City vs. James Martin—But just then a complaint not on file had to be attended to, and Reverent John Walsh, of Las Animas, took the Throne of Justice, while the Judge stepped over to Hoover's. "You are here for horse stealing," says Walsh. "I can clean out the d——d court," says Martin. Then the City Attorney [E. F. Colborn] was banged into a pigeon hole in the desk, the table upset, the windows kicked out and the railing broke down. When order was restored, Joe's thumb was "some chawed," Assistant Marshal Masterson's nose sliced a trifle, and the rantankerous originator of all this, James Martin, Esq., was bleeding from a half dozen

cuts on the head, inflicted by Masterson's revolver. Then Walsh was de-
posed and Judge Frost took his seat, chewing burnt coffee, as his habit,
for his complexion. The evidence was brief and pointed. "Again," said the
Judge, as he rested his alabaster brow on his left paw, "do you appear
within this sacred realm, of which I, and only I, am high muck-i-muck. You
have disturbed the quiet of our lovely village. Why, instead of letting the
demon of passion fever your brain into this fray, did you not shake hands
and call it all a mistake. Then the lion and the lamb would have lain down
together and white-robed peace would have fanned you with her silvery
wings and elevated your thoughts to the good and pure by her smiles of
approbation; but no, you went to chawing and clawing and pulling hair. It is
$10.00 and costs, Mr. Martin."

The "prosecuting witness" in the second case was Carrie
Pembleton, a black prostitute. The confused account in the *Times,*
one of Klaine's more racist and more sexist pieces, reported that
"Miss Carrie, looked 'the last rose of summer all faded and gone'
to ——. Her best heart's blood (pumped from her nose) was freely
bespattering the light folds which but feebly hid her palpitating
bosom. Her starboard eye was closed, and a lump like a burnt bis-
quit ornamented her forehead." Klaine concluded by maligning the
court in much the same manner as he had belittled the plaintiff:

The City Attorney dwelt upon the heinousness of a strong giant man smit-
ing a frail woman. Mr. Morphy, for defendant, told two or three good
stories, bragged on the Court, winked at the witnesses and thought he
had a good case, but the marble jaws of justice snapped with adamantine
firmness, and it was $5.00 and costs. Appeal taken.
    It was Carrie's turn next to the taste the bitter draughts brewed in our
Police Court. She pled "Guilty, your Honor, just to carrying that razor in
my hand. 'Deed, 'deed, your Honor, I never had it under my clothes at
all." Carrie received an eighteen dollar moral lecture and a fine of $5.00
and costs, and Court stood adjourned.

The court carried a far more prosaic statement indicating that
Monroe Henderson had "conducted himself in a riotous and disorderly manner and did beat, wound and bruise this deposant
[Carrie Pembleton] against the peace and disquiet of the city and
contrary to the provision of Sec. II of ordinance no. 16." Such
newspaper accounts were not intended or understood at the time
to be factual reporting but were, in the words of Joseph Snell in his
thoroughly researched account of Kansas gunfighters, "the erup-

tions of humorous journalese." Frontier humor tended to be broad
and could be blatantly sexist and racist. If such accounts were intended to put prostitution in an unfavorable light, the editors failed
miserably. Klaine had condemened open prostitution on many occasions but when presented with a specific case did little to call attention to the dangers and meanness of the prostitute's life. The
courts, at least, treated the victim as an offended person. The
small nonpunitive fine, however, was nearer to Klaine's assessment. Neither the press nor the courts in this and other specific
instances did much to awaken the social consciousness of the community to the plight of the women or to the damaging effect on the
community at large.[17]

Flagrant personal corruption occurred only rarely in the Dodge
City courts. According to Robert Wright, one JP attracted the attention of humorist Bill Nye, who reported that the judge reversed
a decision in favor of the plaintiff when he learned that the defendant was broke and unable to pay the court costs while the plaintiff
had ample funds. The JP, W. Y. McIntosh, later was forced to resign when County Attorney M. W. Sutton brought him to trial for
overcharging the legal limits for fees. However, by the mid-1870s,
even the lower courts of Dodge City were in good hands. Frequently, lawyers held the offices as a means of supplementing their
income. It was rarely the case that the Dodge City courts were not
presided over by one of the local attorneys. All lawyers were called
judge; most who had any rightful claim to the title gained it in one
of the lower courts.

The position of JP or police judge was not taken lightly. Colonel
T. S. Jones, one of the most dignified and respected of the attorneys, won a hard-fought campaign for the position of police judge in
1881. In fact, most judicial elections were hotly contested affairs.
In one of the closest races, Harry Gryden lost by two votes (129 to
127) to D. C. Weaver, a nonlawyer. Four years earlier, the campaign for the position had attracted so much attention that a rostrum was erected in front of the Saratoga House, where Dr. S.
Berry Dorr and Dan Frost held a formal debate amid considerable
heckling that interrupted the speakers with "bright sally[ies] of wit
or sparkling humor [that] electrified the audience with spontaneous
outbursts of applause."[18]

D. M. Frost, R. E. Burns, and H. M. McGarry, all attorneys, served as justices of the peace. The office was considered important enough to Sutton that he went to some pains—as usual, behind the scenes and confidential—to get F. T. M. Wenie appointed JP by the governor at a time when Wenie, although primarily a businessman, was an active attorney. One legal suit that Sutton fought all the way to the Kansas Supreme Court had to do with the jurisdictional rights of a Finney County JP. The JP's status was certainly an honorable one and, because of the nature of most claims and crimes, fairly active.

Records of city-court actions show the proceedings in the lowest courts to be relatively formal, with witnesses present, the accused represented by counsel, and accurate records kept. The individual's rights were ensured even before the bar of the lowly JP's court. Fines were relatively heavy, and some judges took pride in being considered stern and unyielding. In the following instance, the costs totaled $20.75, about three weeks' pay for a laboring man or about three or four nights' work for a prostitute:

Hattie Mauzy Defendent arrested on the complaint of James Masterson charging that on the 5th day of Oct. AD 1878 at the said City of Dodge City,—The said Defendant Hattie Mauzy . . . within the Corporate limits of the said city an inmate and resident of a Certain Brothel Situated on . . . 24 Block on Locust Street in the said City of Dodge City contrary to the provisions of Section II or Ordinance No 42 entitled an Ordinance Relative to houses of ill-fame. Now on this the 8th day of Oct 1878 have this cause for hearing. The Plaintiff appears by its attorney E. F. Colborn and the Deft in person and by her attorney H. E. Gryden. The Defendant waives arraignment and pleads not Guilty. Whereupon *Wyatt S. Earp, James Masterson, Wm Tilghman* and *James R. Ballard* are sworn & testify for the plaintiff and Hattie Mauzy is sworn & testifies in behalf of the Defendant. After hearing the Testimony of both Plaintiff & defendant and listening to the argument of Counsel, the Court does find that the charges contained in the Complaint are true and that the Deft. Hattie Mauzy is *guilty* as charged.

It is there upon considered ordered and adjudged by the Court that the Deft Hattie Mauzy do pay a fine of Ten dollars & the Cost of this prosecution and that she stand committed until the same is paid.

Bond of appeal filed the 8th day of October AD 1878 and Defendant Hattie Mauzy released.[19]

All seemed to be in order and Dodge City's sense of justice seemed served. Although the legal language was a bit strained, the grammar unpolished, and the record preserved in an untidy and disorderly scrawl, the trial process is far from the burlesque Nick Klaine described in "a day in the life of the Dodge City police court."

The court that received the most criticism in Ford County was the probate court, which at times came near to representing stereotypical frontier justice. Having jurisdiction over the probating of wills, the administration of decedents' estates, and the guardianship of minors and incompetents, the court had considerable administrative power. Major abuse lay in its authority to issue writs of habeas corpus. Such a writ could secure release from custody of any imprisoned person on a convincing showing of denial of a constitutional right or other official illegal conduct, such as denial of or excessive requirement of bail or illegal arrest. Considering the frequent informality of arrest and the difficulty of following procedures to the letter of the law because of the distances traveled by the sheriff in transporting prisoners, writs frequently were sought and obtained in probate court.

Judges in the probate courts rarely had legal training: only one of Dodge's probate judges during the cowtown decade was admitted to the bar and another, August Crumberg, was elected under an assumed name because, he said, he wished to "conceal his whereabouts." These judges, more than any other magistrates, would bow to the superior knowledge and glib tongue of an attorney. Part of their willingness to please undoubtedly came from the miserable pay they received. Most of the fees were fixed by law, and those that were not were determined by what the clerk of the district court was allowed. For issuing a subpoena, a judge was allowed twenty-five cents, administering an oath or recording a will a dime, and probating a will or issuing a marriage license a dollar. The highest fee the probate judges could earn was three dollars for a hearing on a writ of habeas corpus. Consequently, the judges were inclined to be overcooperative in setting times for hearings to suit the convenience of an attorney.[20]

On a number of occasions, court was convened late at night without sending notification to all parties involved. A case in point was one dealing with an alleged theft of horses in the Texas Panhandle by W. B. (or B. W.) Rogers and four companions. The owner, Milton Harrison, pursued the thieves, caught them at Hays City, and brought them to Dodge, where they were turned over to Sheriff Bat Masterson for safekeeping. Bat, smarting under his recent defeat for re-election, was at best careless, accepted the prisoners, and locked them in the Dodge City jail. When Mike Sutton, the county attorney, heard they were being held without authorization, he requested a writ of habeas corpus. Obviously, Bat could give no justification for holding the men and, with complete candor, wrote a brief explanation for Probate Judge Nicholas Klaine:

State of Kansas, Co. of Ford
To the Probate Court: I hereby state that I hold the within named parties without any authority whatever; that I have no commitment of them.

W. B. Masterson
Sheriff

Harrison was not informed of the hearing, which was held the next morning, and he was considerably disturbed to find the men he had tracked from Texas released and well out of the country. Masterson's excuse for not informing Harrison was that he couldn't find him and that the one plaintiff he did locate was so drunk "he would not have known the difference between a writ of habeas corpus and a Texas steer."[21]

Other occasions of an overcooperative Dodge City judge's freeing undeserving prisoners were cause for considerable complaint. After one such incident, the *Kinsley Graphic* editorialized, under the headline "Prostitution of the Writ of Habeas Corpus," that the Kansas justice system, "with a carelessness little less than criminal," had allowed criminals to go "unwhipped of justice, and the laws have been set at defiance. The great writ that was intended to be the safeguard of the liberties of the people, bids fair to become the destroyer of peace and welfare of society."[22]

The district courts were far better served than the lower courts. The finest eyewitness accounts of the procedure and atmosphere of the district court in Dodge City were given by Dan Frost. Not only was Frost, an attorney, knowledgeable in the law, he also was a perceptive observer and appreciated the niceties of procedure. Representative of his reporting was coverage of the January 1877 session, which had been a busy one with "a large attendance . . . of interested parties, jurors, witnesses, etc." The court remained in session Tuesday through late Saturday, when it recessed for a week before reconvening to try civil suits. On Saturday, just before adjournment, Judge Samuel R. Peters passed sentence on the six men who had been convicted. Under the headline "The Way of the Transgressor," Frost described the court:

To all who witnessed the scene in the court room last Saturday evening, the proof was positive that "the way of the transgressor is hard." The room was crowded with curious spectators, who had heard that the convicts were to be sentenced that evening, and as sentences in this community have been almost as rare as angels' visits in the past—few and far between—it was natural for the people to assemble as they would to witness a contest in the arena. The Judge was seated at his desk, his grave and solemn countenance told that his thoughts were stern and decisive. Groups of attorneys conversed in low whispers within the railing, all of whom, save one—the prosecutor—had failed to get the ear of the jury, and their spent eloquence was as pearls cast before swine—trampled and trod upon. In a row in front of the Judge sat the six sinners for whom they had labored; all were convicted, and from their features every ray of hope had fled. The whispering was hushed in the room as Judge Peters finished writing, laid aside his pen and reflecting for a moment, said, "James A. Bailey, you may stand up." The first of the six slowly rose to his feet. He was a man of fine appearance, and to questions propounded by the Judge, answered that he was born and raised in New York; was 42 years of age; had received an education, and before coming west was employed as a traveling salesman for his brother. When asked if he had any reason to offer why sentence should not be pronounced, he said he had none, as he had plead guilty; but in view of the fact that he was already advanced in years, he hoped the Judge would not sentence him to a long term, as he would be unable to survive it. He asked that the fact of his being under the influence of liquor be considered in mitigation of his crime. . . .

After the prisoners had all been thus questioned, Messrs. Gryden, Jones and Kellogg, in behalf of their respective convicted clients, argued to the Judge, and directed his attention to the "brightest spots" in the lives and acts of the criminals, and asked that mercy be shown them. The Judge then passed the . . . sentences. . . .

The remarks of Judge Peters on this occasion were very appropriate and the advice he gave should be followed by all who heard it and witnessed this sad scene. It was long after lamplight when court adjourned, and the crowd dispersed, free to go where they pleased, while the doomed six filed out under heavy guard to seek what comfort they might within the narrow bounds of their lonely prison cells.[23]

Not all sentencing appearances were conducted with such efficiency and dispatch. The trial of John S. McCarty, a "confidence man" charged with robbery by use of a "monte game," was a case in point:

The Judge overruled the motion for a new trial, and on Monday evening was the time set for the passing of the sentence. The accused had been admitted to bail in the sum of $8,000, and when his appearance was demanded he was non est. County Attorney Whitelaw, on Monday, moved that the prisoner be taken charge of by an officer, but the court said that the accused was on bail and his custody was not necessary, "or words to that effect." The bonds of McCarty are also missing. It is said that the bond never passed into the hands of the District Clerk, so he informs us. A party started in pursuit of McCarty, supposing that he had gone south in the stage, but they returned without the fugitive, he having taken another course. . . .

The bondsmen are responsible notwithstanding the bonds cannot be found. The bonds can be proven by competent witnesses. A forfeiture of the bond was taken in court on Tuesday morning.[24]

The press was quick to expose the irregularities and to call for an accounting of responsibilities. Nick Klaine wrote in an editorial huff: "Ford County has been at considerable expense . . . and [for] the efforts of justice to be frittered away in this manner is a shame and a mockery. The responsibility will be placed where it belongs." The editor wanted his readers to know that the integrity of the courts was under the careful scrutiny of the press.[25]

The extent to which the rights of the individual were to be preserved and the letter of the law enforced were matters of great concern and occupied much of the court's time. Occasionally, the court was presented with the questions the judge could not answer immediately. In one such instance the judge adjourned the court and spent much of the night researching the problem. The judge, J. C. Strang, had been confronted with the question "Has the court, in the absence of a regular panel, power to order a drawing?" Next morning, he presented "a long and able argument" in which he found that there would be "no jury trial this term except by agreement." During the same session the judge "spent several days" studying the briefs of E. H. Borton as to whether a judgment could be reopened after the statute of limitations had run out. Awareness of the importance of adhering to correct procedures, not haste, motivated the judges.[26]

In one of Dodge's most thoroughly covered trials, Dave Mather's killing of Tom Nixon, the lawyers clashed over several points of procedure in the preliminary hearing. At one point the defense attorney, Sutton, moved that the court require the state to name its witnesses, that they be examined separately, and that all but the witness under examination be excluded from the courtroom. Whitelaw for the state then turned to Sutton, requesting him to name his witnesses. Sutton refused, saying he was not certain of what the necessary defense would be at that point and he might require several witnesses or none in response to the prosecuting actions. He concluded that

there were able attorneys for the State and all the power of the great State of Kansas stood ready to sustain them. To refuse this [the right not to name his witnesses] was to throw upon themselves the imputation that they were afraid of justice. It is an established rule that the defense may or may not introduce testimony and no power can compel them to say at this stage that they will or will not do it. No undue advantage should be taken of the opposing counsel.

The court supported Sutton. Whitelaw then tried to have reporters barred from the court, arguing that if coverage of the trial was published, "nine-tenths of the people of Ford county would read them, and it would be impossible to procure an unprejudiced jury in the county." John Speer, reporter for the *Kansas Cowboy,* who as the Free State editor of the *Kansas Pioneer* in Lawrence was one of the targets of Quantrill's Raid, rose and defended his presence. Speer, seventy at the time, was something of a legend in Kansas journalistic circles as a champion of the rights of the accused. In this instance he won the day and the court overruled Whitelaw's motion. The press carefully and in detail reported all the testimony, cross-examination, and reexamination in the preliminary hearing. Mather eventually was granted a writ of habeas corpus and a change of venue and was found not guilty. The major consideration of the court, obviously, was a fair and impartial trial in which the defendant's legal safeguards were upheld. The judge's decision was not unusual and he certainly was not "prompting" or "guiding" either the prosecution or the defense.[27]

Occasionally, a judge's decision set a precedent. In 1884, at the height of the struggle over prohibition, Judge Strang disqualified a juror. Kansas had been legally dry since 1881, but Dodge City blatantly ignored the constitutional prohibition. When the jury in the widely publicized Bird case was impaneled, the following exchange took place:

In the District Court on Tuesday, Judge Strang made a suggestion which created a slight sensation in court and had considerable effect on the outside of the court room. The precedent has been established that persons engaged in selling liquor are disqualified to sit as jurymen.

In the empaneling of a jury in the Bird case, a barkeeper was proposed for a juror—Judge [N. C.] Sterry, counsel for Bird, propounded the following question to him:

Sterry—What is your business?

Proposed Juror—Barkeeper.

Sterry—Selling liquor?

County Attorney Whitelaw—I object; the counsel has no right to make the juror criminate himself.

Court—That is not your affair.

County Attorney—But I can suggest it to him.

Court—You have no right to do that.

County Attorney—Then the court should do so.

Court—That is not my business, either; and it is not the business of the county attorney to attempt to shield violators of the law, but to prosecute them.[28]

Both Sterry and the judge were fully within their prerogatives to challenge the prospective juror concerning his ability to be fair and impartial. The circumstances of the county attorney's defending an acknowledged lawbreaker must have seemed strange to the judge. Whitelaw, however, represented the community, which had not accepted prohibition and had established other standards of conduct. Sterry from Emporia and Judge Strang from Newton were foreigners in the eyes of most Dodge Citians and in that sense Whitelaw found justification in upholding his constituents' standards. The prohibitionists of Dodge were elated by the judge's action. Editorialized Nick Klaine: "Little by little, prohibition is taking hold in this city." By preventing a barkeeper from serving on a jury, Judge Strang had indicated to the public that "the whiskey selling appeared disreputable." The ruling of the judge no doubt did affect the lifestyle of the town. Sentiments were changing, and the trial of an unrelated matter did much to encourage change.[29]

Usually the lawyers exercised considerable discretion in challenging the validity and decisions of the court, but on occasion such restraint was more than an attorney could bear. This was the case when Harry Gryden referred to a particular trial as comparable to the con games on Front Street. At a little later date, Mike Sutton was able to express his disapproval with more finesse and humor, in fact helping the court through an awkward situation and at the same time pleasing the judge while insulting the jury. William Hutchinson recalled the time the district court was held on Sunday. When the jury brought in a verdict against Sutton's client, Sutton's son, who was inordinately loyal to his father, rose and berated the judge for desecrating the Sabbath. He quoted Scripture at length and refused to be quiet until he sank exhausted into his chair. At that point the father rose and said: "Son, the passages of Scripture you have quoted are correct, and I will also quote you some. 'If the ox or ass fall in the well on the Sabbath, get it out.' Now Judge Hutchinson has twelve asses in the jury box and he wants to get them out." The respect displayed by attorneys was generally shared by the people of the community. In that sense, the court by its example led the town in its quest for progress and the expectation of a more orderly future.[30]

One of the most dramatic and sincere testimonials of faith in the evenhanded nature of justice in Dodge City was given in the dead of night in one of the lime-kiln cells by a black man charged with killing a white cowboy. Earlier in the year, William Allen, a black cowboy from Texas, had quarreled with a white member of a crew in a cow camp on the Cimarron River. Angry words escalated into shooting, and the white cowboy was killed. As a stranger with the added liability of being black, Allen was in a precarious position. During the preliminary hearing before Dodge Justice of the Peace R. G. Cook, witnesses testified for and against Allen, although "the evidence for the defence tended strongly to justification of homicide." But since the evidence was divided, William was bound over to the next session of the district court. He now faced prosecution by hard-driving County Attorney Mike Sutton. Harry Gryden took Allen's case and secured a continuance. While he was awaiting trial, two other prisoners broke jail and tried to persuade Allen to join them. Most cowboys and certainly most blacks in similar circumstances would have taken the opportunity for instant freedom. Allen chose to stay in his cell, preferring to take his chances with the legal system. In that decision, Allen bet his life, at least many years of his life, on the color-blind justice of the district court. It was as strong an endorsement as any man could give.[31]

Equal justice under the rule of law is a basic principle of American democracy. Albeit only imperfectly realized, its attainment is democracy's most cherished goal. The fulfillment of this basic objective is dependent on the community and the laws supporting it, and especially on the procedures of the courts. Dodge City as a cattle town was served well by a court system in place when the Texas trail herds reached the Atchison, Topeka and Santa Fe stockyards on the Arkansas River. Although much of what was found on the frontier in terms of social, economic, and political life was new, untested, and in a state of flux, the process and procedures of the courts had been refined over the centuries, dating back to the earliest English common-law traditions. The courts in the new setting were more effective, more professional, and more attuned to the rest of the United States than any other unit of local government.

Still, the courts, especially the municipal and township courts, responded to the values, standards, and prejudices of the local community. Hence the judicial structure helped perpetuate certain vices, and some of the Dodge City residents who engaged in these necessary frailties were denied full expression of legal rights. Anne Butler found that in spite of this weakness the courts offered prostitutes "a marginal spot within the community" when all other institutions—churches, social clubs, political parties—excluded them. Even the lowest wretch in the social system knew how to use the courts and found "the legal establishment represented the one institution . . . where prostitutes could feel comfortable."[32]

For all their awareness of local responsibilities, the courts were under closer scrutiny from outside the community than other governmental units, such as the school board or the county commission. Challenges of procedures could be, and were, reviewed by the state's highest tribunal. The presence of experienced judges who lived outside the area and the work of attorneys with a variety of experiences and educational backgrounds who came from other towns kept the atmosphere in the district courts far more sophisticated and far less parochial than it was in the other governmental units.

Finally, all courts benefited from the important and searching review of a community. The driving force behind the rule of law comes not merely from constitutions and statutes, but from an informed public conscience. Dodge City was fortunate in having a number of outspoken editors, frequently representing rival newspapers, who were quick to expose any serious deviation from acceptable procedures and practices and who tended to show both sides of a dispute. The courts, charged with the responsibility of putting into operation the compulsory force of the government, had the power to deprive citizens of their liberty, their goods, and even their lives. It was a sobering responsibility that saw the community carefully looking over the court's shoulder, monitoring its actions. If the courts were sometimes less than ideal, they did represent the democratic aspirations of a raw frontier community. As was true of the lawyers, the courts kept alive the hope for a better life with the certainty of personal and social advancement.

# 3. The Bar

*He was me lawyer in thim days when I had wrongs that I didn't pro-*
*pose to have trampled on. . . . He was th' gr-reat man, an' when th'*
*likes iv him were alive 'twas some fun goin' to law.*—Mr. Martin
Dooley

FINLEY PETER DUNNE knew his lawyers. Writing in the late 1890s,
clearly within memory of the florid days of Dodge City as a cattle
town, Dunne knew the power and fascination of a good courtroom
performance. "An' it wasn't all talkin', ayether," the humorist has
his Irish saloonkeeper remind his readers. The lawyer's integrity,
convictions, learning, and faith in the law, in a frontier town of
loose morals and considerable violence, was crucial to the expectations and promise of future civilized society. The Bat Mastersons
could preserve law and order, but it required the golden-throated,
nimble-witted, sometimes flawed logic of the attorney to remind
the rawest cowboy or the most sanctimonious prohibitionist that
civilization was based on rules set down by well-meaning, if somewhat fallible, men. It was the rule of law, not the rule of lawmen
that kept alive the hope of a better and more tolerable life with its
certainty of personal and social advancement. It was a role laden
with heavy responsibilities and serious intent.[1]

The Dodge City attorneys were not necessarily solemn men.
Mainly young, with limited experience, they enjoyed the free-
wheeling atmosphere in which they practiced. They themselves
were known to sidestep the law in minor matters, parody its stuffi-
ness, and entertain their peers in the gin mills and gambling halls as
they contributed to the rough frontier humor and charmed the
whole community. They were also men who on occasion might let

their tempers get the best of them. Robert M. Wright, one of the town's founders and leading merchants who served as mayor and state representative, claimed he had been goaded into firing on Mike Sutton and pistol-whipping William Morphy after violent quarrels with the two attorneys. It was also necessary for Bat Masterson to restrain the fiery Sutton in the courtroom as Sutton and Harry Gryden exchanged blows.

Standing halfway between the crude forces of reality and the dreams of refinement, the lawyers were the unwitting and some-times rebellious harbingers of change. Alternately admired, de-spised, praised, and reviled, they and their shepherding judges were the most conspicuous examples of what progress could hold. While they, as Mr. Dooley observed, were making "a mighty poor livin' by shoutin' at judges that made less" and frequently were forced to move on to other opportunities, they added a certain pa-nache to the town. Few of their names are remembered, but their influence helped to determine the kind of community Dodge City would be. It was a time and setting that made their practice and role unique. There was not to be their like again. Mr. Dooley knew that even by 1900 "th' law is a diff'rent professyon fr'm what it was."

Twenty-seven lawyers lived and practiced law in Dodge City from 1876 to 1886. Only Michael W. ("Mike") Sutton's tenure spanned the entire period, although Daniel M. ("Dan") Frost hung his shingle in 1876 and remained throughout the era, but not as a practicing lawyer, and Harry E. Gryden, who was in practice be-fore 1875, died there in 1884. Five were to be members of the Dodge City bar for seven or more years. Considering that Dodge had only six to fourteen active lawyers in residence at any one time, with the average number being about seven before the land rush of the mid-1880s, this was a fairly stable corps of attorneys. The remainder, some no more than names on a census or a case or two, had short, unprofitable experiences before they moved on to new opportunities.

Although nearly all were the object of a lawsuit, at least a civil suit, three of the fraternity were to experience justice under heavy charges from the other side of the bar: one for murder, two for grand larceny. Three were to abandon the legal profession to be-come newspaper publishers, while three others dabbled in publish-

Tenure of Active Dodge City Lawyers, 1876–1888

| 1876 | 1877 | 1878 | 1879 | 1880 | 1881 | 1882 | 1883 | 1884 | 1885 | 1886 |
|---|---|---|---|---|---|---|---|---|---|---|
| Sutton<br>Gryden<br>Frost<br>Morphy<br>Wyckoff<br>Sells | Sutton<br>Gryden<br>Frost<br>Morphy<br><br>Colborn<br>Holcomb | Sutton<br>Gryden<br>Frost<br>Morphy<br><br>Colborn<br><br>Hardesty | Sutton<br>Gryden<br>Frost<br>Morphy<br><br>Colborn<br><br>Hardesty<br>Jones<br>Kellogg | Sutton<br>Gryden<br>Frost<br>Morphy<br><br>Colborn<br><br>Jones<br>Kellogg<br>Borton<br>Burns | Sutton<br>Gryden<br>Frost<br><br>Jones<br><br>Borton<br>Burns | Sutton<br>Gryden<br><br>Borton<br>Burns<br>Wenie<br>Whitelaw<br>Milton<br>Swan | Sutton<br>Gryden<br><br>Borton<br>Burns<br>Wenie<br>Whitelaw<br>Milton<br>Swan | Sutton<br>Gryden<br><br>Jones<br><br>Borton<br>Burns<br>Wenie<br>Whitelaw<br>Milton<br>Swan<br>Finlay | Sutton<br><br>Jones<br><br>Borton<br><br>Wenie<br>Whitelaw<br>Milton<br>Swan<br>Finlay<br>Hendricks<br>McGarry<br>Pendleton | Sutton<br><br>Jones<br><br>Borton<br><br>Wenie<br>Whitelaw<br>Milton<br>Swan<br><br>Hendricks<br>McGarry<br><br>DePui<br>Soper<br>Wicks<br>Groendyke<br>Frankey |

ing for shorter periods of time, one went into ranching, another became a successful miner, three filled positions with the public schools, and several became real-estate developers. Many simply drifted from the Kansas scene.

Besides the local lawyers, more than sixty "foreign lawyers," the term used by the papers of the day to identify those living outside Dodge City, appeared before or served as a judge of the district court. Many of the foreign lawyers spent so much time in Dodge on district-court duty that the town seemed like a second home. James G. Waters of Topeka expressed his gratitude for the kindnesses of the people of Dodge by donating his services when the city was sued and the case ended in a Topeka court. A few foreign lawyers advertised their services in the Dodge papers, and three—E. N. Wicks of Cimarron, E. D. Swan of Spearville, and Thomas S. Jones of Cottonwood Falls—held residence in two towns at the same time. Dodge City lawyers in turn traveled to other towns and appeared before other district courts and the Kansas Supreme Court. These experiences did much to keep the Dodge bar alert to new trends and increased the stature of the court and the legal combatants. Because of the heavy caseload of the Atchison, Topeka, and Santa Fe Railroad, Topeka furnished more outside attorneys in cases before the district court than any other town. However, the bulk of the work in the justice-of-the-peace, police, probate, and district courts was handled by Dodge lawyers.

Little is known of the formal training in law of many of those appearing in court. At least five read law in Dodge City offices as a means of passing the Kansas bar. The requirements for admission, which were established in 1868, appear relatively unstructured and imprecise, with no formal educational requirements:

Any person [being a] citizen of the United States, who has read law for two years, the last of which must be in the office of a regularly practicing attorney, who shall certify that the said applicant is a person of good moral character, and well qualified to practice law, who is actually an inhabitant of this state, and who satisfies any district court of this state that he possesses the requisite learning, and that he is of good moral character, may, by such court, be permitted to practice in all district and inferior courts of this state, upon taking the oath hereinafter prescribed.[2]

A strict adherence to the reading rule and the rigor of the examination undoubtedly varied from one district court to another. Testimony has been given to the laxness in the Medicine Lodge district court, where Mike Sutton first practiced. The only question asked of one prospective attorney was: "Are you ready and willing to set 'em up?" The examiners accompanied him to the nearest saloon and then reported back to the court that the candidate "had already been admitted to one bar to their personal knowledge and had shown reasonable familiarity with the procedures there." If the story be true, the examiners may have been addressing an admission provision that allowed any practicing attorney from any other state or territory to practice in Kansas.[3]

The Dodge City court would appear to have held to a more rigorous interpretation of state law. All lawyers who were admitted there seemed to have met the standards of time and character requirements. The only exceptions that might suggest a quick fix were schoolmaster John Groendyke, whose admission seemed timed to meet an election deadline, and Martin S. Culver, admitted in the same session, who needed the title to advance a development scheme that was to be beneficial to a number of Dodge Citians. There is no way to determine the extent of the locally instructed attorneys' legal knowledge at the time the candidates were admitted. There is no record of questions asked or answers given.

If the process had been as easy as the Medicine Lodge example, a number of men in Dodge surely would have sought admission to the bar, since they would have profited by the status of attorney. H. P. Myton, L. E. McGarry, and Vine DePui were among those who were closely associated with the courts and who would have achieved more success if they had been attorneys. McGarry's brother did go through the longer process to be admitted by the Dodge district court and DePui served as clerk of the court for a number of years, yet it took the latter some twenty years to be admitted. The other two men never were admitted. Probate Judges Herman J. Fringer and T. J. Vanderslice would have improved their standing also if admission had been granted freely.

The path into law by the mid-1870s usually was not as smooth or easy as was depicted for an earlier time. The experience of Frank Willis, who became a distinguished Texas judge after being admitted to the bar in Liberty, Kansas, was representative of many un-schooled lawyers. Born on a farm in Indiana and orphaned at an early age, Willis took a job as teacher after he had completed the offerings in his rural school. He borrowed law books and read them each day after his stint of teaching. When possible, he accompanied lawyers to court to learn how to conduct a case. Sometimes he sat as a spectator through the entire court session. After several years, he was questioned by a panel of lawyers and was admitted to the bar.[4]

Not all of Dodge City's attorneys were unschooled. E. H. Borton was a graduate of the Iowa University Law School, Colonel Jones's alma mater was Brockenborough Law School in Virginia, W. C. Shinn spent six months attending law lectures in Ann Arbor, Michigan, and E. N. Wicks was in the first class of Valparaiso Law School. Most had practiced at least briefly, and some had consider-able experience, before coming west. The community was gener-ally impressed with their learning, their "gift of gab," and their sophistication. They had no problem with status or professional prestige. Their great disadvantage was that Dodge City was blessed with citizens who were too law abiding and not sufficiently litigious minded to supply a steady stream of lawsuits, which would have provided a comfortable living.

To survive in Dodge City during its cowtown days, a lawyer was required to be more than a legal defender or prosecutor. The role outside the courtroom, if not of equal importance, was at least es-sential for his professional image and occupied many of his working hours. The community expected his presence at public affairs. It was, in the main, pleasant, although unpaid, duty. Far from feeling such activity a waste of time or frivolous, the lawyer knew commu-nity involvement contributed to his professional exposure. Al-though there was no proscription on advertisements and although most attorneys did maintain a small advertising "box" in the news-papers next to the dressmakers, livery operators, and black-smiths, community service was a far better means of becoming known than were the weekly three-liners. Being in the public eye was a cheap way of getting their names before prospective clients and, at the same time, offering a sample of their talents.

The community understood that lawyers, along with preachers

and politicians, were handy wordsmiths. On notable occasions—national holidays, memorials, and celebrations—an attorney was expected to be willing and especially able to "present a few words" that would be entertaining and edifying. There was scarcely a Fourth of July celebration in Dodge City or surrounding towns that one of the attorneys did not rise to the occasion. Other public gatherings, political or civic, also saw them in action. Typical was a "mass meeting," the term was used to indicate a public gathering, called to form a new land district; four of the six speakers presenting arguments were attorneys. When the citizens of Dodge were moved in 1878 by the plight of yellow-fever victims in the southern states, a rally was held on Front Street to collect relief funds. The Dodge City Brass Band (one of the predecessors of the more widely known Dodge City Cowboy Band) attracted the crowd, and Edward F. ("Ed") Colborn, the newest member of the legal fraternity, presented a "well-timed and pointed speech." Then, as if not to give unfair exposure to only one lawyer, W. N. Morphy and D. M. Frost, both attorneys and editors, were called on for impromptu remarks. The same protocol was observed when Harry Gryden, Dodge's most flamboyant orator, gave the major address at the dedication of the new school building in February 1880. At the conclusion of his remarks, Colborn, "being loudly called for," was persuaded to speak, and when he had finished, Colonel T. S. Jones was called upon for his extemporaneous observation.[5]

It should be remembered that forensic ability in the courtroom did not necessarily ensure success. For example, both Colonel Jones and B. F. Milton were praised for giving "stirring addresses" and Jones's effort was judged the "best speech of his life" in the Ben Daniels case, but they lost what appeared to be an easy conviction to a biased jury that was unswayed by their eloquence. Theirs was, however, a grandiloquent age, and most lawyers attempted to follow the model. Outside the courtroom, the lawyers felt less restraint and their hyperbole could reach glowing heights.

Politics also served as an acceptable channel for public service. Since the earliest days of the Republic, lawyers have been noticeably a part of the political system. In his analysis of the American scene, Alexis de Tocqueville found that lawyers filled the legislative assemblies and generally headed administrations. This was just, he believed, because "in all free governments, of whatever form they may be, members of the legal profession will be found at the head of all parties." Therefore, he concluded, they had considerable influence on the creation and execution of the law; however, this influence and power was curbed by public opinion. In Dodge City it was a rare attorney who did not participate in political contests, either as a party worker or a candidate. The lawyers were members of both "the Gang" and the reform faction before these groups drifted into the Republican or Democratic camps. On the state level, they worked in both major parties, and some, for brief periods, labored under the banner of the Independent, Greenback, Labor, Populist, and Prohibitionist parties.[6]

Their political successes were disproportionately high, considering Dodge City's population. D. M. Frost was an unabashedly partisan editor of the *Ford County Globe* while still pursuing a career as attorney and served in the 1875–76 session of the state legislature, representing the 103d District. Colonel Jones had represented the Cottonwood Falls district before coming to Dodge, and E. F. Colborn sat in the Colorado legislature after he left Dodge. At least one other Dodge City lawyer gained statewide prominence and with it considerable political clout. Mike Sutton was to serve in the legislature after the cattle-town era ended; according to Robert Wright, the most reliable of the contemporary authorities:

Mike [Sutton] surely was for many years, the big political boss of the great Southwest, and held the situation in his vest pocket; and he certainly made one United States senator, and came within two votes of making another, besides figuring conspicuously in making and defeating others.[7]

Sutton had been a member of the faction known as the Gang and was a close friend of Bat Masterson, around whom much of the strife revolved. However, he was to become even more committed to the Republican party and the prohibitionist faction than to any local clique, and he eventually found himself opposing his earlier cronies. Among the reasons for the break between Masterson and Sutton, which came with much public exposure and acrimonious name-calling, was Bat's dependency on Mike for political advice. In 1879, Sutton had advised Sheriff Masterson to ignore the rumors and gossip about corruption in his office. The voters, Sutton said, were above listening to such cheap slander; it was better not to dignify it or call attention to it with a public denial. Bat followed the advice and lost his bid for a second term. He blamed Sutton, along with certain newspaper editors, and never forgave them.

Sutton's legal rival was also his most consistent political opponent. Harry Gryden's involvement with politics on both the state and local levels was as frequent and faithful as Sutton's. However Gryden never secured the same confidence of the voters or other party workers that came to Sutton. For one thing, he was affiliated with the wrong party—wrong if success is the criterion. Democrats did not retain offices long in Dodge City. Gryden held positions on the Ford County central committee, was a delegate to the state Democratic and senatorial conventions, and stumped for state and national candidates. He briefly flirted with the Independent party movement, serving as its temporary chairman; ran for county attorney on the People's party ticket (and lost); and tried to steer the People's Greenback party into an alliance with the Democrats. Like Sutton, Gryden was an original member of the Gang but unlike Sutton, he rejected the reform group and its policies He was a persistent maker of motions and grandiloquent speech maker for any and all the groups with which he was associated. Although he frequently was called upon to launch new organizations and preside at their opening sessions, less-controversial figures tended to take over the permanent structures.

If Gryden, Frost, and Sutton were the most active politicians during the cattle-town years, they were by no means the only lawyers to see the advantage of political exposure. E. H. Borton, E. Colborn, James Whitelaw, Frederick T. M. ("Fred") Wenie, and E. N. Wicks all took part in party affairs. For some it was a necessary step in running for one of the public attorney slots; for all it was a means of getting public exposure and their names in the papers. They were always alert to any opportunity to speak, and the political arena was an ideal forum. Shopkeepers had their display windows; political participation was the lawyers' showcase, where they could display their oratorical talents and their ability to maneuver in formal settings. There they also could demonstrate their convictions and entertain the public, from whence came their future clients.

Entertainment was not the least important of the talents political battle revealed. In the minds of the people (i.e., future clients), a dull lawyer outside the courtroom was likely to be unimpressive before a judge and jury. Lawyers were expected to be entertaining. Cleverness in political and legal combat created a reputation that had to be reconfirmed in their daily lives. On cold winter nights after the trail-herd cowboys had returned to Texas, Dodge menfolk gathered around the saloon stove and shared stories of past or imagined exploits. Nick Klaine marveled at Harry Gryden's storytelling talents, even when the stories were obviously lies. "Harry," Nick wrote, "can tell an Indian yarn the width of Texas at the longest way."[8]

Lawyers in all settings have appreciated the possibility of parody in their language and courtroom routine. Harry Gryden was particularly adept at such entertainment. Klaine, editor of the *Times,* delighted in reporting practical jokes and other barroom humor. He told with obvious personal relish how Gryden and Sutton tricked fellow attorney Frost into signing an elaborately drawn bond, replete with double-talk legalese, that resulted in Frost's owing them forty drinks. The story in the paper was far better advertising copy than Gryden and Sutton could have written for a formal ad. Another barroom legal maneuver saw Sutton, ostensibly on behalf of the city of Dodge, bring charges of vagrancy against Gryden. The press reported that there was "considerable comment of a personal nature" before the kangaroo court, but the charge could not be sustained. Drinks all around. Such shenanigans not only helped pass the time but added to their perpetrators' reputations as proficient, clever, and articulate attorneys.[9]

Nor was entertainment left entirely outside the solemn chambers of the law. The biographer of Temple Houston, certainly one of the frontier's most colorful courtroom performers, observed: "The great event [in Mobeetie, Texas] was court week. During the session of district court . . . , people came from throughout the judicial area for unadulterated fun. And Houston obliged, especially if the issue was trivial." In his study *The Western Peace Officers,* Frank Prassel also found the western courts a lively and appreciated source of diversion. "In an era preceding the entertainment provided by mass communications," he writes, "criminal trials served as a source of local amusement." Most sessions of the district court were well attended, and some judges and lawyers, in responding to the crowd, turned courts into theaters, often with sorry results. Although the court sessions in Dodge were not the carnivals that Mobeetie provided, the more spectacular cases did attract considerable attention. The appearance of Dodge characters, such as former marshal Frank Trask or Mysterious Dave Mather; sex-related crimes, such as attorney E. F. Hardesty's killing of a hired hand; or the testimony of soiled doves from the bordellos were major attractions that played to courtrooms "crowded with curious spectators." District-court week in Dodge City always brought new faces to town, and the newspapers made much of the action. [10]

City courts were far more informal than the district court, and the exchanges among lawyers, prisoners, and spectators were frequently colorful. One such instance involved E. F. Colborn, then 21. This was the exchange as reported in the paper:

State vs. Charley [Chalkley] Beeson, shooting with intent to kill—N. R. Gilbert, prosecuting witness; W. N. Morphy and E. F. Colborn, attorneys for defendant. Prosecuting witnesses failed to appear, and defendant was released, on payment of costs. In discussing the case Mr. Colborn made a remark reflecting on the dignity of the Court, which His Honor [Justice of the Peace W. Y. McIntosh] rebuked by leaning over the bench and remarking with great severity of manner: "I will permit no puppy to run this Court!" The attorney retorted by vaguely alluding to His Honor as being himself a relative of a certain variety of canine. The Judge, with his characteristic dignity, ruled that his position as Justice of the Peace in Ford County entitled him to the common courtesy due from one gentleman to another. Mr. Colborn inquired if common courtesy permitted a Judge on the bench to call an attorney a pup. His Honor explained that he did not refer to him in particular, but to all puppies in general. Mr. C. then stated that he was an authorized attorney, and appeared before the Court in behalf of his client. The Court suggested that he would do well to go back to his old business. The lawyer inquired what his old business was. His Honor commenced to state that he had grave suspicions that he was an ex-bullwhacker, when Mrs. McIntosh, the Squire's estimable lady, who did not seem to take a proper pride in the able and masterly manner in which the Judge was getting away with the young attorney, peremptorily ordered him to "shup up!" In the temporary lull that followed Mr. C. fervently thanked God that there was another Justice of the Peace in the county, who would give a lawyer the same rights accorded a "yaller dog" in Court. The Court very appropriately remarked: "You and your d——d Justice may go to h—l for all I care. I don't want the d——d office!"

At this juncture County Attorney Sell and W. N. Morphy interfered and the argument closed. [11]

Newspaper accounts of judical proceedings must be given careful scrutiny. Both D. M. Frost of the *Globe* and Nick Klaine of the *Times* reported insignificant bits of litigation with unbridled imagination, but they intended to entertain more than to inform. This is not to suggest that the Dodge City courtrooms were devoid of humor and drama. In fact, the language of the defendants and witnesses was on occasion too explicit for the press to report, and lawyers, who were entertaining when in their cups at the Lady Gay, were often as clever and quotable in district court.

Some of the offenders described in Klaine's day in police court were to make appearance in the more formal district court, where there were equally frank exchanges. In an oft-quoted case, one of the "nymphs of the prairie" accused another of being a "dirty bitch, a whore and . . . afflicted with the clap." The fight that resulted cost her $20.35; Monroe Henderson, guilty of a like indiscretion, escaped with an $18.00 fine. As ribald as the testimony was in these cases, Gryden for the defense stuck to the unspectacular lawyerese, asking "to quash because the defense was not a public affair" and "not against any ordinance of the city of Dodge City." [12]

Robert Wright reported another engaging response by an irate and frustrated plaintiff as an example of "the wit and humor" of the court:

A good story is told of a Dodge City divorce suit. The jury refused to grant the lady a divorce, and, when the court inquired if she would like to "poll the jury," she said: "That is just what I would delight to do if your honor would give me a pole"; and the glance she gave the jury made the cold chills run up and down their spinal columns. [13]

Obviously, the justice-of-the-peace and police courts did lack the decorum and dignity of the district court, but when Gryden compared the lower court to "the late show-case game" (a confidence game involving the switching of cheap jewelry for the real thing), Klaine suggested that the attorney ought to have been fined for contempt. Generally, however, the editors encouraged levity as a means of holding readers' attention, even when they couldn't print the unexpurgated language. Klaine observed that the July 1879 session of the district court had been fairly routine except for some of the divorce cases. These, he said, had "some racy features" too rough for a "moral newspaper" to use and "shock the readers with detail." Such a teaser was bound to draw spectators at the next court session.[14]

The biggest payoff for cultivated popularity was election to the office of county attorney; a distant second prize was the city attorney's office. Both were always filled by men with legal certification, although that was not required by law until Kansas was nearly eighty years old. Of the two, obviously the county attorney's job was far more important and paid considerably more. In 1877 the city attorney received only $100.00 per year but he also collected fees connected with the performance of his official duties. Equally as important as the pay was the exposure the attorney received, which attracted private clients. The term of office was one year; however, the city attorney was completely under the control of the city council, which not only could determine whether it needed an attorney but could remove him from office at any time. The county attorney's term of office was two years, which provided some stability, and although it was modest by modern terms the compensation made the job a political plum. The fixed salary was based on the size of the population in the county, plus a bonus if unorganized counties were included in its jurisdiction. In 1885 a county attorney in a county with one to five thousand residents was to receive "not more than four hundred dollars" a year, which was increased to $700.00 with the attached areas. Five percent of all monies he collected in favor of the state or county was also part of his compensation, as were certain specific fees. As part of the court costs, a county attorney's fees ranged from $25.00 for a murder trial to $2.50 for drawing an indictment or information for a misdemeanor. In spite of what appears to be a pittance, undoubtedly the pay, more than the honor and power, attracted men to the office. Most of the attorneys in town ran for election at one time or another, even when it required being an independent candidate. In the 1880 election, five of the six active lawyers ran for county attorney.[15]

By statute, the county attorney was required to prosecute or de-

end "all suits, applications or motions, civil or criminal, arising
under the laws of this State, in which the State or their county is a
party or interested." As the population of western Kansas increased, the duties of county attorney at Dodge City also expanded. Jurisdiction extended beyond Ford County, including thirteen unorganized counties as far west as the Colorado line. This
meant the county attorney examined cases and prepared suits origi-
nating 125 miles from his Dodge City base. Travel consumed much
of the county attorney's time. It was not unusual for Mike Sutton to
travel to Coolidge on the state line and to Topeka or Leavenworth
to the east during the same month. The caseload, even without the
travel, could be quite heavy. In the January 1881 district court
session, Sutton prosecuted eleven criminal cases ranging from
second-degree murder and grand larceny to simple assult and petty
larceny. He also was involved in sixteen of the thirty-four civil
cases before the court during the same session. Not all sessions
were as crowded, and the *Ford County Globe* noted with some disappointment that the July 1879 session had seen only one prisoner
sentenced. [16]

Obviously, not all of the county attorney's time was spent in litigation. Among other duties, he was called upon to assist in the capture of fugitives; Sutton even gave Bat Masterson a hand in his
law-enforcement duties. The county attorney occasionally accompanied the peace officers when they delivered prisoners to Leavenworth, as was the case when Sutton accompanied Masterson and
Bat's undersheriff, Charles Bassett, when they had three prisoners
to deliver to the penitentiary. Investigation of reported crimes
away from the city also brought travel to the county attorney.
Gryden rode the Santa Fe train to Coolidge to investigate the murder of Barney Elliott; later, County Attorney Whitelaw made the
same trip to investigate a train robbery there. Attorneys not in city
or county office were sometimes called on by the public attorneys
or private parties for similar services. J. M. Thatcher, agent for
Adams Express Co., took Gryden, who was not then in office,
along with City Marshal Bassett and Chalkley Beeson with him to
Las Vegas, New Mexico, to investigate a train robbery that had
resulted in loss of the express company's goods. Not infrequently
the county attorney attended trials in other jurisdictions in which

the county or state had some interest. These activities were the
result of his role as prosecutor or defender of county and state interests but involved talents not necessarily related to his main
obligations.[17]

The other major responsibility established by law lay entirely
outside the courtroom. The Kansas statute creating the office required the county attorney to be the legal adviser to all county
agencies:

The county attorney shall, without fee or reward, give opinions and advice
to the board of county commissioners, and other civil officers of their respective counties, when requested by such board or officers, upon all
matters in which the county is interested, or relating to the duties of such
board or officers, in which the State or county may have an interest.

Furthermore, this responsibility was his exclusive obligation. For
instance, the attorney general of Kansas would not respond to the
county commissioners if the request did not come through the
county attorney. Editor Frost explained that this made the office
one of the most important in the county, even though little money
passed through the incumbent's hands, because he could "exercise
a controlling influence . . . over his associates, and molds them to
his will." The city attorney exercised much the same authority on
the municipal level. The influence could be seen in some county
and city decisions. When Gryden was city attorney in 1880, he was
directed by the city council to draw up an ordinance relating to the
use of scrip by the city. The *Times* editorialized that the idea and
the "nurture" of it had been Gryden's.[18]

There were occasions when even ordinary citizens expected the
county attorney to provide legal advice. When hotelman G. A. W.
Bodecker of Kinsley found a transient dead in one of his rooms, he
naturally headed for County Attorney Whitelaw's office to find out
what to do. Whitelaw's legal and practical advice was to bury his
guest as soon as possible.[19]

Although the work load was fairly heavy, the county attorney's
position was an enviable one. "Shoutin' at judges," as Mr. Dooley
knew, didn't pay very well, but an even more serious problem for a
lawyer in private practice was attracting clients with cases to take
to court for even a small retainer. Most lawyers found it necessary
to supplement their legal earnings. They advertised themselves as

land agents, notaries public, insurance salesmen, and collection agents. "Law, Loan, Real Estate, Collection and Insurance," read H. M. and L. E. McGarry's 1886 advertisement. Lawyers also filled part-time slots as county and city clerks, held the post of justice of the peace, and served as paid witnesses for legal documents. A number earned their living from other activities and lawyered on the side. Both Frost and Morphy advertised their services as attorneys in the newspaper they edited. Gryden accepted the position of assistant superintendent of schools for a while and held about every minor office connected even remotely with the law. He even worked as a reporter, writing stories for Dodge City and other newspapers—an acceptable addition to his short supply of cash. Even with scratching for odd jobs and using their talents in unrelated activities, lawyers had a hard time of it. Competition was heavy, and there always seemed to be more lawyers waiting in the wings.[20]

From the limited evidence that is available, it is difficult to judge the effectiveness of the Dodge City bar. Only scattered news stories and limited legal documentation remain to suggest the attorneys' legal competency. It would appear from these that some of the lawyers were well grounded in the law, conducted extensive research in important cases, and were considered properly eloquent and persuasive in the courtroom. The press used flattering terms in describing their legal prowess: "vigorous and well-arranged defense," "studious devotion to books," "formidable array of prosecuting talents," "using all fair and honorable means." Many cases—most, in fact—were so cut and dried, to use the *Times*'s expression, there was little any lawyer could do to change the inevitable verdict. "Messrs. Gryden, Jones and Kellogg . . . argued to the Judge and directed his attention to the 'brightest spots' in the lives and acts of the criminals and asked that mercy be shown" was the *Ford County Globe*'s summary of adequate advocacy when the men before the judge had been caught with the goods in the presence of ample and trustworthy witnesses.[21]

If the case warranted the effort, the documentation and argument could be long and exacting. A hurried trial was rarely a goal if the matter was serious. In the case resulting in the only death sentence handed down by the Dodge City district court between 1876 and 1886, forty witnesses were called. Editor Frost, a lawyer himself, reported in another instance that "from the perusal of his [Gryden's] eight-page petition, we rather think the stockmen [the plaintiffs] have the best of both law and the facts in the matter." Argument could be equally long, too long for comfort at times: "Mr. Gryden for the prisoner and Mr. Colborn for the City, opened their batteries and let language fly in every direction. . . . It was near the middle of the night when silence reigned once more." [22]

Gryden was considered by all as the greatest orator—and the most long winded. A reported sample gives some idea of the breadth and depth of his and his colleagues' art:

> Mr. Gryden followed. He argued that where there is a wrong committed, there must be a remedy, that the age of the Seal Chambers of Venice and the Black Hole of Calcutta were past, that if the city could confine an old man in a den of murderers, who had vowed to kill him, they could also incarcerate the maiden with the raving maniac, or employ the thumbscrews and the iron boots of the inquisition as their agents. Mr. Gryden's argument occupied about one hour, and was spoken of by the bar with flattering encomiums. Captain Waters closed the argument for the city, showing by a long list of authorities that a city occupied the position of a State in the regulating of her municipal affairs, that if a liability existed, it was against the agents of the city. That she could be no more liable in this case than would the Warden of the Penitentiary be responsible for the killing of one convict by another. Strong and able arguments were, of course, expected from City Attorney Colborn and Captain Waters and they were in this case fully realized. The court sustained the demurrer, and rendered judgment for costs against Blake, to which plaintiff excepted, and gave notice of appeal to the Supreme Court. [23]

Others, including Sutton and Colonel Jones, relied more on calm, marshaled logic based on precedents and research in the statutes.

Apparently, there was considerable sharing of resources. In the close-knit fraternity, individuals opposed each other literally dozens of times and were partners about as often. When one of the attorneys came into possession of new material and sources, he generously shared the information. E. H. Borton informed the public it might share his new copy of "Copp's Public Land Laws," with some sixteen hundred accounts of decisions on U.S. government land. Borton continued to accumulate books and in 1884 had a library of two hundred volumes, "rich and rare in legal lore." Gryden also became "something of an authority on Texas cattle law" and collected a considerable library which he offered to share with interested parties. [24]

Analysis of actual procedures, tactics, and argument is at this late date difficult to accomplish. There is, however, evidence of individual lawyers' work that gives some indication of professional competence. What is available demonstrates that court procedures have changed somewhat from the cowtown days, but not the attorney's approach to his job. Obviously, certain circumstances and community prejudices and mores are different today and affected the methods and instruments that the attorneys emphasized, but all are recognizable and are applicable in today's courts.

In a setting where emotions could be quicksilver, memories short, and the population highly mobile, the delay of a trial by a few weeks could radically alter the complexion of a jury or the evidence presented. Dodge City's lawyers knew the value of "the law's delay." Change of venue, bond review, and petition for writ of habeas corpus were used frequently to distance the accused from the charge. For any defense attorney, continuance was a prime tool. The extent of its use is reflected in a district-court session that saw twelve cases before the judge; five were continued, and the next session saw at least six more added to the list. It may be unfair to accuse the attorneys of conniving with the defendants in using the time gained in the various delays to flee the district. However, it happened so often that contemporaries at least believed it to be true. On the other hand, a cowboy defendant in a neighboring county, Jim Herron, testified that his lawyer warned him not to run: "I will say only one more thing, Jim, and I give it to you as both your personal friend and as your legal counsel. True to my oath as an attorney, I must caution you to not take this escape route. Don't run. If you do, you will always regret it." But even if the lawyers were not deliberately implicated, their actions resulted in many suspects leaving the state, never to stand trial on the original charges. [25]

How well delaying tactics might work to a client's benefit is illustrated in two cases; both involved Gryden's adroit maneuvering to delay action, and both led to the prisoner's escaping. The first concerned William Bird (or Byrd), who was charged with stealing eight carloads of cattle in August 1883. He was arrested and in pre-

liminary examination his bond was set at six thousand dollars. Not
being able to meet the bond, he was placed in Dodge's crowded jail.
Gryden presented a petition for a writ of habeas corpus to the probate judge, who obligingly called for a special meeting at night without the knowledge of the offended parties. The state was notified
at the last minute and was represented by James T. Whitelaw, the
county attorney. A continuance may work both ways, and in this
instance the prosecuting attorney seemed to have the best of it, at
least for a short time. Whitelaw secured a continuance for ten days
on the basis of his lack of preparation, filed a supplemental petition,
and after considerable debate compromised on a bond of four thousand dollars, still a substantial sum. In the long run, the accused
got the breaks. Bird used the money from the sale of the cattle he
allegedly had stolen to indemnify his bondsman and immediately
left town for the more hospitable plains of Texas. [26]

When his case came before the October 1883 session of the district court, defendant Bird failed to appear. Gryden tried to secure
a change of venue, but the court refused until Bird appeared in person. The bondsman sent Dave Mather to Texas to find Bird, but
Mather failed to persuade Bird to come back to Kansas. "The
Byrd," lamented the *Ford County Globe*, "is still in the bush." In
June 1884 the new sheriff, Pat Sughrue, was more successful and
Bird stood trial in that month's court session. At the trial Gryden
was able to prove to the court's satisfaction that there was insufficient evidence to prosecute. The paucity of evidence was reinforced by a long list of Texas ranchers who swore to Bird's good
character. The Northwest Livestock Association of Texas had
backed Bird from the beginning and had sent a Texas lawyer,
Thomas F. West of Jacksboro, to support Gryden. The Dodge
City–based Western Stock Growers' Association had matched
West with its own Mike Sutton and had added a one-thousand-dollar
reward for Bird's conviction. Surprisingly, Bird was acquitted and
the Texans won. From the Kansas point of view, "the actions of the
attorneys in this case look a little cloudy." An important factor in
"clouding" the issue was the passage of time, which had dimmed
memories of tallies and sales. What had appeared clear and certain
became questionable. Bird returned to his Texas bush. [27]

In the second case, George U. Holcomb used the time gained in
delays to escape twice. He was never brought to trial, and his case

was dropped. The court action, however, was not forgotten in Dodge City. When delay maneuvers were attempted again in 1883, editor Frost reminded his readers of Holcomb, "who wore the State out on bonds and was never brought to trial nor even had his bond declared forfeit."[28]

Delaying tactics did not always work for the defense, and Gryden was lectured on more than one occasion for seeking a writ of habeas corpus when the case was considered frivolous. But in most instances, the court responded favorably to such petitions, which invariably resulted in delay.[29]

The failure of a witness to appear was another frequent cause for a petition of continuance. With communications difficult and some witnesses members of a transient population, people often failed to appear when subpoenaed. The difficulty was illustrated in the highly publicized case against the Cheyenne leaders of Dull Knife's 1878 raid. Sutton, who had brought the suit, was finally forced to enter a plea of nolle prosequi since he could not get a continuance. Three of his witnesses were unavailable, he informed the court. One was in Texas, another in Nebraska, and a third in Arizona. Usually, judges were tolerant and cooperative when faced with missing witnesses, but there was a limit to their patience. When Jack Bridges, city marshal of Dodge, failed to appear as a witness, the presiding judge ordered him arrested and denied access to a writ of habeas corpus if he should petition. The problem of missing witnesses remained a fairly serious one throughout the period. To what extent attorneys encouraged this practice cannot be determined.[30]

The art of favorable jury selection was developed as much as could be expected with limited numbers and types of jurymen available. When selection became routine, carelessness crept into the impaneling chore. In 1885 an entire jury was "thrown out owing to an informality in its selection." Discriminating selection was generally unnecessary. In fact, most juries were chosen quickly with few challenges. However, in what the *Ford County Globe* considered "the big case" for the October 1883 session of the district court, selection took one and a half days. Usually, the procedure was more perfunctory, since there was little to be gained by choosing one settler over another. Exceptions were cases involving cattle rustlers or horse thieves in which the defense attorney would try to eliminate farmers and ranchers. Wrote Nick Klaine, Dodge City's master of doggerel:

> Both the counsel and the judge
> Saw with eyes in a fury
> That the man wouldn't budge
> Who sat on a granger jury.
> I want to be a granger
> And with the granger's stand;
> With hay seed in my hair
> And a pitchfork in my hand.[31]

After the Western Kansas Cattle Growers' Association was formed, the county attorney had his task considerably lightened when the association hired Harry Gryden to assist in the prosecution of cattle thieves. Gryden had been a tough opponent before his appointment and, much to the association's consternation, had secured the release of William Bird, who had stolen cattle from association members. Gryden demonstrated his jury-selection artistry in the acquittal of the "most notorious horse thief operating in the border country." Henry Born(e), known throughout the frontier as Dutch Henry, had been charged with stealing two mules. Bat Masterson hunted him down and returned him to Dodge City to face trial. Confronted with a panel about equally divided between townspeople and farmers, Gryden opened the proceedings by alleging that the statute of limitations had been reached. A jury was impaneled to judge that contention rather than to determine the guilt or innocence of Dutch Henry. Gryden succeeded in getting the first jury chosen from "the horny-handed grangers." The *Ford County Globe* explained the strategy:

In allowing the farmers to sit to try the plea in bar, the defense had an object in view. They hardly expected the plea to be entertained, but it disqualified the farmers sitting in the trial of main issue—it being the opinion of the defense that farmers who, as a class, had suffered from horse thieves, would be more likely to convict than parties not so directly interested.

The new jury, consisting mainly of residents of the city, found Borne not guilty. Apparently, that was enough for members of the association. They hired Gryden to represent them in future cases. His conviction record proved the wisdom of their choice.[32]

Most of the time, even the cleverest, most persuasive lawyer
had no choice in his selection of jurymen. If only farmers were
called or only ranchers were called, juror challenges were mean-
ingless. Mike Sutton was confronted with such a case when he
faced a jury loaded with farmers:

At that time, the railroad was plagued by the theft of ties from the right of
way. They decided to put a stop to it. Their special officers staked out a
pile of ties, saw a man load up a wagon load of them and haul them off.
They apprehended him in his yard, chopping one of them for fire wood. He
was arrested for stealing ties.

When Mike was notified of the fact, he told the Superintendent [of the
Atchison, Topeka and Santa Fe Railroad] that he would do the best he
could, but it would be impossible to get a conviction.

At the trial the evidence was dead against the defendant, no question
about it. The jury was out about fifteen minutes and returned with a verdict of not guilty. The Superintendent said to Mike, "You told me but I
didn't believe it. Now why was that man not convicted?" Mike said, "Well,
you see it is like this: every man on that jury was using railroad ties for
fuel."[33]

The particular circumstances of practicing law in Dodge City
during the glory days of the Texas trail-herd business led to an influx of attorneys who became rich in experience and influence if
somewhat pinched in economic rewards. Since the town and the
High Plains in general (the Great Southwest as labeled by Robert
Wright) were in transition, the successful lawyer was obliged to
keep pace, drop out, or move on. The general caliber of the attorneys tended to improve over the years, but the dominant legal
leaders remained the old-timers, such as Mike Sutton and Colonel
Jones, who lived through the change and adapted to it.

The professional ability of men like Gryden and Sutton cannot be
denied. Generally, they served their clients well. Their knowledge
of the law tended to be in the area of practical application, although
they could discuss legal theory with some competence. The community also benefited by their presence and undoubtedly had more
confidence in them than the results would warrant. Still, without
the orderly process of the justice system, which the attorneys
helped to forge, there would have been less progress achieved and
at a higher social and economic cost to the community.

Outside the courtroom and legal office, the cowtown lawyers' impact was of much significance to Dodge City and the West. There is no denying the civilizing influence of these men with their active minds, articulate leadership, and more cultured approach to life. In politics, their role in defining issues and channeling debate is hard to overestimate. Politics remained emotional, personality oriented, and explosive almost to the end, but the attorneys were among those who tried to direct political thinking into issue considerations and a more orderly adversary relationship. Their leadership role made the political process far less chaotic than it would have been if the cowtown lawyers had remained neutral.

Their influence on the total life of Dodge, not just the legal system, was far greater than their numbers and their wealth would have suggested. Although few were, like Colonel Jones, cut from aristocratic cloth, they tended to view matters from a higher level of consideration than their peers. Alexis de Tocqueville observed: "The profession of law is the only aristocratic element which can be amalgamated without violence with the natural elements of democracy, and which can be advantageously and permanently combined with them." Little on Gospel Ridge and much less on Front Street bore the marks of aristocracy, but the democracy that was developing in Dodge City was nearer a positive resolution than it would have been if Shakespeare's admonition "to kill all the lawyers" or Bat Masterson's brand of law enforcement had been the final decision. Cattle-town Dodge owed much to the lawyers; the future was to be indebted even more.[34]

# 4. For the Defense: Harry E. Gryden

THE WESTERN THEME in literature and cinema is based on the triplex system of the hero, the adventure, and the law—all adapted to a westward movement intent on conquering an unproductive wilderness and establishing a society based on an improved model of the old, jaded East. Western movies, television adaptations, and novels are basically morality plays in which good contends with evil. The heroes, whether cowboy or sheriff, are free spirits, bold and resolute, who dominate the adventure in the name of law and order. The law, as defined in the western theme, has little to do with the subtleties of legal procedures or the niceties of statutory definitions but is interpreted broadly as embodying the principles of fair play and the advancement of the common good. *The law* usually meant *the lawman* and his gun. Eventually, however, if the story is carried beyond the dramatic confrontation, even the boldest lawman had to admit that the courts had final jurisdiction and the lawyers, not the lawmen, were to be the ultimate champions, contending in some improvised courtroom for truth and justice.[1]

The contestants in the legal community of the early days of cowtown Dodge City who served most frequently as the ultimate champions were Mike Sutton and Harry Gryden. The rivalry between the two took on something of the symbolic characteristics of the western theme. Unfortunately, the allegory is flawed. The discordant note in their drama is struck because the casting office was not manned by professional Hollywood veterans, for neither Gryden nor Sutton fit exactly the white-hat or black-hat image. Miscasting aside, the rest of the morality play conforms to the theme.

As in all good western adventures, the rivals were a near match

69

*Harry E. Gryden. If anyone was prepared by nature and circumstance for a wide-open cattle town, it was Harry Gryden. Courtesy Kansas State Historical Society.*

n talent and cunning. They began as friends and ended as enemies, with reconciliation only at the graveside. Each had his moments of triumph and defeat. But in the end the good prevailed and the righteous lived to see a fair if somewhat diminished version of his dreams come true. Mike lived on into the twentieth century to bask in honor; Gryden staggered to an early grave before the cattle-town era ended. Old, exciting cowtown Dodge died and a placid country mart replaced it. The morality play is complete. And so to Harry Gryden, the vanquished.

## Harry E. Gryden: 1875–1884*

If anyone was prepared by nature and circumstance for a wide-open cattle town, it was Harry Gryden. Life, which had not always been kind to him, had knocked him about the world enough for him to have experienced the uncertain joys of respectable living, the dubious virtues of violence, and the shallow satisfactions of a bohemian lifestyle. He had adopted a profession that transferred to the controlled environment of the courtroom the civilized contest of human will and wit. He found in the law a safe harbor for his cynicism, verbal abilities, and adversarial talents. His glib tongue, which spoke with a blending of Swedish-French inflection and a soft southern charm, was the perfect instrument for an unpolished frontier courtroom. To the less sophisticated folk of a Kansas cattle town, his personality was uniquely fascinating. They liked him on first meeting, and he responded with equal appreciation. The manly, adventurous sort he found in the bars on Front Street stimulated him, and he held a special compassion for the common sinners who shared his own shortcomings. His sense of humor, including a wry view of himself, found a favorite target in those who took themselves too seriously or who desired to direct other people's lives for what was perceived as everyone's good. Possessing enough learning and polished culture to impress a frontier community, he was the town's favorite black sheep. The talents he possessed were enough to make a modest living with minimal labor. He had no great ambition.

*Dates indicate years practicing law in Dodge City.

Gryden was born in Stockholm, Sweden, in 1840 and received part of his education there. His father had been an officer in the French army corps of Marshal Jean Bernadotte, a favored but mercurial general of Napoleon. In 1810, when Bernadotte was elected Charles XIV, King of Sweden, Gryden's father left France to become a Swedish citizen and an official in the king's civil service. The family emigrated to the United States in the 1850s, settled in Virginia, and moved to Greensburg, Indiana, just before the Civil War. Gryden enlisted in the Union Army signal corps and was promoted to the rank of lieutenant. The high point of his army service came when he wigwagged this message from General William Tecumseh Sherman to Brigadier General John Murray Corse at Altoona, Georgia: "General Sherman says hold fast for I am coming." The words inspired evangelist P. P. Bliss to write the hymn *Hold the Fort, For We Are Coming,* which became a favorite in camp meetings and frontier churches. Over the years, Harry, in the retelling of his adventure in the saloons of Dodge, added a few earthy details to the message: "I am badly wounded. I've got an ear cut off, but can whip hell out of them yet." It was a snappier version, even though it might not inspire a hymn.[2]

Gryden married shortly after the war, and two children were born before he and his wife separated; after the divorce his wife remarried and reared the children in Kentucky. However, at the time of Gryden's death, his former wife and children were living in Baxter Springs, Kansas. While in Indiana, Gryden held several civil positions, was admitted to the bar, and served as a U.S. revenue officer. During this time, he visited Kansas on occasion, then moved to Leavenworth, where he practiced law, and eventually settled in Dodge City in the early 1870s.

He had left behind his first failed effort at settled responsibility; the divorce had cut him free of all past ties, and he was to make the most of the Beautiful, Bibulous Babylon of the Frontier. For the next dozen years, he amused himself in the gambling and drinking establishments of the town, enjoying the company of the most prosperous and respectable as well as the truly wayward citizens of the West. Harry was always ready for a drink, a card game, a practical joke, or a lawsuit. If his dissolute habits were to "soon wreck his name and fame," as Deacon Klaine tut-tutted at the time of

Harry's funeral, he also was remembered as "the most genial and companionable fellow that . . . ever resided" in Dodge City and his casket was followed to Prairie Grove Cemetery "by one of the largest processions which ever fell in line."[3]

There is no question about his drinking. It was something he worked at with a dedication that carried well into the late hours of most evenings. Friends preached, nagged, and badgered him about his destructive vice—and then bought the next round of drinks. But mostly they marveled at his capacity and joked about his consistency. When editor Frost reported Harry's recovery of a good-luck charm, "his koo-i-noor," he described Harry's reaction as "never happier since the day he gagged down his first barrel of rye in the rural district of Indiany." When Gryden was elected to represent Dodge City at a state political convention, the editors of both the *Ford County Globe* and the *Times* noted that Harry made certain he would be well supplied with liquor while in Topeka. "His grip-sack contained six bottles of rye and a boiled shirt," confided the *Times;* the *Globe* thought the weight of the grip was due to one brick from "Webster's brick pile, while the remaining space contained bottles of liquor, a la gin sling." On at least one occasion, Gryden's indulgence was immortalized in pure frontier doggerel, parodying a letter he sent to Bat Masterson:

> *Dear Bat: I am sitting in Kelley's*
> *And we are filling our bellies*
> *With something to drink:*
> *That is fair, we think.*

It was hardly a parody of Gryden, however, sounding precisely like the Harry everyone knew.[4]

As for gambling, where could he have found more congenial companions? Or, for that matter, more prospective clients? A visitor to Dodge City in Gryden's time reported that "every saloon in the city has one or more gambling tables. Faro, monte, and the other usual games are dealt openly, and most of the saloons have a private room for the votaries of draw poker." There were more opportunities than the visitor could have guessed. To make certain there was always a game in town, the legal fraternity fashioned its own casino. "The game," Dan Frost reported, "over the city bastille is promptly opened each morning at 9 o'clock with Judge [R. E.] Burns as dealer, H. E. Gryden in the lookout chair, and [Frank] Chapman as case keeper. The game has never been beaten, as anyone knows, and the managers don't intend that it shall be. Judicially speaking, it is the only one of the kind in the city."[5]

America's black sheep are always attractive, well-dressed rogues. Harry fit the pattern. All judged him handsome, and the surviving portrait shows him in fashionable dress, with a head of wavy hair and a full mustache. When the press wanted a picture of Dutch Henry Borne, that camera-shy, notorious horse thief suggested that the reporter would do better with a portrait of his attorney, Gryden. Frost thought Gryden should be flattered by Borne's suggestion, since Dutch Henry was "conceded to be a very handsome man." When someone sent the editor Gryden's picture, labeled "Murderer, outlaw and thief, Dutch Henry," Frost first thought to publish it in his paper, "knowing Gryden could take a joke," but on further reflection, Frost confessed that he "didn't know which gentleman would be insulted," so he felt it the better part of wisdom not to print the portrait over either man's name. In spite of his attractiveness, Gryden apparently was not a ladies' man, at least among the respectable ladies. There is only one hint that there might have been a spark of romance left after his failed marriage. The *Ford County Globe* reported as a matter of news that Harry had traveled to Chillicothe, Missouri, to propose marriage to "a French lady" residing there. But by then Harry had perpetrated and been the victim of so many hoaxes and practical jokes that in all likelihood editor Klaine was simply getting back at Gryden for some recent stunt.[6]

As for the demimondes, again there are only hints and bits of information. He did know them, had bailed many of them out of jail, and he represented them in court. An anonymous correspondent wrote of the adventures of a number of Dodge Citians visiting Las Vegas, New Mexico. A grand ball was given by the community leaders and all the proper visitors attended:

In the meantime Harry Gryden was not idle—although a dancer he was not seen at the ball—having attended a very select ball in the "new town" [where the saloons and brothels were located], but he soon left as the air was too close for him, and too light for his pocketbook. He became infatuated with a Castilian lady, who navigated under the nom de plume of "Steamboat." He lavished favors on her recklessly and even made her a present of a fine gold cross that usually ornaments Harry's shirt bosom— afterward he stole it back and once again Mexico was cheated out of her rights. The last seen of Harry he was leaning against a "jacale" [shack] going through his pockets for wealth he never had. Forgive me Harry, I will never tell the truth about you again.

His cronies at the Lady Gay, if not Harry, must have enjoyed what is undoubtedly the gentlest description in American journalism of a respected citizen getting rolled in a sleazy part of town.[7]

The broad frontier humor of a town catering to the unsophisticated male delighted Harry. Newsman Klaine was Harry's target more than once, and before he turned "reform-sour," Klaine returned the favor. One of Gryden's harmless hoaxes, however, disturbed Nick more than a little. The *Times* ran a notice of the death of C. C. Pepperd, a Comanche County rancher and troublemaker, along with some appropriately frank remarks on the dead man's exploits in Dodge City. Within the week Klaine received a postal card from Pepperd protesting the falseness of the story. The *Times* immediately printed a retraction, considerably longer than the original story, as well it should have been. Pepperd was no man to rile. He had killed at least one man at Fort Griffin and was involved in a number of shooting scrapes in and around Dodge. Klaine did his best to clear his skirts before Pepperd appeared in town:

Furthermore, the herebefore mentioned postal card [from Pepperd] goes on to state, with considerable and unmistakeable emphasis, that he'd settled the bill usually charged for the publication of obituary notices with us when the first opportunity offers. Of course, the time is now approaching . . . when overcoats are a necessity, but we don't want to wear such an article of apparel made of mahogany or pine, we hasten to pen this retraction and let our readers know that Mr. Pepperd is not dead. . . . Whether with malice aforethought and intent to get us into trouble, Mr. Gryden gave us the alleged report . . . [and] an individual craving further particulars regarding the killing which did not occur . . . will apply to Mr. Gryden.

Gryden and the boys at the Lady Gay and Alhambra must have laughed through a dozen drinks to see Klaine fume and twitch.[8]

Another of Gryden's drinking partners was John ("Red") Clarke of the Boss Ranch in Clark County. Together, this time with

Klaine's cooperation, they advertised samples in Charles Rath's store of a snuff discovery in a snuff mine on Clarke's ranch, a miraculous lode that, under the promotion of the three, at one time or another yielded alum, cinnamon, and pure castile soap. Before the mine reached its most fabled proportions, Bill Jones was one greenhorn who fell for the snuff line. He and several others started out on foot for the diggings and an assured job in the only snuff mine in Kansas. After walking nearly a hundred miles going and coming, spraining an ankle, hiding out at night in a plum thicket, and quaking in mortal fear of nonexistent marauding Indians, Jones arrived back in Dodge, bruised and considerably wiser, to face the taunts of the saloon crowd.[9]

It was fortunate that Gryden did have a sense of humor, for he frequently was to be the target of other people's barbs and the butt of other pranksters' jokes. Many comments were made in the press about his stylish dress and "sartorial splendor," emphasizing his penchant for hats. When the town sent him off to a big-city convention in Topeka, Klaine observed that, with his new white necktie and derby, Gryden would "make a creditable showing." The *Ford County Globe* advised him to take a big, heavy bag so that the hotel management wouldn't throw him out as a hick lawyer from "coyote country." On another occasion, Nick Klaine noted in the *Times* that Harry had attended the Sunday evening prayer meeting at the Presbyterian Church and had sat in the front pew, a unique event worthy of journalistic note. "Gryden's hair stood on its end when the melodious air of the choir rang out 'Come ye sinner, poor and needed'—and Gryden's heart rose and almost choked the thoughts within him." A number of the jibes that appeared in the papers were in jokes now long past the remembering, but Klaine's question "Who's afraid of Gryden? You tam dogs; all you tam dogs" must have brought to mind some embarrassing incident.[10]

Gryden's sense of humor was also useful to him as an attorney. During the early days, the cases he was given to defend were generally indefensible. His victories then were rare. Furthermore, the type of situations he defended were often more humorous than tragic. In defending one combatant arrested for fighting over a laundry bill, Harry's only defense was a straight-faced admonishment to the judge that the case ought to be thrown out because "wash bills should never be brought to the 'bar' for collection." If there was a pickpocket to defend, Gryden drew the chore: vagabonds, con artists, and drunks sought Harry's help and legal guidance. One of his cases inspired Joseph G. ("Joe") Waters of Topeka to put the affair to rhyme:

> *"The State vs. Jesus Perea," the court now calls;*
> *"I appear for Jesus," Gryden bawls;*
> *"His last name you will please to state,*
> *Or Harry, I will fine you, sure as fate."*
> *"Perea," says Gryden, so low the court could hardly hear,*
> *"He is the man for whom I appear;"*
> *Says the court, sotto voce, "When the savior employs such as him,*
> *Our chances for heaven are getting quite slim."*[11]

In most instances, the judges took even the frivolous cases seriously; the press, however, tended to play them for laughs and to get even with Gryden for past embarrassments. Klaine used such reporting opportunities on a number of occasions. In one instance, Gryden tried to keep an inebriated client, perhaps his drinking partner for the evening, out of jail. Klaine caught the mood of the law at its least serious level and provided good copy for his faithful readers:

The prisoner, Mr. James Dalton, had been arrested by a police officer and brought before Police Judge Frost for trial at the 4 o'clock session of his court, but the Judge gave it as his opinion that Mr. Dalton was not sufficiently sober to be heard in open court, and ordered him taken back to the calaboose, there to remain overnight, unless bail came to his relief. Bail failed to come, but Mr. Gryden, with deep feelings of compassion at the idea of Dalton's having to spend the night in such an uncanny place as the calaboose, consented to take the matter before the Probate Judge without promise of reward in either gold or scrip. A writ of habeas corpus was issued, and the case set for hearing at 9 o'clock in the evening. The Judge and Sheriffs and Marshals and witnesses and policemen and learned counsel, and "the prisoner at the bar," all assembled at the appointed hour, and from the air of importance and dignity that prevailed, a stranger might have thought something of rare occurrence had happened. But all these machinery wheels of justice had been set in motion because a police court prisoner wanted to avoid the horrors of twelve hours in the calaboose.

The Judge took his seat, and the witnesses laid themselves down to sleep, while the attorneys, Mr. Gryden for the prisoner and Mr. Colborn for the City, opened their batteries, and let language fly in every direction. It was a novel spectacle. The poorly trimmed lamps shed a ghost-like flicker over the room, and the silvery notes of the law expounders ceased not for a moment. Never in Ford county has two limbs of Blackstone talked more over a case of such small importance, or more properly speaking, where fees of such pecuniary smallness were involved. It was near the middle of the night when silence reigned once more and Judge Fringer was enabled to get his work in. He ordered the prisoner sent to the dog house. [12]

Later, when the jibes became less friendly, Klaine's humor took on a cruel edge. In 1882, Gryden apparently became discouraged with his lack of progress in Dodge City. With considerable fanfare he let it be known he was leaving, hoping to find Colorado more congenial. In December 1881, his law office had been attached for a forty-dollar debt. He was in sad shape financially, with ground rent of two hundred dollars past due and a mortgage of fifty dollars on his office, which was estimated to be worth only seventy-five. The *Times* observed that "to meet all these claims will leave Mr. Gryden without visible means of support." When Harry left, Klaine noted his desertion with jibes and poetry:

> *Deal gently with thy brother man;*
> *Still gentler, sister woman.*
> *Though they may gang a kennen wrong,*
> *To step aside is human.*
> *One thing must still be greatly dark,*
> *The moving why they do it;*
> *And just as lamely can ye mark*
> *How far perhaps they rue it.*

Rue it he did. The *Times* kept track of his progress and reported him stranded in Pueblo "on the rock of impecuniosity." Harry did not find wealth or position in Colorado, and within a month he was back to face the hazing of his friends and the press. His only explanation was that the "altitude was too high." As a good sport, he was open to good-natured ribbing almost to his last breath. A progress report on his condition during his final illness noted that he was "able to sit up, eats somewhat, and swears quite naturally in four different languages." [13]

Cases involving women fighting or prostitutes in any embarrassing or chastening situation were described in derisive tones by the
local papers. Since Gryden was a favored counselor of Dodge's
prostitutes and its black community, he was often included in what
was intended to be humorous reporting:

The office of City Attorney was thrown into extatic convulsions at precisely 4:30 P.M., Monday, by the appearance of Fannie. (Fannie is a
beauty, and the color of a Colorado Claro, as found at Beatty & Kelly's.)
She complained of one James Cowan (Maduro color) and on the case being
tried Mr. Gryden developed the following facts: That Fanny was peace-
fully ironing at the residence of Mrs. Curly, when James entered (three-
sheets-in-the-wind drunk) called Fannie a soldier b——, throwed her on
the floor, elevated her paraphernalia, spanked her, and finally busted her a
left hander in the right eye, accompanying the same with a kick in the
stomache. The City Attorney went to the court and for the defendant,
touched up the Louisiana and South Carolina questions, and closed by
flinging the star spangled banner over the contraband female, sending the
defendant to the regions of the unjust—$5 and costs.

Klaine's well-documented bigotry, which on one occasion provoked
a "colored delegation" to call on him demanding a retraction, did
not reflect the full or only sentiments of the community. The col-
lective attitude of cowtown Dodge toward blacks was far more am-
bivalent, being a mixture of respect for the economic contributions
of the black cowboys as well as the traditional stereotyping that
permeated American prejudices.[14]

Black prostitutes held a place of special contempt. Soiled doves
of any color or race were considered both disgusting and intriguing
creatures who paid for their pathetic and exotic lives with social
ostracism and public ridicule. That violence was part of the penalty
for living beyond accepted behavior was understood. Beatings, especially by those within their own caste, were frequently treated
by the papers not only as sources of amusement but as one of the
normal consequences of an abnormal life. What was true for white
prostitutes was doubly true for their black sisters. Society, courts,
and the women themselves regarded violence as routine. Carrying
such matters to court was considered frivolous at best. Once in
court, an assault victim, such as Fannie, could not be ignored, but
the judge could support Klaine's perception by levying a small, triv-

ial fine on her attacker. Gryden's contribution helped maintain that "marginal spot" as citizen for one individual for that one limited occasion, while the court and press either directly or by inference presented the business of prostitution to the public as a loathsome community blight. The dynamics of the system, as long as there were lawyers like Gryden and editors like Klaine, would make for slow progress toward reform. In the words of Anne Butler: "The convergence of . . . many forces served to enlarge the legal system and to stabilize western social order. In no small measure frontier prostitutes [and, it could be added, the lawyers who defended them] assisted in this process. The mighty legal structure and the early frontier prostitutes? Strange bedfellows indeed."[15]

Gryden's clientele did not consist only of the misfits and outcasts. As was true of the other Dodge City lawyers, routine matters troubling the ordinary citizen filled most of Harry's working hours. In court most of his cases were civil in nature, usually dealing with small sums of money and garnering even smaller fees. As there was little specialization, except in real-estate matters, Gryden accepted any litigation offered him. In the January 1874 session of the district court, he was involved in eighteen of the thirty-one civil suits, and in 1884 he was attorney of record in twenty of forty-one such suits.[16]

Typical civil actions were the Mix-Hoover case and the Sawyer divorce suit. In the latter, Gryden stood for the plaintiff, Mary Sawyer, and Kellogg, Sutton, and Colborn for Nathan D. Sawyer. The plaintiff charged extreme cruelty and gross neglect; the defense responded by claiming that Mary had proved her unfitness to be a wife and mother of their child by committing adultery with Harry Farwell and "diverse persons" at "diverse other times." Witnesses and depositions for both sides rebutted each other's claims. The plaintiff's position was considerably strengthened when testimony indicated that life in the Dodge City dugout was "little better than living outside." Gryden then presented an audit of property amounting to $6,000 held by Nathan Sawyer during the marriage but not revealed to Mary. This property included a comfortable stone house. Nathan was given sixty days to show why an alimony payment of $2,500 and a monthly payment of $30 should not be granted. It had been an unpleasant, name-calling affair with the kind

FOR THE DEFENSE: HARRY E. GRYDEN

of sleazy details the press usually found attractive. Neither paper carried the story because the criminal docket overshadowed it with more exciting cases featuring notorious horse thief Dutch Henry Borne; cattle-rustling hometown lawyer G. U. Holcomb; Thomas O'Haran, the man accused of killing of Deputy U.S. Marshal Harry T. McCarty; Henry Gould, alias Skunk Curley, charged with assault with intent to kill; and an assortment of less spectacular thieves and rustlers. A lawyer's reputation was built on the more sensational action; his bread and butter, however thinly spread, came from the routine legal chores and civil suits. Unfortunately, the aspiring attorney needed the criminal cases to attract attention and to lure clients to his office.[17]

Gryden had his share and more of the more publicized criminal cases. Frequently they brought him clients who placed him on "the wrong side," or at least on the less popular side, of the law. In the notorious killing of Ed Masterson, Gryden, aided by Dan Frost and William N. Morphy, defended the cowboys involved. Few shootings disturbed the community more than Marshal Masterson's assassination at the hands of drunken cowboys. Gryden was not present when Masterson was shot, being occupied across the tracks in George M. Hoover's saloon. "I saw him coming," Gryden later reported, "and in the darkness of the evening he seemed to be carrying a lighted cigar in his hand. I remarked to a friend that the cigar burned in a remarkably lively manner, but as the man [Ed Masterson] drew near we saw that the fire was not at the end of a cigar, but in the wadding of his coat. He fell dead at our feet." Gryden assumed the unpopular duty of defending the men charged as accessories. Considering the agitated state of the Dodge City folk, about all that could be done was to delay action until emotions calmed down. The inquest had produced no witnesses with sufficient evidence to hold the unwounded cowboys for complicity in the shooting. The major defendant, Alfred M. Walker, lay near death for some time. He died in June after suffering long enough for new matters to occupy the community's attention.[18]

Grievous wounds seemed to satisfy most people's desire for punishment. At least it held true when Fannie Keenan, alias Dora Hand, was killed by mistake. Dora had returned to Dodge to have Gryden file divorce papers against her estranged husband. Dora's

alleged slayer, James ("Spike") Kennedy, was hunted down by a
posse led by Bat Masterson and suffered a shattered arm in the
ambush Bat set for him. He languished in jail for some time, was
finally released for lack of evidence, and never quite recovered from
his wounds, dying from complications within two years. Apparently,
the community looked philosophically on such matters. They approved the results since the punishment represented faster and
more certain justice than the courts furnished.[19]

The spring of 1878 was a busy one for all Dodge City lawyers,
and Gryden was busier than most. In May he was called to Kinsley
to defend Dedrig White in the killing of Fred Seilig. Gryden made
"such a vigorous and well arranged defense" that the bail was set
low and trial delayed. Also that spring, for the second time within
the year, Bill Tilghman needed Gryden's services. Tilghman had
been a suspect in the abortive Kinsley train robbery in February,
and now, in April, he was arrested again by Bat Masterson on a
charge of horse stealing. In both instances, Gryden got the charges
dropped. He was not as successful with Henry Markling, who was
arrested on a similar charge, stood trial, and was convicted.
Gryden also took on "the town establishment" when two clients,
George B. Cox and Albert Boyd, sued Masterson, Wright, and
Mayor James H. ("Dog") Kelley for damages caused by prisoners
who they charged carelessly had been allowed to escape. Harry
outdueled Sutton in this instance and won an award of forty dollars
for the plaintiff.[20]

In general, 1879 was an equally troubled year and a busy one for
Harry: of forty-four cases in the January term of the district court,
Gryden was attorney of record in thirty-nine. It was also a good
year for Gryden's clients, although he began the season back on
the unpopular and losing side when he defended Arista H. Webb for
a brutal and senseless killing. Gryden's defense, innocent by reason of insanity, was no doubt correct, even if he was unable to con-
vince the jury. He and Colborn continued to follow the case and
eventually got Webb transferred to the Kansas Insane Asylum.
After additional testimony by doctors and friends in Virginia concerning his mental state, Webb was pardoned and returned to the
care of his family. Other cases that year saw Gryden defending
some of the West's most well-known gunmen.[21]

Frank Trask, who had been a popular policeman in Dodge, was charged with stealing two government mules. Gryden secured his release for lack of substantial evidence. Trask was rearrested immediately by state authorities, who believed his popularity had blinded the Dodge City jury. Eventually he was taken to Topeka to appear before the U.S. commissioner, where Gryden's previous questioning apparently had sufficiently tarnished the testimony of witnesses to cause Trask again to be discharged.[22]

Gryden's biggest case that season found him defending Dutch Henry Borne, one of the most talented and elusive horse thieves in the West. Borne had escaped the Dodge City jail, and Bat Masterson pursued him to Las Animas, Colorado, where he found him in custody and charged with another crime. After considerable sparring and a bold bluff, Bat gained custody of the prisoner and brought him back to Dodge City's jail. In the trial that followed, County Attorney Sutton excused himself from prosecution because of previous legal business with the prisoner. The stand-ins, T. S. Jones and E. F. Colborn, were no match for Gryden. He used his knowledge of the jurors to exhaust the list of grangers and ranchers on the jury panel in settling a peripheral question. A second trial by "a special venire empaneled to judge guilt or innocence of the prisoner" was far more sympathetic to Gryden's pleadings. It must be noted, however, that Dutch Henry was his own best mouthpiece. An imposing, genteel-appearing man, Gryden led his client into telling a brave tale of his life, which moved the *Ford County Globe* to characterize him as the "Rob Roy of the Plains." To the surprise and consternation of nearly everyone, including the judge, Borne was found not guilty. The victory added to Gryden's reputation as a clever attorney, but it could not have won him many free drinks from his cattlemen cronies.[23]

A few years later, he was to defend successfully another unpopular cattle thief, William M. Bird. His legal maneuvering in the Bird case again led to criticism. The *Dodge City Ford County Globe* concluded that "the action of the attorney in the case looks a little cloudy." The Western Kansas Cattle Growers' Association had invested considerable money in capturing and prosecuting Bird in the hope of making an example of him. Its members' disappointed reaction to the verdict was far more bitter than the *Globe*'s. To add to their chagrin, Bird sued the association for false arrest. The association decided that if it could not beat Gryden, it had better join him, so Gryden was employed as its official attorney. On learning of the appointment, Frost predicted that "no more guilty cow thieves will escape the penitentiary." Although somewhat overoptimistic, the arrangement did work well. [24]

Gryden's record as an attorney was spotted with both victories and defeats. His record was better when he was prosecutor, but even then his most publicized cases, the Nixon-Mather and Holcomb killings, saw him unable to convict. Unfortunately for him, he faced Sutton, a superb craftsman, in many instances; adding to his handicap, Gryden willingly took cases he had little chance of winning. The rivalry between Sutton and Gryden was very real. The fiery Irishman was involved in more than one scuffle outside the courtroom, but the closest Sutton came to losing his professional decorum before a judge occurred when he was provoked by Harry. In a minor suit in Judge Frost's police court, Gryden accused Sutton's client of not paying his honest debts. Since it was a matter unrelated to the case, Sutton interrupted Gryden to ask Frost to strike the statement. According to the *Times,* before the judge could reply, "Gryden broke loose again, saying with great emphasis, 'I repeat it. They would swear to any ——.' 'Mr. Gryden, you are a liar,' broke in Sutton, as he bent forward from his position and leered at his opponent. 'You're another, and you would swear to any ——,' but that sentence was never finished." The two men exchanged blows and had to be restrained by one of the participating attorneys and Special Policeman Bat Masterson, with the judge threatening contempt citations for both combatants. For genial Harry to arouse professionally cool Mike reflected a deep-seated animosity that went beyond courtroom bickering and was to take its most bitter form in the political arena. [25]

Gryden can be judged to have been a good frontier lawyer. Even his most bitter critic, Deacon Klaine, granted him that. On occasion he prepared extensive, well-disciplined petitions, briefs, and summaries. He was knowledgeable in the law and thoroughly attuned to the passions of the community. Unfortunately, he tended to rely on his considerable oratorical skills too heavily and, in the face of Sutton's knowledge of the law and his clever marshaling of facts, was likely not to carry the day.

Gryden's oratorical powers were not always a liability. His reputation as a speaker carried over into the social and cultural life of the community, making him a frequent patriotic speaker on the Fourth of July and keynoter and promoter for political conventions. On one occasion he even found himself in the uncharacteristic posture of being a fund raiser for a preacher. In an "Evening Musicale" dedicated to supplying a salary for Ormond W. Wright, pastor of nondenominational Union Church, Gryden presented a number of "readings." His recitation of "Wounded, that famous dying dialogue of the battle-scarred soldier . . . [left] the audience listening in breathless silence." Harry enjoyed being on center stage. In one of its lighter moments, the *Times* paid extravagant tribute to his oratorical style:

Mr. Gryden succeeded in getting command of the situation. As is his style whenever he has the judge's attention, he began to spread himself. The fierce tone of his voice rent the air causing little children on the street to run and scream with terror, and frisky longhorns miles away to sniff the air, curl their tails toward the clouds, and then scatter as when a storm strikes them. Kelley's dogs sought shelter under the sidewalks. The festive gambler, thinking the great Gabriel had come, bet his last chip and cared not whether it won or lost. At last, the power of the speaker's fury came down upon frail mankind, and he gave vent to bitter insinuations.

Obviously, Gryden was enjoying putting on a show before a police judge in a civil suit that the reporter considered so unimportant that he forgot the cause of debate.[26]

Harry wrote free-lance copy for a number of newspapers, both in Dodge and elsewhere. Most of his pieces did not carry a byline, so the extent of his writing is impossible to determine. His journalistic style was nearly as colorful as his speech. The following passage, taken from the *Ford County Globe* of December 2, 1880, indicates something of his approach and talent:

### A Hunt in the Pan-Handle

We had been asked on an average of 57 times a day if we knew who Hancock was, and had reduced ourselves to a skeleton weeping and wailing with [W. F.] Petillon, Jones and Swan over the degeneracy of Ford county democracy, when (there being no guardian angel to whisper a "no" in our ear), we snapped with avidity at an invitation to join Sheriff [George T.] Hinkle and Mr. Geo. Anderson in a two weeks hunt at the latter's ranch in the Pan Handle of Texas. It was a lovely Monday morning, when

perched on the bacon and buffalo robes, with the little brown jugs (2 gals.)
in the most secure place, we bid a long (16 days) farewell to the scenes of
our childhood, to hot stoves, buckwheat cakes, cocktails, and lager beer.
The teams provided by Col. James Anderson were of the pure Arabian
blood, and, in the language of James, "All you got to do is to hold on to
the ribbons, you'll be there before you know it." We made 41 miles to
[George W.] Hoodoo Brown's by 5 p.m. Brown's is the commercial metropolis of Meade county, its inhabitants consisting of Mr. and Mrs. B., a
crazy Dutchman and a hobbled bull calf. We here fried our bacon, pitched
our tent, turned in at 7 p.m., and slept the sleep of innocence until
2 o'clock, when "the beautiful snow" gathering too muchly on the High
Sheriff's skating rink, compelled him to evacuate. A half hour later, there
being but three pins holding the tent, and the wind and snow increasing,
yours truly became discouraged, and fled to the unfinished adobe in which
Hinkle was trying to walk 300 consecutive miles in 300 consecutive
minutes to keep warm. We joined him in this invigorating exercise, and
had ample time to ruminate on the wisdom and cussedness of Bob Inger-
soll's god—Nature—which let loose the snow and wind, but tied the kin-
dling wood furnished by the longhorn of Texas beyond the power of our
long fingers, lovingly to mother earth. At 7 a.m. we were joined by
George, who had, a la Grant, fought it out on that line, tent or no tent.
Tuesday we were mainly occupied in concocting choice biblical quotations
applicable to the weather—Mr. Anderson having had superior advantages
in bible matters while occupying the position of U.S. wagon master, had
considerable the best of the contest. We occupied comfortable quarters
the following night in the chicken house, the only inconvenience being experienced by Mr. H., on whose cranium a black Poland hen insisted on
roosting. Wednesday morning, with fresh courage and a close inspection
of the little brown jug, we sallied out for Beaver Creek Ranch, 35 miles
through the snow drifts. There were no incidents except the tumbling of
Mr. A. into Beaver creek while crossing, and then sweet Hellen Blazes
how we froze. At Beaver the fiery Arabian was completely played out, and
we exchanged him for a fine looking sorrel, whose half circle S denoted
him once the property of Mr. [R. J. ("Jack")] Hardesty.

The sufferings of the following days we fear would prove too much for
this edition, hence we will continue in our next.                    G. [27]

No doubt Gryden's least characteristic role in Dodge City was in
serving as assistant superintendent of public instruction. His financial plight apparently had reached a desperate state in 1877, and for
three years the county paid his salary as he struggled to upgrade
the county school system. He organized new districts (Offerle and
Spearville were established under his leadership), visited schools,

gave teacher's examinations, and spoke at school functions. The job kept beer on his table and a roof over his head. Besides, he still had his private practice and his jobs as city attorney and clerk of the town council.[28]

Of his part-time jobs, that of city attorney was the most important, providing him with opportunities for many useful services. Among other duties, he drew up the first ordinance providing Dodge with legal scrip. The cash flow in a town dependent on seasonal trail-herd trade and end-of-the-year tax assessments was such that employees could not always be paid or goods purchased at other times of the year. As a stopgap measure, Gryden drafted an ordinance with provisions for issuing scrip to keep the local government functioning while the council attempted to solve the basic issue of insufficient revenue. Dodge City merchants accepted the scrip, usually at only a slight reduction from face value, to be redeemed when tax collections replenished the city's coffers. Gryden also worked out a compromise with the city's general merchants, the most powerful group in town, to provide a fifteen-dollar annual license tax. As in other compromises, not everyone was happy, but the tax, eventually levied on all business concerns, became an important and steady source of revenue. By 1886, thirty-two categories of businesses, including ice dealers, stationers, attorneys, and livery operators, paid a license fee each year and the general merchants' tax, which yielded the largest return, had risen to forty dollars.[29]

Although struggling to make ends meet, Gryden continued to scrape together bits and pieces of odd jobs, mostly legally oriented, until the Luke Short affair alienated him from the in-office politicians. After that episode, he lost his public offices and his lifestyle financed by his private practice alone would have suffered considerably had he not been able to replace the lost positions with an appointment as legal counsel for the Western Kansas Cattle Growers' Association. Still, at the time of his death, the *Kansas Cowboy* noted that he was "in moderate circumstances," able to leave only a few hundred dollars to be distributed between his two children.[30]

For Gryden, life's greatest rewards did not require a fat salary. With no family obligations, he needed only enough income to sus-

tain him while he indulged his true passion: politics. He seems to
have edged into the political arena by the back door, finding it difficult to commit himself totally to any of the contending cliques. The
initial political factions in Dodge City were just that: combinations
of individuals or cliques of contentious self-interest. None of the
groups was motivated by goals other than gaining office. The outs
opposed the ins, and the ins opposed the outs. Robert Wright,
merchant, and James H. ("Dog") Kelley, saloonkeeper, headed the
earliest recognizable political contingent, which came to be called
the Gang. When opposition arose, it did so casually and without
identifying marks. The Gang liked its label and kept it; the opposition never was given a name—at least a printable one. Neither the
Gang nor the opposition developed the slightest resemblance to an
organization. Since all nominating meetings were open, it was always difficult to tell exactly who belonged to which group. It was
clear to all, however, that Dan Frost of the *Ford County Globe,*
through his antagonism to the Gang, was the spokesman for (if not
creator of) the first opposition faction. Because of Frost's stand,
his rival editor, Nick Klaine of the *Times,* was forced into a position
of support for the Gang if he was not to become merely a journalistic echo. Mike Sutton, new in town and hungry, saw little future in casting his talents with the outs and consequently became
the Gang's legal counselor and the confidant of its leadership.
Gryden was slow in choosing sides, since he was friendly with the
individual members of the Gang and their opponents, but finding
himself in much the same position as Klaine, there was little choice
but to join the faction that did not have an attorney as a member.

The early elections went to the Gang by default. Its domination
seemed uncontested when Dog Kelley was elected mayor in 1877.
For the next three elections, his was an easy win. But as in all political machines, no matter how small the arena, internal friction
developed. In Dodge the first trouble came in the form of personal
quarrels between Mayor Kelley and Marshal Lawrence E. ("Larry")
Deger. Kelley and his pack of dogs came to Dodge in 1872, where
the former freighter established a saloon, restaurant, and eventually an opera house. Deger, also an old freighter who had been
with Custer's wagon train, was an impressive figure weighing in at
three hundred pounds. Deger and Kelley shared the common back-

ground and attitudes of the other Gang members and all had similar philosophical positions. The quarrel that grew between Deger and Kelley was strictly personal but by no means private. In the open "People's Mass Meeting" of November 1877, held in the Lady Gay, the Kelley supporters proposed to dump Deger by nominating the popular Bat Masterson for sheriff in place of Kelley. Sutton seconded the nomination. Since Sutton had taken his stand, Gryden had no choice but to do likewise for the opposition, and backed Deger. As was usually the case in clashes between Sutton and Gryden, Sutton's side won.[31]

Members of the Frost faction realized that they could not successfully contest the Gang's dominance until they found a new constituency. Thinking to broaden the faction's base, they turned to the county elections and found a new contingent of voters in the incoming German homesteaders. Meeting in the Spearville schoolhouse in October 1878, Gryden opened the caucus with a major address. Only a paraphrase of the speech exists, but it clearly reveals a call for the new homesteaders to join in opposing the town-based Gang. "The time had been," Gryden reminded the meeting, "when Dodge City [had not] considered Ford county a part and portion of the city, but . . . some of the citizens [have] 'tumbled' to the fact that there were people outside of its sacred walks whose opinions in choosing our county offices should be consulted." The "People's Ticket" was approved, featuring Frost for county attorney and Richard W. Evans, owner of a general store, for state representative, but the rest of the slate was filled with non-Dodge residents. Gryden became chairman of the campaign committee, taking over the task of defeating the establishment.[32]

The Gang members took the new threat seriously. They established the "Independent Ticket" in opposition, called on their most respected member, Robert Wright, to oppose Evans, and they, too, made overtures to the rural voters. In spite of Gryden's initiative and effort, the Gang won handily at the polls. Gryden as the farmer's friend was out of his element. Lifestyle, friendships, and conviction ought to have placed him on the Gang's side; only chance and Sutton's role kept him in opposition. There would be change, but not until Sutton came to feel uncomfortable with the Gang's convictions. When Sutton changed affiliations, Gryden quickly and happily moved into the Gang's camp, but only after Sutton had made clear his new position. But for the moment, in 1878, the Gang without Gryden's affiliation seemed securely in power.

Frost kept up a barrage of abuse in his newspaper, directing it mainly at Sheriff Masterson, whom he believed to be the weakest link in the Gang's personnel. When Sutton failed to convict the Cheyenne leaders after Dull Knife's Raid and when other prisoners in Masterson's custody awaiting trial escaped while Bat was busy with the Indians, Frost poured on the abuse. Bat's temper got the better of him and he reacted in his typical blunt and direct style. The result was that Frost had more stories about Bat's high-handed and unprofessional conduct to fill his paper. As the November 1879 election approached, rumors on Front Street were added to Frost's tales, rumors of fraud and careless handling of money. His political advisers, Sutton and Klaine, encouraged Bat to ignore the gossip, but when the votes were in, Bat failed to be reelected. He blamed his defeat on bad advice from the Gang's leaders and never forgave them. It was the beginning of the realignment of factional affiliation.[33]

Other forces also were affecting political loyalties, not the least of which was the influence of national parties on city and county elections. The *Times,* under Klaine's editorship, was still staunchly pro-Gang but was even more ardently Republican. Sutton supported Klaine and the GOP; Gryden, who came to Dodge as a southern Democrat, was happy to extend his personal and professional rivalries with Sutton through party action. In August 1878, Gryden was elected delegate to the Democratic state convention in Topeka, and as secretary of the Ford County central committee he was named delegate to the district senatorial convention. In September he attended the Democratic convention in Leavenworth, and in October he was one of the major speakers for the fifteen hundred delegates assembled in Wichita's Eagle Hall. He was by far the most active Democrat in Dodge City; unfortunately, he was to pay a price for his role. As his political importance increased, he was gradually stripped of his part-time political-patronage jobs. In the elections of 1879 and 1880, he lost both the county attorney and police judge contests.[34]

As the national party organization grew in effectiveness, the local elections became increasingly bitter, and for the first time issues as well as personalities figured in the voters' decisions. It was also clear by 1879 that Sutton, Klaine, and the Republicans were looking to a future less dependent on Texas cattle interests and cattle-town ways. If they gained control of local offices, the nature of Dodge's social and economic life would be changed drastically. The Frost faction had a hard time dealing with this development. Not being able to embrace the Democrats, the members remained champions of the status quo, strongly supporting the established cattle interests while remaining in the Republican party. The Klaine-Frost feud was to remain an intraparty affair. Those individuals left in the Gang continued opposition to Sutton and Klaine and came to feel more comfortable in the Democratic fold, even when they did not agree with all of the national issues. With both leading editors in the Republican ranks, part of the early problem of Democratic organizations was that they did not find an editorial spokesman of the caliber of Klaine or Frost until the *Dodge City Democrat* was established in 1884 (actually, the first issue was dated December 29, 1883) and W. F. Petillon became its partisan editor.

It took several years to solidify the two-party alignment, but each election saw the pattern become clearer. Meanwhile, the local picture was briefly complicated by the appearance of strong third parties. By 1880, the major national party organizations were in almost as much disarray as the local ones in Dodge City. "Half-Breeds" belabored "Stalwarts" in the Grand Old Party, and the Democrats chose as their presidential candidate an authentic war hero, Winfield S. Hancock, who promptly announced that he favored sound money and a protective tariff. The Greenback party reaped enough reaction from this conservative and traditional Republican stand to poll 308,000 votes in the 1880 presidential election.

In Dodge City, Gryden was persuaded to call a Greenback and/or Independent party convention and to serve as its temporary chairman. The Greenbacks, seeking the grass roots of debtor states such as Kansas, had designated Ford County as an area to be cultivated and appeared willing to consider cooperating with the Independents. Gryden and others saw this as a highly disruptive development that would split the Democratic vote. He chose to try to persuade the soft-money advocates and the Democrats to join forces. As a result, he played a significant if frustrating role in the initial Greenback convention. The hard-line opponents in the Republican party, especially Frost, saw this new coalition of Greenbacks and Democrats as a serious threat and pummeled Gryden and the convention in the press. Gryden "was aspiring to be a Chieftain," Frost wrote, confusing the issues in an attempt to persuade Greenbacks and Democrats to compromise on delegates to the state convention. At one point, Frost observed, "the great mass convention appeared about to lose its grip and sink into apathy, but Mr. Gryden, the ex-sachem of Democracy of Ford county, came to the rescue with a resolution that all candidates nominated by the convention be required to pledge their support to [the Democratic candidates] Hancock and English." Harry was unable to carry the convention, but what he did bring about had much the same desired results. The Greenbacks ended their meeting by nominating a short ticket, endorsing only a few individuals, and leaving the voting, both national and local, to individual conscience. The Republicans won nationally and overwhelmingly in the local contests that followed. Obviously, what Harry attempted to do was to keep the faint-hearted Democrats from deserting a national candidate who looked and sounded like a Republican. Greenbackers nationally had leaned more to Democrats than Republicans, and Harry had tried to hold that affinity in Ford County. He failed and Republican domination of Dodge City and southwest Kansas was ensured. If political success is the measure of correctness, Harry had backed the wrong party.[35]

The 1881 local elections saw the end of the unchallenged rule of the Gang when Dog Kelley was beaten. Nick Klaine's campaign to lift the town out of its gaudy and violent ways was stepped up, and he became more specific in his editorials as to what needed to be done. The new mayor, Alonzo B. ("Ab") Webster, took a firm position against saloons, gambling, and prostitution by making life more difficult for them and by making certain the license fees were paid. More encouragement for reform arrived when a temperance society was organized and added its emotional demands to the growing opposition to the status quo. Reform sentiments seemed to become more popular with more Dodge Citians, and even Deacon (the new title awarded by the opposition to the reform-conscious editor) Klaine thought he could sense a change in the moral and social atmosphere of the place. Bill Jones, that teller of tall tales, reported that the town was going "soft and cozy." Said he: "Dodge is sure becoming civilized. . . . You boys can believe me or not, but here was Mike Sutton, D. M. Frost, Nick Klaine and Bobby Gill pitching horse-shoes for the soda."[36]

But the town was not so tame that shots were not exchanged occasionally on Front Street, and the saloons continued to flourish. The differences in opinion of how wide open or how civilized Dodge should be were rapidly dividing the town into irreconcilable factions. The clash of philosophies was symbolized in people's reaction to the return of Bat Masterson, who had left town in a huff after his political defeat. A distress signal had called him back to protect his brother Jim's interest. He landed in town on April 16, 1881, looking for trouble and found it before he could leave the train tracks. Al Updegraff, who may or may not have been waiting for Bat, came face to face with him shortly after Bat stepped down from the train. Who fired the first shot was never determined, but during the melee that followed, Updegraff was dropped with a bullet in the lung. Bat was arrested and paid a fine of eight dollars. To many it seemed Dodge had not advanced much beyond the old and wicked days; others felt that Updegraff had gone looking for trouble and got what he deserved. Both Klaine and Frost criticized Bat for his reckless behavior and berated the court for putting a value of eight dollars on a man's lung. As usual, Gryden stuck with his old friends and said Bat should not have been fined even eight dollars for acting in self-defense.[37]

In June, Klaine printed a letter reported to have been sent to Bat by Gryden:

Dear Bat: I am sitting in Kelley's; we have just took a drink, and Jim says to drop you a word—the damn town has been torn up over the telegram of your coming. Webster telegraphed to Sargent and the shot gun brigade was up all night. They consisted of Webster, Singer, Bill Miller, Deger, Tom Bugg, Boyd, Emerson, Bud Driskill, Hi Collar, Peacock, Updegraff and others. Nate Hudson refused to support them. Kelley and myself will be up one of these days to see you. I have an annual [rail-

road pass] and have written a pass for Kelley. Don't give away what I tell
you Bat; it is damn hard for me now to stay here, because I have pronounced myself in your favor; so has Kelley and Phillips, Mose Barber,
Dave Morrow and several others. You ought to hear Old Dave ROAR.
Charley Powell is here, the same good fellow as of old. Kelley is looking over my shoulder and says "tell him Sutton is at the bottom of it all,
damn him."

> Yours as ever,
> H. E. Gryden

The message, whether Harry's or not, was clear: antagonisms
were beginning to solidify into identifiable factions; names were
named, with issues as well as personalities in contention.[38]

Dodge's new mayor, A. B. Webster, earned a quick reputation
as a fighting mayor who would not tolerate gunplay or other violent
behavior. The result was that the year 1882 was one of the quietest
on Dodge City's record. The trail herds, however, were still coming in and business in the saloons and joints was steady. Vice, as
the folks back east knew it, flourished.

The election of 1883 showed how far the reformers had come. In
March the usual mass meeting had picked W. H. Harris, part
owner of the Long Branch, as its mayoral candidate. He was supported by the remnants of the old Gang and the *Ford County Globe*.
If elected, his administration would have been business as usual,
catering to the cattle trade and the sporting ways of cowboys and
gamblers. An opposition slate was put together by another group
of citizens with Larry Deger as its candidate for mayor and a number of prominent businessmen, including Robert Wright, Ham Bell,
H. M. Beverley, George S. Emerson, and Henry Sturm, running
for the council positions. This ticket was vociferously and intem-
perately supported by Nick Klaine and the *Dodge City Times*. It
was a reform ticket, so much so that the early contender for the
mayor's spot, Ab Webster, withdrew because he was associated
with the liquor business and it was felt that this was an inappropri-
ate credential. Deger and crew won the election by a comfortable
margin and immediately pushed reform measures through the city
council. It was the spark that ignited the comic-opera affair known
as the Dodge City Saloon War.[39]

As was true of almost everyone in Dodge, Gryden was caught in the Saloon War in a way that altered forever his friendships and professional life. Few men, Robert Wright being an exception, could remain in amicable contact with representatives of both factions. Events of that episode not only heightened personal animosities but did much to destroy the old cattle-town Dodge that Gryden had known.

The issues in the conflict were far greater than saloon rivalries, being in fact compounded of past political animosities, economic conflicts, differences in attitudes as to what constituted proper moral standards and social life for the community, and disparate visions of the future. At the beginning of the affair, Dodge was still dominated by the Texas cattle trade and was catering to the needs and pleasures of free-spirited cowboys. At war's end, it was a railroad town seeking a broader but more localized economic base to accommodate a settled community of families. Harry Gryden stood firm with the older conceptions—with the Dodge City he had helped to create and had enjoyed to the fullest.

The overtones of change were well under way when Luke Short entered the picture. The Texas ticks; the granger fences; the increased city population, including women and children; the flaws in open-range ranching; and the hardening political rivalries already had threatened the town's frontier cattle-town dominance. In supporting a dying past, Gryden was once again on the losing side, and the political faction he supported moved deeper and deeper into the settled position of opposition and the status of the outs.

Luke Short picked this time, February 1883, to attempt to escalate Dodge's high life for the coming cattle season. Chalkley M. ("Chalk") Beeson sold Short his half of the Long Branch, and the partners—the recently defeated mayoral candidate, W. H. Harris, owned the other half—installed a new piano player with obvious feminine charms, plus a number of new "lady entertainers." Meanwhile, encouraged by community support, the city council passed additional reform measures against drunkenness, prostitution, and gambling. The Long Branch was singled out for enforcement of these new ordinances. As representatives of the old-time Texas cattle interests, Luke and Beeson would have been obvious targets even if they had not been political and business rivals of some members of the council. The blend of personal, economic, and social animosities reached an explosive point when Luke learned that his "singers" had been arrested as prostitutes and that entertainers in other saloons had not. He resisted in the time-honored Dodge City fashion: with guns. The reformers, believing they had community support, decided it was time for a showdown. Short was arrested, jailed, bonded, and eventually hustled out of town.[40]

While in jail, Luke had tried to make contact with Gryden to ask him to serve as his attorney. Responding to his call, Gryden "attempted to interview [Luke] through the grating, but was driven off by an armed policeman, and notified that he could not see him, and was further informed by the mayor and Webster that he must leave the street or the top of his head would be blown off." Luke's partner then wired Nelson Adams to come to help, but the Larned lawyer was met at the depot by an informal posse and was not allowed to get off the train.[41]

By this time the world was aware of the Dodge City War, which featured Bat and a number of old gunmen cronies determined to secure with six-guns what had been denied Luke by civil authorities. Dodge's image as a lawless town was back in the headlines. What began as an effort to secure law and order had backfired. Gryden's sympathy was with Luke and Masterson, and he accompanied them to Topeka and Kansas City as they sought redress through state offices.

As negative publicity spread, both sides in the quarrel began backpedaling. In late summer, Gryden drew up a resolution, approved by a mass meeting at "Kelley's Hall," and presented it to the mayor, urging a return to law and order. But by then state officials had become thoroughly alarmed because the waywardness of Dodge City was being spread with alarming exaggeration throughout the nation on the front pages of newspapers. Governor George W. Glick thought things had gotten completely out of hand and alerted two companies of the state militia to be prepared to move to Dodge. For immediate emergencies, he decided that a militia unit in Dodge, composed of local citizens who could act promptly, was essential. He directed Gryden, the town's leading Democrat, to form the company. Gryden wired back:

Company has been organized and mustered by me. There are forty-two men. [H]ave seen sheriff & R. M. Wright, both say they have not a gun in their possession belonging to the state and do not know what has become of them. It is evident that they are being held out. I apprehend things have been grossly misrepresented to you. I know they are distributed over the City.

H. Gryden

The governor immediately furnished the necessary accoutrements and guns.[42]

Glick's Guards, under the command of Major Harry Gryden, was never required to suppress violence, since none developed, but the special state militia unit was kept as a permanent "independent cavalry company" just in case something did happen. At full strength, it consisted of fifty men with Gryden in command and Pat Sughrue as captain, Peter Harding as first lieutenant, and Dog Kelley as second lieutenant. The men furnished their own horses. Glick's Guards was the first cavalry unit of the militia organized in the state.[43]

As was true of most Dodge Citians, Gryden was disturbed by the state's intervention and the bad publicity. Since he was now acting under the direction of Adjutant General Thomas Moonlight, he tried to calm the fears of Topeka authorities by wiring Moonlight: "Everything here settled. Parties shook hands across the bloody chasm. A number of men with records are here but all is lovely." The governor, however, had received a number of reports to the contrary indicating that the town was overrun by desperadoes who were drifting in from all over the West. He ordered the adjutant general to catch the next train to Dodge and find out at first hand what the situation was. Moonlight wired his reply to Gryden's calm assurance with a message that must have made Harry think his telegram had been lost in transit: "Keep the peace at all hazards—will be in Dodge tonight—meet me." After an uneventful twenty-four-hour visit, Moonlight's inspection seemed to verify Gryden's assessment and he returned to Topeka. Peace, if not tranquility, settled over the town.[44]

When Luke and Bat eventually retreated to Fort Worth, Texas, it was a symbolic move: the Texas cattle interest had returned home, leaving the reform-minded businessmen in charge of Front Street. In September, all businesses were required to close on Sunday. Klaine gloated in the *Times:* "The last relic of the frontier has given up the ghost." It took several more years to tame the town, but the bloodless Dodge City Saloon War was a major factor in attracting settled business interests to replace the gunmen, cowboys, and prostitutes of the earlier and more exciting cowtown. The Dodge City that was dominated by the cattle trade was to become a lively memory, but, nonetheless, only a memory.[45]

It was also a symbolic turning point for Gryden. His effort to bring calm to the troubled town was to be his last official contribution. He continued his routine as attorney for the city and the Western Kansas Stock Growers' Association and as a member of the volunteer fire department and Glick's Guards, but during the winter he became ill and remained incapacitated until his death on August 29, 1884. The diagnosis of his illness depended on one's political persuasion. His bitter enemy, Klaine, had no doubt that it was "his dissolute habits," meaning drink. Frost's diagnosis was more honorable, death being attributed to "softening of the brain and hemorrhage." The *Kansas Cowboy* found an even more sympathetic and socially acceptable cause: "His disease was consumption." Whatever the cause, death came slowly and painfully. Klaine even found it in his heart to report, while Harry was still alive, that Gryden was "dying with the cold charity of the world around him." More friendly folk found his circumstances less cruel. He had been moved to the county poorhouse for the last few days, where "he died in the hands of his friends, with all the kind ministrations and attention which true hands and loving hearts could give."[46] The funeral was all that Harry could have expected:

His remains were followed to the Dodge City cemetery by the members of the bar in a body, the city fire company, the city council, the Glick Guards, and the Post of the Grand Army. He was buried with military honors, the usual salute being fired over his grave. The pall bearers were selected from the different organizations of the city with which he was so long and prominently identified; to wit, from the Glick Guards, I. J. Collier, W. F. Petillion; from the Grand Army, M. Sughrue, E. Deinst; from the firemen, Fred Singer, R. E. Rice; from the Bar, J. T. Whitelaw, T. S. Jones.

The remains were taken to the City Hall, and remained in state during the portion of the day preceding the funeral rites, the City Hall being appropriately draped in mourning. From the City Hall they were followed to the Union Church and thence to the burial ground by one of the largest processions which ever fell in line in this place. The order of procession was as follows:

The Drum Corps.
The Glick Guards.
The hearse with the body.
The horse of the deceased, decorated in mourning, with the military accoutrements of his late rider.
Pallbearers.
Fireman's Organization.
Members of the Bar.
Officiating Ministers of the Gospel.
Mayor and City Council.
Citizens in carriages.

The Dead March was played on the way to the last resting place. At the Union Church very appropriate and touching ceremonies occurred, Rev. Mr. [N. G.] Collins officiating, assisted by Rev. Mr. Elliott. Their discourses were admirably delivered and the language chosen exceedingly appropriate to the circumstances of the deceased without kindred but with such marks of sorrow as to impress all with a deep sense of the solemnity of the occasion. At the grave, Rev. Mr. Collins again addressed the audience in a very sympathetic manner, alluding to his death among strangers without kindred, and yet with such marked evidences of esteem and emotion as was worthy of a true humanity. He thanked in a beautifully expressed language the different organizations who had taken the place of mourners to a citizen departed without kindred, and yet with hearts so impressed that a whole community become mourners.[47]

Memorials were published and Gryden's seven legal colleagues, including Mike Sutton, testified to their loss. "Seldom has death visited our city in which there was so general a manifestation of sorrow," was the *Kansas Cowboy*'s summation of the community's sentiments. During the following year, a fund for a monument was raised and a seven-foot shaft was erected. Of the many honors paid him, Harry undoubtedly would have appreciated most the action of the city council. After directing a committee to draw up an appropriate memorial, the council members moved to revoke a five-dollar fine standing against Harry Logue because Logue had volunteered his services as a musician for Gryden's funeral. That even in death he was responsible for having the judgment of the court set aside would have appealed to Harry's sense of irony and poetic justice.[48]

Gryden's passing, apparently mourned by all save Deacon Klaine, signaled the beginning of the decline of those who had gloried in the Beautiful, Bibulous Babylon of the Frontier. In his day he had defended murderers, cattle thieves, cattlemen, prostitutes, bunko artists, and drunks; his colleagues would have to look to a different clientele in the future. Harry had brought to his calling a charm and grace that removed some of the rough edges of frontier sin and violence. His humor brightened what would have been merely drab, boring, or sordid. Because he was an ineffectual politician, a sometimes brilliant lawyer, Harry's mark lay outside his professional life. In the hearts of old-time Dodge Citians, there was always to be a comfortable feeling for that "most genial and companionable fellow."

# 5. For the Prosecution: Michael W. Sutton

THE VICTOR in the Dodge City "real life morality play" starring Harry Gryden and Mike Sutton bore few early marks of distinction. Sutton was typical of those rootless sons of poverty who came west seeking opportunity and stayed to build a community. His ancestors left Ireland believing they could improve their lives in a new land; once uprooted, they were never content with their latest home, wherever that home might be. Mike's parents first settled in one of the seaboard states but slowly moved west, never remaining long in any one settlement. The Suttons both died young, living long enough, however, to pass on to their son their discontent and their dreams of a better life. Mike, in turn, became a part of the post–Civil War flood of migrants who believed there was abundant opportunity in the West, or at least the promise of stable and improved livelihood. He came to Kansas with no material wealth and no status. Possessing a sharp, orderly mind, a strong work ethic, reasonable ambition, and a license to practice law, he found Dodge City a likely place for advancement. He was to be rewarded by his fellow citizens with leadership roles and an active career. Unfortunately, he was unable to pass on to his descendants the motivations of his parents or the fruits of his own labor. The community he adopted as his own, however, was to be the richer for his presence and was to profit from his motivation.

*Michael Westernhouse ("Mike") Sutton: 1876–1886*

Known formally as M. W. and informally as Mike, Sutton was born in Deer Park Township, Orange County, New York, on January 8, 1848. The family moved to Tompkins County while he was "still a

*Letterhead of Michael W. ("Mike") Sutton, a tough customer for any-
one in the legal profession. Courtesy Kansas State Historical Society.*

*Mike Sutton in his law office. The spacious room filled in a hurry
when political maneuverings were planned. Courtesy Kansas State
Historical Society.*

babe in arms," and he grew up on a farm there. His mother died when he was six and his father died sometime after the beginning of the Civil War. Sutton attended public school in Tompkins County until 1863.[1]

Since he was orphaned, Sutton found it easy to quit school and join the Union Army. He enlisted in Company B of the Sixth New York Heavy Artillery on February 12, 1863, and saw considerable action but escaped injury, although he spent some time in the hospital with a case of child's measles. Sutton's own description of his service revealed that he survived some of the bloodiest engagements of the war:

I went to the war of '61 to '65. I was a private—carried a musket always.

I participated in the Battle of the Wilderness, two days; in the Battle of Spottsylvania, three days and did my part at the "bloody angle;" was at the Battle of Northanna [North Anna, Virginia], shared in the terrific slaughter at Cold Harbor; was in the charge at Petersburg on the 16th, 17th and 18th days of June 1864; stayed with the Army of the Potomac to the end and participated in all its struggles. On the 30th day of July, 1864, I stood in line of battle (early in the morning). What we were to do I knew not. Suddenly the earth rumbled and groaned very much louder than distant thunder; it swayed under my feet like a light boat in a rough sea, while in front of me, an acre or two of earth arose hundreds of feet in the air. Mingled in that great mass were great field pieces of artillery, indiscriminately mixed with men and horses. It flashed thru my mind that God's anger with his people was so great that he had concluded to destroy the world, and that all things were at an end. That thought has recurred to me many times since and I record it here—known as the crater or mine blown up before Petersburg, Va.[2]

At the end of the war he returned home and attended Trumansburg Academy for two years. In November 1867 he moved to a farm near Warrensburg, Missouri, where he taught school "and employed his leisure hours in studying law in the office of White and Baldwin." He was admitted to the bar in March 1872. Attracted by prospects of greater opportunities on the frontier, he set up practice in Wellington, Kansas, but in the fall of 1872 he moved to Medicine Lodge. There he formed a partnership with James T. Whitelaw, an equally footloose and ambitious newcomer to the West.[3]

"Business for a lawyer," T. A. McNeal testifies in *When Kansas Was Young,* "was decidedly scarce and the pickings slim." So slim that Mike owned only one shirt, which he laundered in "the clear, soft waters of Elm Creek," waiting patiently while it dried on the sandhill plum bushes that then flourished in Barber County. None of his efforts to improve his pecunious state seemed to work. The usual channel of advancement for a lawyer unsuccessful in practice was to run for political office, but when Mike tried to capture a minor post, he lost convincingly at the polls. Just how tough times were is illustrated in a McNeal story. The firm of Sutton and Whitelaw had taken a case to be prosecuted in Hutchinson:

As the time of trial approached Mike, for the first time since his settlement in the town, appeared to be somewhat worried. "Jim," said he to his partner, "one of us has to go to Hutchinson and try that case. I really haven't clothes fitting to appear in court, but you have a pair of overalls, nearly new, and a shirt that you haven't been wearing more than six months. You also have a pair of socks and your toes are not sticking out of your shoes. You will have to go and show the court that this firm has some style and dignity."[4]

Attracted by the boomtown rumors and the presence of a district court, Sutton moved to Dodge City in 1876. He came unencumbered with worldly goods, riding on a freight wagon part of the way and walking across the countryside on foot the rest. Later he claimed that he "had no coat, and wore one boot and one shoe" and that "his wardrobe consisted of one pair of overalls, one calico shirt . . . and a straw hat." He was, when he arrived in Dodge, a small man, approximately five feet, six inches tall, with fair complexion and gray eyes. Although he was plagued with a weight problem in later life, in 1876 he was lean, intense, and superbly healthy. For a time he hired out, counting buffalo hides, but his new home brought an almost immediate change in fortune. He first was appointed city attorney, then, on November 1, 1876, county attorney. Both positions were reconfirmed in April 1877. The city council's agenda began noting payments due him of $125 and $135 and special fees of as much as $189 for duties outside Dodge City. In the spring of 1877, Sutton was joined in his practice by another young bachelor, Edward F. Colborn, and when Sutton resigned as city attorney, Mayor James H. Kelley appointed Colborn to the vacated position. For a time the firm of Sutton and Colborn had the public legal offices of Ford County to itself, and the two were recognized as a formidable prosecuting team.[5]

By 1877, Dodge City was fully established in the Texas cattle trade and was earning a just reputation as the "wickedest town in the West," if not the most violent. In the spring and summer months, Dodge was wide open with saloons, dance halls, and brothels. In such a setting, there were bound to be law violations that even a sympathetic community could not tolerate. Then, too, the town was growing, the railroad was testing its privileges and obligations, and settlers were contesting disputed land claims arising from confusing laws and questionable homesteading practices. It was a good town and a good time for an untried lawyer to begin his practice.

The social life of Dodge was ideal for young, carefree, unattached males. Sutton joined the fun and contributed his share to the excitement. Involved in the rough humor of frontier practical jokes, he was an accepted member of the sporting crowd. Never as wild as his rival Harry Gryden, Sutton spent less time in the bars and put more effort into his assigned duties. But he did have time to make a trip to Las Animas, Colorado, for no more serious purpose than viewing an eclipse, plus several trips back to Medicine Lodge to court "a fair lady." He was also a close friend of Bat Masterson, one of the gayest blades in the bachelor crowd. Masterson chose Sutton to accompany him to Topeka when he accepted appointment as deputy United States marshal and when he went home to tell his parents that their son Ed had been slain. In the early days, Mike worked closely with Bat in fulfilling the duties of their offices.[6]

Sutton was also a member of the Gang, and he ran for county attorney on the same slate that listed Masterson for sheriff and Robert M. Wright for state representative. Sutton's seconding of the nomination at the Lady Gay meeting put Bat on the ballot. Both Bat and Mike spent considerable time at the Alhambra, political headquarters for anyone interested in politics. In 1878, when Mike made his first bid for elective office, the Gang's slate was unopposed and received the uncritical support of the *Dodge City Times* and the vociferous opposition of the *Ford County Globe*. The

Gang not only won but seemed solidly in power until saloonkeeper George T. Hinkle, a conservative property owner, challenged and defeated Masterson in the November 1879 election. That revolt had not been without cost, according to the *Dodge City Times:*

The election in this county last Tuesday was characterized with about the usual activity, but the polls closed with only a few fights on record for the day, although a vigorous skirmish was kept up all along the line, and considerable ammunition expended on both sides. . . . It is the defeat of the Independent ticket, representing the influences that have controlled the politics of Ford county since its organization, and the triumph of a new element, the successful candidates running on what was known as the "People's" ticket. . . . The "Gang" is no more in existence. It failed to "get to the joint" last Tuesday and has lost its grip forever.[7]

Like Mark Twain's death, the prediction of the Gang's demise was premature. The following April, the city election re-established Kelley in the mayor's office. Sutton, Dan Frost wrote in the *Ford County Globe,* was responsible:

The old gang element was apparently discouraged and demoralized from its defeat of last fall, and its most sagacious advisors and leaders, Messrs. Sutton, Klaine and others, endeavored, as a dernier resort, to make a compromise with [Dr. T. L.] McCarty's friends. . . . A meeting was called at Kelley's the day before election and a love-feast and communion was indulged in. . . . "Put up our old leader, James H. Kelley and, if die we must, let us die game!" . . . was the general response, and the silent warrior, St. Michael [Sutton], he of the smoothe and oily tongue, wrote out the ticket as follows: For Mayor, James H. Kelley. . . . The "communion of the saints" broke up, each with a decided knowledge of the work he had to do; and they went forth seeking scalps. From that hour until the polls were opened the Kelley men were everywhere.[8]

Sutton's reputation as a political wheeler-dealer was just beginning. Robert Wright confessed that from the start Sutton was "behind me, as advisor, in all my deals and undertakings." In Wright's judgment, Sutton eventually was to hold the political strings of "the great Southwest" in his "vest pocket." Unfortunately for Wright and the Gang, Mike was having second thoughts about his old friends and had begun to shift allegiance from the informal and unconventional methods of the Gang to the more ordered structure of the Republican party. Sutton broke with the Gang when it became clear that many of the business leaders in Dodge were also taking a different tack.[9]

Local politics became considerably more contentious during Mayor Kelley's third and last term. H. M. Beverley, George Randall, and Dr. Samuel Galland all resigned from the city council during a heated meeting on June 8, 1880. In a public assembly called to discuss the conditions of city government, the three businessmen aired their grievances and charged the Kelley administration with exercising "dictatorial powers," establishing grossly "exorbitant salaries," and giving "encouragement of profligacy and vice." That evening after the council meeting, Sutton resigned as city attorney in a public gesture of disapproval of Kelley's rule. The mayor appointed Gryden in Sutton's place. In the next county election, Gryden unsuccessfully challenged Sutton for county attorney. Sutton won handily and remained in office until February 28, 1882, when he resigned and the position went to an old Gang stalwart, Colonel T. C. Jones, by appointment of Judge Jeremiah C. Strang.[10]

Just how far Sutton had moved from his old associates was shown by his action in the Saloon War of 1883. During that fracas he signed none of the petitions sent to Governor George W. Glick, and he remained inconspicuously in the background, away from the various posses and mass meetings. Many, however, considered him the real leader—"the Judas," the opposition said, who perfected the plan for Short's "assassination." In the election that helped trigger the conflict, Sutton was accused of stuffing the ballot box by importing voters through his generous use of Atchison, Topeka and Santa Fe rail passes. As far as Bat was concerned, this was the final betrayal. The break had started with Bat's defeat in 1879, when Sutton gave him bad advice. Bat believed that it was deliberately intended to remove him from office, and his animosity exploded in unrestrained abuse. Bat was not one to hide his grievances, and his venture into newspaper publishing with *Vox Populi* was a declaration of political war upon those who had "gone over to the enemy." Sutton, a major target in Masterson's bestiary, became

a marvelous, amphibious creature known as Sutton-a-cuss Gymnatus or the electrical. To whatever object it comes in contact, it transmits a shock such that the victim seldom recovers (in his purse). . . . [The creature] is also allied to the chameleon, changing its color to correspond to the object it approaches. It has been known to be one day red like wine and on the next allied to water.

Only with Mike's death in 1918 did Bat relent. In response to the telegram telling of Mike's passing, he wired back: "Dear, good Mike, the last of life-long friends is no more. Peace to his ashes."[11]

Bat had a difficult time understanding and explaining the changed relationship between Mike and the Gang. The two men had worked so well together that Robert Wright referred to them while they were in public office simultaneously as "Catch 'em & convict 'em." In an editorial, Nick Klaine praised their law-enforcement efforts as "a great combination" and especially commended Sutton, who, Klaine said, had "crowned himself in glory." Masterson certainly had not changed. He was the same generous, emotional friend and defender of the cattlemen, the same nemesis of lawbreakers that he had been the day he stepped off the train. It was Sutton who had changed. And Dodge City was in the process. There were new rail lines to the south, Texas ticks on the range, granger fences on the homesteads, and civilizing influences in town. Anyone who was to become a permanent part of the new Dodge would have to change with the times, and Sutton intended to stay. New circumstances required new attitudes and new friends, and for Mike the adjustment paid off with higher social status and financial rewards.[12]

The business of lawyering had brought the firm of Sutton and Colborn limited prosperity, at least enough for Mike to acquire a more complete wardrobe and a better office. When Herman Fringer added to the post office, the firm moved into new facilities there, but the major change in Mike's lifestyle came when A. B. Webster's niece, from Gloversville, New York, arrived for an extended visit. It was a brief courtship and in October 1879, Mike and Florence Estelle Clemmons were married in a simple home wedding. They settled into a house just east of the courthouse, close to Mike's work.[13]

Not only did marriage end Mike's frivolous evenings at the Alhambra, but Florence had brought with her strong, unbending prohibitionist convictions. In a short time her husband came around to her persuasion. However, Mike's public stance toward the saloon business was tempered by the economic realities of the time and by his public position as county attorney. No official could survive opposing the public demand to look the other way in the matter of the saloons catering to the Texas cattle trade. Such private convictions were kept from public airing. Consequently, Sutton first appeared to Albert Griffin, editor of the *Manhattan Nationalist* and aggressive officer in the Kansas Temperance Union, as merely one of the hypocritical city officials who were thwarting the enforcement of Kansas liquor laws. Griffin lumped Mike in with Masterson as a vicious, disreputable member of the "sporting fraternity," responsible for keeping saloons open and prohibitionists silenced. [14]

Griffin completely misjudged Sutton. Certainly by 1883 Sutton was a committed prohibitionist, doing what he could to change saloon domination of local policies and practices, a fact Griffin publicly recognized later. When the saloons were finally closed in 1886, Sutton wrote a "private and confidential" letter to Kansas Attorney General S. B. Bradford castigating both Masterson and his old friend Robert Wright for keeping the liquor establishments open as long as they had. "The Prohibitionist crowd to which I belong," he wrote, had finally managed to close down the saloons, "and prohibition reigns supreme." But he feared that Masterson, Wright, and their cronies would soon circumvent the laws and start the liquor flowing. The attorney general should be aware, he warned, of Masterson's maneuvering and be prepared to intervene. [15]

Sutton's actions were not restricted to working behind the scenes, and most Dodge Citians were aware of his prohibitionist convictions. Dan Frost, his longtime political antagonist, informed readers of the *Globe* that Sutton was behind the new prohibitionist campaign for mayor, George S. Emerson. Emerson's opponent, incumbent Robert Wright, was far too tolerant of the old days and the old ways for Sutton; consequently, the friendship went the way of Masterson's. In August 1886, Sutton represented the Seventh District at the National Republican Anti-Saloon Convention, and editor Frost reported that Mike's presence there emphasized the prohibition crowd's plot to run Emerson as "a figurehead to repeat, parrotlike, the decrees issued by Sutton." Sutton's stand on liquor was so well known by the mid-1880s that he came close to being shot because of his convictions. There were conflicting stories of what happened, but most people believed Sutton's version rather than Wright's:

Bob Wright, mayor of Dodge City, arrested on Monday [December 14], charged with felonious assault on Mike Sutton, formerly of the Lodge [Medicine Lodge], but for several years past a prominent attorney of Dodge City. We have heard the story of the assault from a friend of Bob Wright, which was in substance as follows: After the second fire [December 6, 1885] the rumor was started that the prohibitionists had fired the town and friends of Mr. Sutton feared that an attempt would be made to assassinate him and went to Mayor Wright and asked him to send an extra police to guard the residence of Mr. Sutton. Instead of sending the policeman the mayor said he would go himself, and accordingly armed himself with a revolver and went to Sutton's house. He saw some one moving about in the shadow of the building as he says and ordered him to halt. Instead of that the man started to run around the house and Mike, supposing that somebody was trying to shoot him pulled his freight. Even putting the most favorable construction upon this story, it seems to us that it is not at all surprising that Mike should suppose that an attempt was being made upon his life and further more if that is the way the Dodge City mayor has of guarding people we don't want him for a bodyguard of ours.

Before the comedy of errors—if they were errors—ended, a warrant was obtained against Wright for "making a felonious assault on M. W. Sutton." A hearing on January 4, 1886, apparently cleared up the matter, but prohibition agitation had so strained the friendship that it was never quite the same again.[16]

In July 1880, Sutton became a father and the next month moved to a new residence on Gospel Ridge, the designation Front Street scoffers gave to the hill area between First Avenue and Railroad Avenue in which two churches and several fine residences were located. He was by then a member of the city council, financially and socially secure, enjoying a positive reputation as a prosecuting attorney. His private practice was growing, and he could afford to be one of the pillars of the community. Apparently, Florence exerted other "civilizing influences" on Mike besides her prohibition convictions. A literary society, a must for any frontier community aspiring to cultural respectability, was organized in his office. When Sutton and Whitelaw acquired an injunction against a ribald "variety show," Frost reported that "probably their wives wouldn't let them go so they shut the show down." It was an unusually cruel jibe even for Frost, for not all of Sutton's new life was going positively for him.[17]

Florence's sister had come to visit and help with the new baby. One pleasant afternoon, Mrs. Sutton bundled the baby in a warm blanket and went for a drive with her sister. The horse became frightened, lunged, and overturned the buggy. The child, Stuart, less than a month old, was injured seriously and did not regain consciousness for more than a week; he was never to recover completely. Stuart was the Suttons' only child and remained a burden to his parents and occasionally an embarrassment. When he grew older, his father constructed an addition to their home that Stuart named the Sutton Photograph Gallery. He took pictures of trains and appeared in and around town as a simple soul who sometimes gave quick, humorous, and occasionally profound responses to the teasing he received.[18]

Perhaps as important as Mrs. Sutton's presence in fixing Sutton's changed attitude toward his former political and social allies was Mike's new legal position. In February 1882, after being elected to the office three times, Sutton resigned as county attorney to accept a position on the legal staff of the Atchison, Topeka and Santa Fe Railroad. He had acted on behalf of the Santa Fe from time to time, and even more frequently he was attorney of record in opposition. The cases were generally small damage suits involving the death of some farm animal that had strayed onto the tracks or the setting afire of a grain field by a spark from a locomotive, but some were more significant. Sutton had conducted the prosecution with impressive ability in the more costly ventures, including "action to enjoin unpaid taxes of 1875" and a similar suit brought by the Santa Fe in 1877 to escape new school and township levies. These cases involved substantial amounts of money, as much as $9,747 in one dispute.[19]

Not only his legal skill but also his knowledge of local conditions and moods made Sutton a formidable opponent. Apparently, officials in the Santa Fe central office at Topeka concluded that he would be a good man to have in western Kansas, where litigation was frequent. After his appointment, criminal cases involving the railroad were prosecuted in the district court by the county attorney, with Sutton assisting. The number of convictions increased and the penalties became more severe. Typical was the action brought against two cowboys, Jacob Cobb and John Rivers. Their crime at an earlier date would have been considered no more than mischief, high spirits, or what Dan Frost believed to be, even at that time, "a little innocent fun." After an evening on the town, the two cowboys finished their spree by galloping along the railroad tracks and emptying their pistols into a Santa Fe caboose. The Santa Fe officials saw the incident as more than innocent fun, and the cowboys were charged with "mutilating railroad property." With Whitelaw and Sutton prosecuting, a conviction was obtained and the now sober cowboys were sentenced to one year in the penitentiary. [20]

Sutton's association with the railroad coincided with his growing interest in ending the lawlessness of the old cattle town. Furthermore, it gave him considerable clout as a representative of Dodge's major source of economic strength. He did not hesitate to use his new advantage. His most successful use of power came at the end of the Saloon War, which had resulted in a tenuous and shaky compromise. Luke Short was allowed to return to town and manage his property, the reform measures were kept on the books unenforced, and the militant posturing of Glick's Guards ended for the moment. Most businessmen were willing to see the saloons and gambling continue as long as there was law, order, peace, and profit; Sutton did not concede quite so easily. Although cowboys were still an important economic factor to most merchants, he looked beyond their immediate contribution to Dodge's economy. In August 1883 he helped bring together a number of the more reputable businessmen to meet with C. C. Wheeler, general manager of the Atchison, Topeka and Santa Fe. Wheeler told the men that if Dodge City did not make a serious effort to "suppress vice," a proposed rail facility valued at about one hundred thousand dollars would be located either east or west of Dodge. The railroad, he said, no longer was interested in a town where law and order could not be guaranteed. The threat, couched in understandable dollar-and-cents terms, convinced those who were wavering that the time had come to change Dodge City's reputation. It was the beginning of the end of the legendary wickedest town in the West. Sutton's role, again mostly behind the scenes, was a prime factor in the change. [21]

Local politics, of which the Saloon War was a highly visible example, seemed to occupy more and more of Sutton's time. His initial ventures with the Gang had been purely practical politics designed to put bread on the table and a shirt on his back. He belonged to "the Kelley faction" and ran against most of the other active lawyers for the office of city or county attorney as a matter of expediency. Along with Robert Wright and Bat Masterson, he had electioneered "through the east end of the county" and had achieved grudging respect from his enemies as a "Pirate Captain" who acquired votes even if it meant applying "lashings of free whiskey." As early as 1878 he campaigned hard for Judge Samuel R. Peters of Newton and spent some "Senator lobbying" time in Topeka. His easy victories at the local polls, however, did not attract much support beyond the county. Gang politics was not identified with a major party and could not call on loyalties outside western Kansas. When the new bill carving the Sixteenth Judicial District out of the old Ninth District was pending, Sutton apparently made "a quiet, dignified, indifferent canvas" for the new judgeship, to no avail. These early efforts laid the base for later, broader influence.[22]

Only when he left the Gang and became a confirmed Republican did Sutton's influence mature. Once committed, he was an active member of the Republican party and eventually had considerable clout in Kansas political affairs. The groundwork was laid in his early service on several committees, including the nominating caucus, the Republican county central committee, and the United States Senatorial Committee.[23]

Sutton's reputation was not based primarily on his official party position. Depending on the describer's politics, Sutton was described as either a valued political adviser or a conniving and secretive "operator behind the scenes." Harry Gryden, his old friend turned political as well as legal opponent, saw him as a devious string puller and passed on to an acquaintance Mayor Kelley's judgment of politics in Dodge: "Tell him Sutton is at the bottom of it all, damn him." Dan Frost was even more specific, at one point charging Sutton with directing the undersheriff to post fifty deputies to "bulldoze unwanted voters who were brave enough to approach the polls." Frost even saw Sutton's Republican hand in the growth of the People's party. The Populists, he claimed, under Sutton's leadership, divided the Democrats and eventually attracted enough voters away from the Democratic party to guarantee Republican victory. Bat Masterson and Luke Short thought Sutton, motivated by political consideration of the basest kind, was the real brains behind the harassment of Short that resulted in the Saloon War. They backed suspicions with threats to kill Sutton. Mike knew Bat well enough to take the threats to heart, and when a friend told him Bat was gunning for him, Mike found reasons to check on "business in Kinsley," getting out of town as soon as possible. It is doubtful that Sutton was more involved in the Luke Short affair than a dozen other businessmen. However, he was adroit at working behind the scenes, as all knew, so Bat and Luke easily concluded that Sutton was the ringleader.[24]

Certainly Mike was not above concealing the truth while working out the details. A skillful maneuver is revealed in a March 1886 letter to Attorney General Simon Briggs Bradford:

Dear Sir.

The City of Dodge City has been declared a city of the 2″ class proclamation of Gov. John A. Martin and that takes it out of the township of Dodge. The two Justices of the Peace of Dodge Tp. reside in the City and therefore Dodge Tp. proper is without—in fact not only Justices of the Peace but any other officer as they all live in the city. I can not go to the Clerk and get certificate for that would let the cat out of the bag, and if you can get Gov. John A. [Martin] to appoint John Groendyke J. P. a commission as such officer will not only please him but delight the law abiding citizens.[25]

If Sutton was not "the high muck-a-muck" of Frost's convictions or the grand strategist of Wright's reminiscences, all recognized his ability to pull strings. The longer he operated in the Republican party, the more sources of power he cultivated and the greater became his influence. Wright's judgment, although generous, was close to accuracy for the years after Dodge had ceased to be a cattle town. However, during the 1870s and 1880s, Sutton was far too busy to spend much time plotting and politicking. Holding the political fortunes of the area in his vest pocket was, in the early days, a treasure not worth the price.

Above all else, Sutton was a lawyer. Prohibition, literary societies, and Republican-party activities were all secondary to his life as a lawyer. His record in the several hundred cases with which he was connected was an enviable one. Most were instances of minor litigation that were quickly resolved and required no extensive preparation. There were, however, major suits that tested his skill and revealed his knowledge of law, people, and courts.

His legal reputation was established solidly in those early years as county attorney. During the time when he still enjoyed the friendship of editor Frost, the *Ford County Globe* boasted that Mike had never lost a criminal case. Later Frost was complimentary of Sutton the lawyer even when he criticized him as a politician. Under the heading "Court Notes," Frost's paper reported that "Judge Sutton was very successful with his state cases, as also with all his civil ones. He came out with fresh laurels and, in all probability, handsome fees. There is no doubt about his being a good lawyer, and by studious application to books and business, he is constantly improving." Frost was so impressed that he added an editorial:

> When looking up the cases tried during the last term of the district court, curiosity enticed us away back among the musty pages of the past, to 1877, and led us to take a glance at the criminal record of our county. It was in the above year that M. W. Sutton, Esq., became our county attorney, and since then, some seventy men have been arraigned before the district court charged with every crime under the law, from cold-blooded murder down to petty larceny. The disposition of the cases is not complete, but so far as the records show were as follows: Six were dismissed, seven found not guilty, twenty guilty, fourteen plead guilty, two had a change of venue granted, and one forfeited his bond. . . . We should congratulate ourselves that, through the instrumentality of our efficient county attorney, our laws have been so well enforced and faithfully executed.[26]

While it is not true, even by Frost's accounting, that Sutton won all his cases, his was a remarkable record. Not only did his victories add to his "laurels" and "handsome fees," they were to become part of Dodge City legend. Among the characters touched by Sutton's skills were John Gill, Bill Tilghman, Mysterious Dave Mather, Henry Gould (Skunk Curley), Tom Nixon, George T. Hinkle, Joe Sparrow, and Dutch Henry Borne. A number of the suits attracted statewide and even national attention. The county attorney's office in a wide-open cattle town was a good base for building a legal career, or at least an enviable reputation.

The case that captured the most extensive coverage at the time was to be one of Sutton's least successful ventures. In fact, Mike's image has since been portrayed as that of a love-sick incompetent who wasted the taxpayers' funds and neglected his duty. The problem lay in Dull Knife's raid of 1878. The band of Northern Cheyennes who broke from their reservation in Indian Territory on September 9 of that year fled across Kansas with U.S. Army regulars and civilian amateurs attempting to corral them. Dull Knife's leadership kept the Indians moving at such a tiring pace that the army and local contingents of cowboys and volunteers either could not keep up or were outmaneuvered. Living off the land and frustrated by the relentless pursuit, the Indians vented their anger in death and destruction. The army's inability to make contact with the Cheyennes left townspeople, ranchers, and soldiers uncertain of where the Indians would attack next, which made the ordeal all the more frightening for white settlers. Dodge City and the rest of western Kansas were caught in a frenzy of fear, and the final death count of more than forty Kansans indicates that there was ample cause for alarm. When the Cheyennes were captured, the citizens of Dodge City were relieved; they also demanded retribution, and Sutton was one of the first public officials to act.[27]

In January 1879, Sutton swore out warrants for the arrest of the Indian leaders, citing the specific murders of five people in the Dodge City area. Bat Masterson and others who had personal and unpleasant knowledge of the leaders were dispatched to identify those cited in the warrants. The army had been mulling over the problem of jurisdiction for some time, and in late December it gave permission for transfer of authority to civil courts. Bat supervised the prisoners' return to Dodge City to answer Sutton's charges. The Indians were incarcerated, photographed, and exhibited as a kind of community prize. After languishing in jail some four months, they were brought before Judge Samuel R. Peters for a preliminary hearing. The court, acting on advice of J. G. Mohler of Salina, attorney for the defense and another of Frost's "wily, oily" lawyers, granted a change of venue because of the judge's and the frontier community's prejudices. Masterson and A. J. Peacock, filing in amicus, denied that such prejudice existed. Peters, however, knew his own mind and the community's mood better than Bat did and changed the site of the trial.[28]

In the new setting at Lawrence, Sutton ran into the old problem of distance and delay and the Indians found a far more congenial climate. Mohler had no difficulty in lining up forty sympathetic witnesses. Sutton, on the other hand, found his witnesses scattered. Confiding in the attorney general, he feared he could not persuade his witnesses to go to Lawrence for a long and costly stay, and without witnesses he could not bring sufficient evidence to bear to warrant prosecution. It seemed hardly worth the effort to work up a brief. Mike also may have had other, more pleasant distractions: he had been married on October 1 and had honeymooned in Kansas City for nine days. When the trial opened on October 13, Mike was back in Dodge City and there was no one in Lawrence to head the prosecution. A substitute was appointed at the last minute, but by then the case was in shambles. Mike's substitute called for a continuance. When the judge refused, the prosecution entered a plea of nolle prosequi. The judge turned the prisoners back to federal authorities.[29]

Both Dodge City papers were critical of the proceedings, which had wasted tax money and officials' time only to have the Cheyennes receive a "free and nice pleasure trip" home to their agency. However, bringing the suit was far from being a "hasty" and "indiscreet" act, as was charged. On the positive side, the trial settled an important question of criminal jurisdiction and was applauded by those who had experienced the terror caused by the raid. The people in Dodge had welcomed the trial; they just did not like the results. Frost hung the incident as a political albatross around Bat Masterson's neck when prisoners in the Dodge City jail escaped while Bat was occupied with Cheyenne affairs. Frost roasted him to a fare-thee-well. The community's greater indignation, in spite of Frost's efforts, was reserved for the way the case ended. Sutton, who knew the suit was lost when the trial was moved to Lawrence, seemed to come out of the affair with sympathy rather than blame. He had tried to secure justice; the system simply had thwarted him. Despite Frost's chiding Mike about his romantic absence, Sutton was kept in office at the next election; the case was to have no ill effects on his career.[30]

If Dodge Citians were disappointed at the time, the case does have special interest today, throwing a different light on frontier justice from that usually shown. In this instance, Indians who had pillaged, raped, and killed found themselves in a white man's court. They received all the legal safeguards: legal counsel, change of venue, the right to confront witnesses, and the right to subpoena. The result was that the Indians escaped punishment—not the usual picture of the white man's frontier justice dealing with the red man. [31]

As would be expected, some of Sutton's more spectacular cases involved murder. The first death sentence in the Ninth Judicial District court was imposed with Sutton, assisted by L. W. B. Johnson, prosecuting. In December 1878, Sutton had appointed Johnson deputy county attorney for Foote County (now Gray County), which was attached to Ford County for administrative and judicial purposes. Sutton called on his new appointee for aid in preparing the case. The crime, a particularly brutal and senseless one, resembled the stereotype of Dodge showdowns only in that it had occurred on Front Street after a quarrel in a saloon. Arista H. Webb had bullied Barney Martin, a Dodge tailor, during a drunken spree and had forced Martin to apologize for some imagined wrong. Not satisfied with Martin's words, Webb staggered back to his home. There he picked up his rifle and, still in a rage, returned to find Martin seated on a bench in front of the saloon. By far the larger of the two men, Webb used the rifle as a club to crush Martin's skull. For that day and time, the trial was a long one, with forty witnesses called and the jury deliberating for several hours. Found guilty of first-degree murder, Webb was sentenced to be confined at Leavenworth for one year at hard labor, at the end of which the governor was to set the date for execution. In this instance, Sutton may have been too efficient in his prosecution. Webb had displayed signs of insanity before the trial and the attack certainly appeared irrational. The community, however, was so incensed by the brutality and arrogance of the act that it would have been difficult to negotiate a plea of innocent by reason of insanity. [32]

An equally shocking murder was that in which Thomas O'Haran killed H. T. McCarty, deputy U.S. marshal and former county surveyor, the third marshal in Dodge City to be killed in the line of duty. After some legal maneuvering by the defense, which attempted to move the trial to a less hostile setting, Sutton secured a denial of a change of venue. With the trial to be held in Dodge City, it was easy to predict the outcome. O'Haran, a slow-witted "quarrel-some wretch," while in a drunken fog had shot McCarty with no apparent provocation. He was found guilty of first-degree man-slaughter and sentenced to twelve years and three months in the penitentiary.[33]

One of the gaudier murder cases prosecuted by Sutton followed John Gill's killing of Henry Heck. The description of the circumstances of the killing by the *Ford County Globe* (probably written by Dan Frost) is undoubtedly the best of that genre by a frontier newsman. Heck, it would seem, was a hardworking and peaceful man who established a small ranch south of Dodge on the Fort Supply Trail. For a while he captured the affections of Callie Moore, "a woman of easy virtue," who lived with him as a "faithful companion, according to the approved method of this class of Dodge City lotus eaters." Then she met tall, dark, and handsome John Gill, alias Concho, who was a gambler. Callie shifted her affections to the more glamorous man. Heck did not forgive and forget. Instead, late one night he went to the gambler's domicile, kicked down the door, and received a fatal bullet from Concho's gun when he burst into the room. Sutton prosecuted. In spite of the fact that there was intrusion and fear of mortal harm, Concho was found guilty. Under normal circumstances, a verdict of justifiable homicide would have appeared certain. Compared to Edward F. Hardesty's pre-meditated execution of his hired hand, Concho seemed well within his rights of self-defense, but in a cattle town a rancher of "industry and prudence" had the edge over prostitutes and gamblers. Mari Sandoz's contention that the law favored the rancher was confirmed. "Only halfwits and greenhorns," she wrote, failed to realize that western gunmen avoided shooting "important people" because the officers of the law, courts, and citizens were all on the side of cattlemen. This was true even when the cattleman came looking for trouble. In this case Gill was found guilty of murder in the second degree and received a long term in the penitentiary. Bat had another passenger headed for Leavenworth.[34]

Less-reckless killings were prosecuted with equal vigor. James Allen, who killed a Clark County rancher; the slayer of an Atchison, Topeka and Santa Fe conductor; and Henry Kellum, who robbed the train and killed the engineer at Coolidge, all received long sentences. One of Sutton's successful convictions should have put one of the more notorious gunmen in the West behind bars, but through the tactics of securing repeated delays the conviction was reversed and the culprit went free. Joe Sparrow, a young Texas cowboy and saloon owner in Trail City, Colorado, shot and killed unarmed I. P. ("Print") Olive, one of Dodge City's toughest cattlemen. Print himself had killed rustlers in Texas and Nebraska and had seen various members of his own family gunned down. Sparrow ambushed Print, firing his last shot while the old man lay on his back. Sutton assisted in the prosecution at Las Animas, where Sparrow was found guilty. Three years and three trials later, the decision was reversed. Olive's own record, which included burning the bodies of three men he had helped lynch, and the state's unwillingness to sink more money into legal action, undoubtedly saved Sparrow's life. [35]

Out of office, Sutton was as successful in defending individuals accused of murder as he had been in prosecuting them. Two confessed clients escaped without convictions: E. F. Hardesty and J. J. Webb. Webb, a former Dodge dance-hall owner and lawman, was tried in Las Vegas, New Mexico. Sutton managed to delay trial long enough for Webb to break out of jail twice. The last escape was so successful that Webb was never recaptured and brought to trial. [36]

Sutton had a turn at train robbers as well. The spectacular holdup attempt at Kinsley in 1878 led to a long, highly publicized search for the would-be robbers before they were apprehended. The Santa Fe central office spared no expense in securing a conviction and setting an example. The company marshaled a "formidable array of prosecuting talent," including Sutton. After one of the gang, Dave Rudabaugh, turned state's evidence, two others changed their pleas to guilty. The judge used the sentencing statement to express an opinion worthy of today's deprived-culture environmentalists. He saw the young cowboys as victims of hard times and urged the businessmen of the state to give such unemployed men jobs so that they would not turn to crime in order to survive. For a time, young Bill Tilghman, the popular part-owner of the Crystal Palace saloon who was well known to Sutton, was considered an accomplice but eventually was cleared. Sutton had not spared

Tilghman and no doubt would have prosecuted him with the same impartiality he had shown others he did not know.[37]

Sutton's caseload was always heavy. During his terms as county attorney, court dockets were extremely full. The January 1879 docket was particularly crowded and Sutton missed the most notable case—one involving Dutch Henry Borne—by removing himself from the prosecution. Borne was the only defendant that session to gain acquittal. Other successfully prosecuted cases included those of Henry Gould (Skunk Curley) and Dan Woodward, both convicted of assault with intent to kill, and Frank Jennings, M. A. Sebastian, Bill Brown, Jim Bailey, and Jim Skelly, who were found guilty of various thefts. Their sentences ranged from eighteen months to two years and six months. A number of cases were continued or the record would have been even more impressive. Sutton did follow up on the delayed suits, and eventually O'Haran, one of those who received a continuance, was found guilty and sentenced. The case involving Woodward gave Sutton an opportunity to present "a vigorous and able argument" against the "pistol practices of Dodge City." His efforts to bring a more orderly and peaceful climate to Dodge were in keeping with the sentiments of the jury and the majority of the townsfolk. Sutton received most of the credit for the convictions of that session:

The energy of the indomitable and untiring worker, County Attorney Sutton, is manifested in the successful prosecution of these cases. Mike certainly "got to the point" in his accustomed and able manner, and is deserving of many good words spoken in his behalf for his efficient services in the cause of justice.[38]

Obviously, most of Sutton's cases were less spectacular: land suits, morals cases ("keeping a bawdy house and a house of 'ill shape'"), various degrees of battery, cattle rustling, horse stealing, mortgage and debt disputes, and matters involving county business, such as taxes and disputes over public property. The variety is remarkable. Like Gryden, Sutton handled more civil suits than criminal cases. In one session (1885) after he was out of the county attorney's office, Sutton was attorney of record in nineteen instances (two criminal and seventeen civil). Not all of these cases required extensive preparation, but at least one had broad implications. That case, T. J. Philipin et al. vs. Thomas L. McCarty was carried to the Kansas Supreme Court and affected a large number of people.[39]

The matter in dispute concerned the sale of school lands where no government existed in the unorganized counties attached to Ford County for judical purposes. A writ of mandamus was sought to compel the superintendent of schools to sell the established school land. With Sutton and C. M. Walters of Garden City prosecuting and Gryden in opposition, the court ruled that the land had to be offered for sale. The importance of the decision lay in transferring the land to the tax rolls and making it available for immediate ownership outside the homesteading restrictions. Sutton contended that the issue of Ford County jurisdiction over the attached but unorganized counties had been settled in the G. U. Holcomb case. This second victory certainly proved the point, and the issue, which involved some 9,500 square miles of southwestern Kansas, was put to rest.[40]

Sutton's loyalty to friends occasionally put him in awkward positions that seemed on the surface to run counter to his commitment to build a more progressive Dodge City. When George T. Hinkle was charged with illegally selling whiskey in Garden City, Sutton, by then an avowed prohibitionist, came to his defense. There was more to the Hinkle-Sutton relationship than the question of liquor. As the apparently confused sheriff during the Luke Short affair, Hinkle had been cagier than Governor Glick realized. Hinkle had placed his authority on the side of the reform faction and had worked with Sutton and the other businessmen to discourage Short, Bat Masterson, and their gun-toting pals. Since the governor's orders were favorable to Short, Hinkle had to appear confused or not altogether bright in order to circumvent them. The ruse had worked, although Hinkle had been put in an unpleasant position. Once the affair was over, he must have thought the prohibitionist owed him tit for tat. Naturally, he called on Sutton when the whiskey charge was made; naturally, Sutton responded. After all, the whiskey was in Garden City, not Dodge. Using the time-gaining legal maneuver of delay, Sutton raised the question of jurisdiction and won a favorable ruling for a change of venue. The case eventually landed in the Kansas Supreme Court, where Hinkle petitioned for a writ of habeas corpus. Gryden was Sutton's partner for the plaintiff and the court responded favorably to their petition, which indicated that the justice of peace and the constable had acted without authority in making the arrest since the township they represented had been abolished. "If there be no township, there are no township offices to fill; and if there are no township offices, there can be no justice of the peace" was the court's unanimous decision. Hinkle was released.[41]

Sutton appeared to have no difficulty squaring his prohibitionist conscience with his professional obligation. He was interviewed as he stepped from the train when he returned home from Topeka after arguing the Hinkle case. He was asked whether he had seen the Reverend A. B. Campbell of the Kansas Temperance Union. Admitting that he had spent some time with Campbell, he denied that he had been employed to prosecute the whiskey violation cases in Dodge City—at least "not yet." The cases would be pressed, he said, but he was not involved at the moment.[42]

At the same time he was dealing with Hinkle's problem, Sutton took on Dr. Samuel Galland's quarrel with Orlando ("Brick") Bond and Thomas C. Nixon. The doctor, an ardent prohibitionist, sued Bond and Nixon for maintaining a disreputable establishment next to his hotel, the Western House. The initial petition to close the dance hall indicated that Galland's business had been injured and his "family denied social privilege in consequence of the proximity of the dance hall." The *Times*, fully in support of the doctor, indicated that as long as the hall existed it would be "a source of litigation and disorder." The problem, the *Times* insisted, was that whiskey and traffic in prostitution had taken over, with "the dancing part being left out altogether." A contest pitting respectability against whiskey undoubtedly was more to Sutton's liking than the defense of a bootlegger, even if he were an old friend. An injunction was granted, which solved the immediate problem favorably to Galland, and that spring an ordinance was passed prohibiting dance halls within the city limits. A neighboring city editor commented: "Dr. Galland's work begins to bear fruit."[43]

The relentless pressure of the reform faction was gradually pushing the disreputable element out of business, which in turn drove them out of town. Prohibition was not only drying up liquor

124 COWTOWN LAWYERS

consumption but was having a chastening effect, just as its advocates claimed, on the total social climate. Each year saw Sutton becoming an increasingly more ardent supporter of the prohibitionists' cause. The year after Galland's victory, Sutton and Galland went together as delegates to the state prohibition convention in Topeka. Many Dodge Citians remembered the more tolerant Mike of earlier times and found his new crusading zeal hard to understand. The charge, frequently made, that Sutton still enjoyed a convivial glass of spirits may or may not be true, but it was completely beside the point. Sutton supported the dry forces as a means of cleaning up the town and putting the lawless-cowtown image to rest. Liquor was a convenient symbol—one that proved to be increasingly useful.

Tom Nixon figured in another case that was awkward for Sutton. On July 21, 1884, Assistant Marshal Nixon was shot and killed by Dave Mather as the result of a long-running feud. A few days earlier (July 18), Nixon had shot at Mather, leaving him with a bad powder burn but no serious injury. Mysterious Dave was a bad target to be shooting at, especially if the shots were not fatal. He had been a lawman in other dangerous frontier towns and was reputed to have killed men in Las Vegas, New Mexico, and Mobeetie, Texas. Sutton took the case, supported by T. S. Haun of Jetmore and E. D. Swan. Gryden, as usual, was in opposition.[44]

Because both men involved in the shooting were well known and connected with law enforcement, the case attracted much interest and was covered thoroughly by the press. After an exhaustive preliminary hearing, Sutton, Haun, and Swan, armed with money supplied by several prominent businessmen in Dodge, got Mather out of jail on bail. A change of venue put the trial in Kinsley. The proceedings there lasted two and a half days, but the jury took only a few minutes to return a not-guilty verdict. Sutton and Haun (Swan had dropped out) were praised for their "defense and their indefatigable and successful efforts." Whether friendship entered into Sutton's acceptance or only his professional obligation is a matter of speculation, but he did know Mather well; in fact, that spring, Mather had accompanied Sutton to Topeka on "railroad business." Mather had stood for law and order in an acceptable and respectable manner while in office, and Sutton had not approved of Nixon and his dance hall next to the good Dr. Galland's property. Whatever his motives, the Nixon killing added to the image of Dodge as a lawless town and Sutton could not have been happy about that. To add to the indignity, a year later Mather was involved in another shooting in which one man was killed and three wounded. Sutton did not come to his defense.[45]

Since cattle-trail activities were largely responsible for Dodge's reputation as a dangerous town, Sutton hoped to see the town develop into a more civilized center of trade. As a consequence he frequently opposed the Texas cattle interests, but not all ranchers or all cattlemen. As was true of other Dodge Citians, Sutton saw Dodge's future in a broad-based economy maintained by transportation facilities. Ranchers in the trade area were a welcome and perhaps even essential part of the diversified economy he envisioned. The Western Kansas Cattle Growers' Association, based in Dodge and composed of large ranch owners, clearly understood the distinction and played an important role in diverting Texas cattle from the state.

J. L. Driskill and his sons were the type of cattlemen who were acceptable to the Dodge City reformers. They put imported Shorthorn bulls on their Cimarron ranch in 1880 and established respectable contributions to the new order of cattle business. Sutton did not hesitate to undertake the defense of Driskill's cowboys who violated the Kansas quarantine law by driving cattle across Ness County, even though the law did more to break the Texas cattle interests in Dodge than any other single factor. Sutton was equally willing to take on the association as an opponent. In one instance involving a popular young Meade-Ford County rancher, William Schmoker, in a cattle-stealing charge, he pursued the case as prosecuting attorney through two trials in the Larned district court. Like a latter-day Theodore Roosevelt who distinguished between good and bad trusts, for Sutton there were clearly good cattlemen (meaning substantial Kansas ranchers) and bad cattlemen (the Texas trail-herd bosses).[46]

The Kansas ranching interests tried to keep Sutton on their side and were pleased when he attended the Western Kansas Cattle Growers' Association meetings. In 1883 he was asked by the group to give a major address. It was such a new role that his

old friend Nick Klaine found it advisable to clarify Mike's credentials. "Mr. Sutton," he wrote, "knows a few things about law and
cattle." He then cited Sutton's early experience of driving oxen in
Missouri until he traded them to finance his move to Kansas. Two
years later, when Sutton again attended the convention, the *Globe
Live Stock Journal,* which had not quite accepted the sophisticated
distinction between good and bad cattlemen, reported Sutton's
knowledge of cattle as marginal. All the livestock Sutton ever
owned, the editor insisted, was a bull calf that he sold after waiting
"for the expected increase" and becoming indignant when the
grown bull failed to give birth to a calf. Actually, Sutton and the
association had much in common. For different reasons, both
wanted to keep the Texas cattle out of Kansas. The reform faction
of which Sutton was a member saw it as a means of curbing the
lawless ways of cowboys that had given Dodge its sorry reputation. The association members were trying to avoid Texas competition and Texas fever. In 1886, as a gesture of reconciliation and
recognition of his influence, Sutton was sent as a delegate to the
Western Kansas Stockmen's convention in Wichita; by then, their
common goal had been achieved. The marriage of convenience between Sutton and the association was consummated when the *Globe
Live Stock Journal* was consolidated in 1889 with the *Ford County
Republican,* founded in 1886 by Rush E. Deardorff and Sutton. [47]
The old cattle interest had died hard, but by 1885 the wisdom of
relying on more established regional ranchers was widely accepted
in Dodge City. Even the *Dodge City Kansas Cowboy,* created exclusively as a journalistic spokesman for the cattle industry, acknowledged "the days of the cowboy in his pristine glory at Dodge
are almost numbered now." Mike would have agreed. [48]

   Sutton was a man who accumulated both long-lasting friends and
enduring enemies. His reputation as a successful lawyer gained
him the nickname *St. Michael of the Oily Tongue* and his political
dealings the label *high muck-a-muck of Dodge City.* [49] These were
not terms of endearment. On a number of occasions he found it
expedient to leave town or at least stay off Front Street. The
*Dodge City Ford County Globe* explained: "As soon as Bat Masterson alighted from the train on his late arrival into this city, Mike
Sutton started for his cyclone building on Gospel Ridge, where he

remained until a truce was made." At one point there was an attempt to have Larned declared off limits to him by the citizens of that town. The move was in retaliation for the treatment a Larned resident, Nelson ("Net") Adams, received at the time of the Luke Short affair. Luke had asked Adams to come to Dodge to defend him. The "foreign" lawyer was met at the station by an unorganized posse of Dodge Citians who would not let him off the train. People in Larned accused Sutton of masterminding the action. The affair led to prolonged litigation and a barroom confrontation between Adams and Sutton in which, as the *Larned Optic* explained, Adams "shot him with a 44-caliber beer bottle and Mike went home badly wounded in the neck." Adams obtained a $4,500 judgment against the city of Dodge but wisely did not try to implicate Mike.[50]

Sutton lived to see the old cow town as only an exciting memory. He remained active in politics, was elected to the state legislature in 1888 and 1892, lost the nomination to Chester I. Long at the Republican senatorial convention in 1894, was appointed collector of internal revenue for Kansas by President William McKinley, worked in the Grand Army of the Republic, helped to secure the establishment of Fort Dodge as a soldiers' home, served on the home's board of managers, and continued his law practice.[51]

Although Dodge became nearly as civilized as Mike had hoped and although he reaped the rewards of political labor, his last days were not without pain and disappointment. In spite of his success and heavy caseload, he had not accumulated much in the way of material wealth. In 1887 he had been cited by the *Times* as an example of a man who had come to Dodge penniless and accumulated wealth in a short time. He was estimated at that time to be worth forty thousand dollars. But, like other Dodge Citians, he was hurt by the depressed economic conditions of the 1890s, which had disastrous effects on the town, especially its real-estate values. Sutton had been involved during the land boom in several land deals that did not pay off. He purchased a half section of land on the Soule Irrigation Canal; invested in the speculative town lots of Rio Junction, which failed to develop beyond the paper stage; purchased town lots in Hartland and Pierceville, both of which failed after an initial boom; and made several abortive attempts, including costly purchase of land, to move to Kinsley before he settled for building a "magnificent residence," an expensive one, in Dodge. When ill health came with old age, he and those dependent upon him faced hard times. Mrs. Sutton died July 6, 1888, and her sister, Jessie Clemmons, who had joined Florence in the ill-fated buggy ride with baby Stuart, lived with the family for a while and cared for Stuart. For the last twenty-five years of Mike's life, an unmarried sister, Hattie Sutton, lived with them. In 1912, Sutton applied for a veteran's pension, indicating illness and obesity as the reasons he was no longer able to work. He died at his home June 12, 1918. After his death, a pension was sought for his son. The application indicated that Stuart's total annual support was six hundred to seven hundred dollars from the trust fund established by his father. His aunt was still looking after him.[52]

Sutton's contributions to Dodge City were of a high order. Robert Wright, in spite of his many differences with Mike, praised his skill as an attorney and politician who deserved "the respect and esteem of his community." In the cattle-town years, Sutton's efforts in developing a more stable, law-abiding community based on the advantages received from the Atchison, Topeka and Santa Fe Railroad were his most important contribution. Yet many of his actions appeared opportunistic and self-serving. His desertion of his old friends in the Gang, for instance, seemed to many to be callous, even perfidious. At the time it was difficult for some to understand the extent of his commitment to the progress of Dodge City. But his rejection of Bat Masterson and Bob Wright must be judged in the same light as his willingness to come to the aid of friends, such as George Hinkle and Dave Mather, when in doing so he appeared to be betraying his own principles. His consistency was not always easy to follow. Then, too, he appeared at times to be too clever, too slick, too successful. Many felt he used rather than served the law and that his political influence was too sub rosa, too manipulative. Where Gryden was enjoyed and loved, Sutton was given grudging and discreet respect. The final judgment, however, stands: Mike Sutton, as much as any man, put to rest the image of Dodge City as a lawless and tainted cowtown and replaced it with the reality of a community suited to the peace, dignity, and prosperity needed for the nurturing of family and personal well-being.[53]

# 6. Mike's Boys

IN THE BEST of western morality plays, the hero does not stand alone facing the advancing villains in the middle of Front Street. Because of the example of his character, his unflinching bravery, and his tenacious adherence to principle, the citizenry rallies to his side and the whole community profits by the inevitable victory. The morality play proves that democracy in action, when the majority of good "little people" are pitted against the few "evil minions" of power and corruption, will be successful. As the miscast hero, Sutton, in a considerably watered-down version of that scenario, attracted to his side, usually in his office just off Front Street, a number of able men who shared his convictions, profited by the association, and stood by him as he faced his adversaries.

During the cattle-town decade, he had four law partners: Edward F. ("Ed") Colborn, 1876–80; James T. ("Jimmie") Whitelaw, 1882–83; Frederick T. M. ("Fred") Wenie, 1883–84; and L. K. Soper, 1886. Two other attorneys followed Sutton's lead, did many of his chores, and conformed to his convictions but were never partners. Robert E. ("Bobby") Burns, 1880–84, was clearly one of Sutton's crowd, an even more faithful disciple, once converted, than the partners. The other, Ezra D. ("Ed") Swan, 1883–86, began his association with Sutton when he settled in Spearville and continued to support Sutton's principles after he finally moved into Dodge. All profited from the association with Sutton; none regretted the role they were assigned or the villification that came with the label *Mike's Boys*.

*Edward F. Colborn: 1876–1880*

Mike Sutton's first partner, Edward F. Colborn, arrived in Dodge from Fort Hays, Kansas, about six months after Mike hiked into town across the prairie. Colborn was born in Ohio in 1855 and was Mike's junior by some eight years. While in Dodge, he never lost his boyish stature and appearance, a handicap frequently noted by opposing attorneys and the press, being referred to at one point as the "lawyer of mighty brain but small body." For a while, Colborn continued a previous relationship with another attorney in Cottonwood Falls, S. N. Wood. Joining Mike in 1876 in Dodge City made for a new arrangement that was an advantage for Colborn, not only because of Mike's reputation and legal influence but also because Sutton held both the city- and county-attorney offices. Sutton's first recorded political deal in Dodge was in persuading Mayor James H. Kelley to appoint Colborn to the city post that Sutton proposed to resign. Kelley agreed. Colborn became city attorney and city clerk on April 28, 1877, and the law firm of Sutton and Colborn became known for its aggressive prosecuting team handling all public prosecution in the region. The *Ford County Globe* gave him high praise when it testified that with Colborn as city attorney "an offender might as well be beneath the nether stone."[1]

The partners established themselves in the new post office, boasting the "most attractively furnished and neatly arranged office in Western Kansas." There were obvious advantages to letting a "bright young lawyer" have access to the courts and to clients supplied by Sutton, even though the income from the menial offices that Sutton had obtained for Colborn was small. In one of his earliest cases involving Hattie Mauzy, frequently cited as an example of the cowtown's handling of people charged with disturbing of the peace and one involving a number of witnesses, including Bat Masterson, Wyatt Earp, and Bill Tilghman, Colborn's fee was $3.50. The partnership arrangement was also advantageous to Sutton, who shifted some of the smaller nuisance cases to his partner. When Louis Snizek was adjudged insane after an original charge of horse stealing, Colborn conducted the hearing as acting county attorney. His early cases were all of a minor nature: suits to collect wages, disorderly conduct, land claims. He got his most im-

*Edward F. Colborn, Mike Sutton's first partner, was described as "the lawyer of mighty brain but small body." Courtesy Boot Hill Museum, Dodge City.*

portant case that first year when the city was sued for $5,000 by a prisoner who lost an eye in a scuffle while imprisoned in Dodge's notoriously inadequate jail. In none of these cases was there much in the way of fees and income, except in the last suit, which required a trip to Topeka to seek advice on proper procedure. In 1878, Colborn held the part-time offices of city clerk, city attorney, deputy county clerk, deputy county attorney, and deputy county treasurer, yet the combined fees were barely enough to cover living expenses.[2]

Colborn's first big chance for favorable public notice came in January 1879 when Sutton withdrew from the prosecution of Dutch Henry Borne and appointed Colborn to take his place. Working with T. S. Jones, the prosecuting team had what appeared to be an easy victory, but through manipulation of the impaneling process the defense received a favorable verdict. Colborn might have received even more publicity in defending the cowboys arrested as accomplices in the killing of Ed Masterson, if they had been brought to trial, but there was insufficient evidence to hold them. In defending A. H. Webb in a brutal murder case with racial overtones and community prejudices, Colborn and Gryden, acting as co-defenders, lost to Sutton, who undoubtedly was overzealous in his prosecution of an obviously demented person. In the formal language of the defense, Webb was "now and has been for a long time immediately prior hereto, a person of unsound mind and understanding wholly unable to comprehend his situation or understand the solemnity or purpose of the proceedings against him to the extent necessary to enable him to receive the trial for his life in the sense the law intended." Colborn continued to follow Webb through the justice system and eventually secured Webb's release by virtue of insanity.[3]

Although his record in court reflected more defeats than victories, the citizens of Dodge did not consider Colborn incompetent. He was, in fact, quite popular as a young lawyer—just twenty-one when he began practice—and frequently was called upon to speak at public functions. He was appointed clerk of the city council through Sutton's efforts but was reelected on his own in May 1880. He seemed to be well established by then, but he must have been aware that he would remain in Sutton's shadow as long as he practiced in Dodge City.[4]

In the summer of 1880, Colborn caught the gold fever that had infected many of his fellow Dodge Citians and joined the rush to Colorado. He spent the summer and fall exploring for gold and anthracite coal in and around Gunnison and Irwin, eventually purchasing a gold mine for ten thousand dollars. The prospect of spending a winter in the Colorado snows apparently was too much for him, however, and in November he passed through Dodge on his way east. On December 29, 1880, he married Lizzie L. Dygert in Ann Arbor, Michigan.[5]

He continued to maintain contact with Dodge City, especially with Sutton, for instance, reporting back on former Dodge Citian James Hanrahan's trial in Gunnison, Colorado. For a time he continued his mining contracts but gradually shifted his interests back to law, establishing practice in Ruby and then in Gunnison. In 1883 he ran for county attorney of Gunnison County and won. He was to live out his life in Colorado and in the legal profession.[6]

Colborn's association with Mike was during the time Sutton was getting his legal feet on the ground and while he was still identified with the Gang. Consequently, Colborn does not reflect any of Mike's later reform zeal, nor is he part of Mike's political manipulations. There is no reason to believe that he would not have gone along with Sutton's later activities or, for that matter, that he would not have revolted. From all that can be garnered, theirs was strictly a straightforward business relationship and Colborn profited in a professional way by the association.

*James T. ("Jimmie") Whitelaw: 1882–1886*

By far the closest friend Sutton had in Dodge City was James T. Whitelaw. Other partners and associates were to be nearer Sutton's philosophical position, certainly politically, than Whitelaw, but for sincere friendship, none touched Sutton as did the man who shared those first poverty-ridden days in Kansas. James T. Whitelaw was born in Brownsville, Tennessee, on May 23, 1845. His parents then moved to Salem, Missouri, where he attended school. He served in the Confederate Army and fought at Gettysburg. After the war he returned to Salem, studied law, and farmed. On April 3, 1867, he married Emma Julia Arthur at her parents' farm in Dent County. After being admitted to the bar, he and his family

*James T. Whitelaw was Mike Sutton's law partner in both Medicine Lodge and Dodge City. In his younger days, the* Dodge City Democrat *judged him to be the "Handsomest unmarried, free for all, catch as catch can attorney in Kansas." Courtesy Boot Hill Museum, Dodge City.*

moved to Medicine Lodge, Kansas, in 1873. Although well known nationally because of the treaty signed with the Indians there, the town, less than a year old when he arrived, was scarcely a wide spot on the trail. Derrick Updegraff had established a trading post on the site during the winter of 1872 and later added a sawmill and a one-room log house. The country was just beginning to attract settlers, and during the summer of 1873 a town company (Bemis, Hutchinson & Company) platted the town and a board of commissioners began meeting. By the end of 1873, however, there were no more than two hundred people in Barber County.[7]

Whitelaw entered into a partnership with M. W. Sutton, who had arrived a month or two before him. With one other lawyer, a member of the town company, in a town of four stores and three dwellings, Medicine Lodge was amply supplied with counselors. In spite of the legal presence, it was to begin life with a major bond swindle and a resulting debt that put on the county a heavy tax burden that was not to be paid off for sixty years. Although Whitelaw and Sutton, as partners, both ran for office, neither was successful; it was a defeat they boasted of in later years when the swindle by the winners was widely publicized.

The partnership resulted in a lifelong friendship between two markedly different personalities. Their nationality, upbringing, political affiliation, and service in opposing armies during the Civil War made for interesting debates and public exchanges. They did have common interests, however: both fought at Gettysburg, and they shared the poverty of early law practice. When Sutton moved on, Whitelaw remained, but only briefly. There was for Whitelaw a partnership with Henry Van Trees in Sun City, a town about twenty miles northeast of Medicine Lodge, which was platted the year before Medicine Lodge was founded and began attracting settlers about the same time. Although its early history was marred by Indian scares and stockades were erected for protection, it missed the county-seat prominence that Medicine Lodge enjoyed. Sun City grew rapidly, however, as a cattle town and boasted a population of fifteen hundred. Legal business in 1878 was even less lucrative than that in the Barber County seat, even counting the few dollars Whitelaw brought in as a justice of the peace. At least one of his cases in Medicine Lodge had traveled all the way to the

Kansas Supreme Court, where his client won on the basis of
Whitelaw's preparation of the case.[8]

To improve his economic position, he purchased a general store
in Lake City, an even smaller ranch community two miles west of
Sun City. Lake City was never to enjoy even the brief boom that
came to its neighbor. While there, Whitelaw continued a minimal
legal practice, devoting most of his time to the store. Business was
disappointing and Whitelaw was obliged to advertise that produce
would be exchanged for goods. Meanwhile, his former partner,
Mike Sutton, who was prospering in Ford County as county attorney, made certain Whitelaw knew of his good fortune.

The former partners had kept in touch, and Mike made several
trips back to his old haunts, where the closeness of their friendship
was widely recognized. When Whitelaw narrowly missed being
struck by lightning, the local paper, the *Barbour County Mail*, described the event in a poetic conversation between the two friends:

> *SUTTON TO WHITELAW*
> *Come take my hand old fellow.*
> *Lay it there and tell us how*
> *You escaped the firey furnace.*
> *And not a wrinkle on your brow.*
>
> *I have heard that lightning struck you*
> *That your checks were handed in.*
> *And that on earth Jim Whitelaw*
> *Would not be known again.*
>
> . . .
>
> *W[H]ITELAW TO SUTTON*
> *Here it is and thank my fortune*
> *That this noble brow of mine,*
> *Lives and moves and has its being*
> *All unscared except by time.*
>
> . . .
>
> *I was standing on the prairie,*
> *Not a living thing in sight,*
> *Save a mule that was a grazing*
> *Just a little to my right.*
>
> . . .

*For it flashed across the heavens,*
*Till it got to a spot o'er my head,*
*Then it dropped upon my forehead*
*Like a hundred ton of lead.*

*But this head of mine old fellow,*
*Is agin the general rule,*
*For that lightening failed in its object*
*And glanced off and killed that mule.*[9]

Following Sutton's lead, Whitelaw ran for county attorney and was elected in November 1880. During his term he joined C. W. Ellis in legal partnership. In the middle of his term, after a visit to Sutton, he resigned on April 13, 1882, moved to Dodge City, and, undoubtedly at Sutton's coaxing, reestablished the partnership. Whitelaw explained that his reasons for the move were based on the obvious prosperity of Dodge, which was experiencing considerable growth in population. Furthermore, it was a railroad town with a much "wider field for the practice of law" and better opportunities for his children. But it is clear that the friendship with Sutton was the major reason for the move. Sutton did open many doors for his friend. Through his association with Sutton, Whitelaw became recognized and accepted by the community through the public exposure he received in his appearance as Sutton's assistant in important cases, including the highly publicized defense of Ed Hardesty. He not only appeared in court as Sutton's partner, but when Mike felt himself disqualified to handle a case, Whitelaw acted as county attorney. A story told by Heinie Schmidt, Dodge City's chronicler of legend, fact, and conjecture, may be apocryphal, but it does illustrate the kind of relationship the two had established:

One day while a very sensational case was being tried, Whitelaw was appointed to preside [serving in Sutton's place]. He became very angry and said to Sutton, "Mike why in the devil is it that every time a case comes up that the judge doesn't want to try, you use your political influence and have me appointed?" With a twinkle in his eye, Mike replied, "Jimmy, you don't know how much good it does my Irish heart to see an old rebel like you raise up his hand and swear allegiance to the constitution and the flag!"[10]

From the beginning of his stay in Dodge, Whitelaw entered into the political wars with enthusiasm and to the surprise of some as a

Democrat, in opposition to his partner. His first political test came when he ran for county attorney on the Independent-party ticket in November 1882. Local candidates did not use national party labels, but the Independents were Democratic in sentiment and Harry Gryden, a solid Democratic leader, had called the mass meeting and presided as temporary chairman when Whitelaw was selected. Editor Frost saw Whitelaw's candidacy as a ploy on the part of Sutton to control all political activities in Dodge, Republican and Democrat, through a typical Sutton behind-the-scenes maneuver. Whitelaw denied the charge and made a public promise: "If I am elected to office it will necessitate a dissolution of the partnership between us." He was as good as his word and in January, after his election, he set up a separate law office. This did not mean an end to their close ties, nor did it end Frost's carping. For instance, when Whitelaw, as county attorney, closed a variety show, Frost saw Mike's influence being exerted through the office of county attorney. [11]

As a matter of record, Whitelaw frequently called on Sutton for assistance and probably would have been prudent to have used him even more often. Jimmie, as folks were now calling him, got off to a very shaky start as county attorney, and his two-year record in public service was far from the success Mike had achieved during his first two years. Among Whitelaw's early failures was his dealings with the elusive William Bird, accused cattle thief, who kept law officers busy trying to run him down because Whitelaw could not keep him before a court once he had been captured. In the Coolidge train robbery, Gryden and Swan for the defense negotiated continuances until they could get charges dismissed for want of evidence. In the Mather killing, which looked like an "open and shut case," Whitelaw made a major blunder in attempting to keep reporters out of the courtroom during the preliminary examination, then lost control of the case to a change of venue. When he suggested that reports of the proceedings would prejudice prospective jurors, he in fact was doing the work of the defendant's attorneys. In the McCarty case, even with Sutton's assistance, the prisoner was never convicted; he died of smallpox while out on bail, but what was worse in the eyes of the community, the bond was lost in a bureaucratic shuffle.

To make the first sorry season more traumatic, Mrs. Whitelaw died October 22, 1883, leaving Jimmie to care for the three children, Bessie, Correy, and Harold. After the funeral, the children went back to Dent County with their grandparents, but in the spring they returned to Dodge, where various relatives took turns looking after the family. By the time Bessie was seventeen, she had taken over the care of the home.[12]

The county attorney's caseload was never light. The winter session of the district court in 1884 had forty-four cases, of which Whitelaw was involved in fifteen. Unfortunately, Gryden was the opposing attorney in most instances, being the attorney of record in sixteen cases. Much of Whitelaw's term during the years 1883 and 1884 was taken up with the Saloon War.[13] The first shots in that bloodless affair were fired on April 28, 1883, by Luke Short and L. C. Hartman, but before it ended with the final exchanges in out-of-court settlements during the winter of 1884, nearly everyone in Dodge—certainly every public official—had been threatened, sued, or slandered. The press, including papers on the East Coast, were in on the fun from the beginning. Although Luke, Bat Masterson, and their gunslinging acquaintances paraded up and down Front Street in menacing fashion, the real action moved to Kansas City, Topeka, and points east as Luke sought redress at the state level.

Dodge City, especially local-government officials, had remained fairly isolated and brashly independent of state governmental interference from the beginning and city and county officials now became alarmed that their authority would be usurped. As the affair wore on, some began to wonder whether such independence was not a liability, so they solicited help from any available source. A bigger concern, however, one shared by all permanent residents, was revival of Dodge's image as a lawless town where vigilantes clashed with gunmen. Whitelaw, aware of the unfavorable publicity generated by Bat and Luke, quickly joined those seeking to keep local control and a curb on violent action. He became a major figure in countering Luke's attempt to bring Governor George W. Glick and state forces into the fracas.

The governor was not anxious to intervene in a purely local squabble, but he could not ignore his duty to maintain law and order. When confronted with conflicting reports concerning the violence in Dodge, he sought an on-the-scene personal account of what was actually happening, naturally turning to a known politician of his own party. In response to a telegram from Glick, W. F. Petillon, leader of and spokesman for the Democratic party in Dodge, left for Topeka on May 10 to confer with the governor. The city council, primarily Republican, was certain that because of Petillon's Democratic leanings he would not present their side of the story in a favorable light. As clerk of the court, he had endorsed the statement Luke sent the governor describing his abuse and the breakdown of authority. Knowing that Luke was to get in touch with the governor personally, Sheriff Hinkle asked Whitelaw to go to Topeka and present the "true" version. It can be assumed that the Dodge City Republicans chose Whitelaw because they felt it wise to produce their own Democrat to deal with Democratic Governor Glick. At any rate, Whitelaw wired ahead, indicating that he would call on the governor on the fifteenth, and made a hurried trip to Topeka. By the end of Petillon's and Whitelaw's visits, the governor must have been thoroughly confused. Additional reports from telegrams, letters, and personal accounts did little to clear the picture. Adding to the confusion were Dan Frost's reports and editorials in the *Ford County Globe,* which opposed the city council and supported those Frost believed to be the old Gang members. The governor and the *Topeka Commonwealth* had tended to accept Frost's accounts, which backed the first reports they heard, and consequently cleared Short of wrongdoing. On May 13, after seeing the governor, Whitelaw was back in Dodge in time to add his name to a telegram warning Glick that he had been misinformed. Apparently, Whitelaw persuaded the governor to meet with a delegation of twelve Dodge City businessmen. The committee, known as the Twelve Apostles, went to Topeka on the seventeenth and was introduced to Governor Glick by Whitelaw. The burden of its message was that Dodge City wanted to be: "Let alone! The people were a distinct municipality for local purposes and local government; with sufficient power to protect themselves against internal discord."[14]

By then, Atchison, Topeka and Santa Fe Railroad officials, including Whitelaw's good friend Sutton, the railroad's legal representative in Dodge, saw to it that the railroad was brought into the affair. The governor's understanding seemed to clear with the more lucid messages coming from the Santa Fe's central office. Finally, with the personal intervention of Adjutant General Thomas Moonlight, matters did calm down. There were, however, continuing repercussions. The final determination of the case in favor of the champions of reform was made when the Santa Fe threatened to move facilities from Dodge. Whitelaw was one of the men to whom General Manager C. C. Wheeler spoke in Topeka. He came back to Dodge to convert the fence straddlers to the new order, which would mean embracing prohibition, Deacon Klaine, and closed saloons. It was to be a bitter submission for many.[15]

Whitelaw was brought into two late lawsuits against Dodge City that were related to the affair and that were initiated by Luke Short and Nelson Adams. Gryden was city attorney at the time, and in each case Whitelaw acted in conjunction with him. Adams's charges caught both attorneys off guard, and they did not arrive in Larned, where the district court was to hear the case, before a judgment unfavorable to Dodge City had been rendered. They requested a new trial, and the motion was granted. Adams kept the case alive for several months and eventually settled out of court, accepting as part of the settlement some bonds that were to be paid out over a ten-year period.[16]

In the second case, Short sued the city for $15,000 in damages. The city council employed Whitelaw to appear for it with an interesting remuneration agreement: he was to receive a retainer of $250 and an additional $740 if he won the case or got the judgment reduced to no more than $500. The case eventually was settled out of court, as were the final fees. The Short affair had cost the town dearly in cash, disruption, and, by far the most burdensome, a tarnished reputation. The city of sin and fun was back in the headlines of papers throughout the nation, more firmly fixed than ever before. In the end, however, Dodge citizens were so appalled by the nation's perception and expectation of lawlessness that they redoubled their efforts to achieve reform and a calmer, less exciting lifestyle. When reform came, Whitelaw was to be on the side of the angels—or at least on the side of the Deacons and the saints on Gospel Ridge.

After the excitement of the Luke Short affair, it would seem things might ease in the county attorney's office. The 1884 cattle season was a profitable one, and the Fourth of July celebration, with its Mexican-style bullfight, was to be unequaled in cowtown celebrations. The next day, July 5, H. B. ("Bing") Choate, the 25-year-old son of a prominent Texas cattleman, was shot and killed in A. B. Webster's Old House Saloon by Dave St. Clair, a gambler. Since the shooting had occurred before a full house of witnesses, Whitelaw did not attempt to push the case after the initial investigation showed self-defense. His explanation reflects the frontier prosecutor's respect for public opinion unless it ran clearly against the law. His statement also indicates his continued reliance on Sutton and an awareness of Mike's influence:

This is a sad case—sad to defendant and his family, sad to the public generally, to Dodge City in particular, and infinitely and immeasurably sad to deceased and his family. I have given the evidence the careful consideration which was due on account of its importance. Public feeling and excitement has run high in regard to this matter, and it has been intimated that the County Attorney might be influenced by such a consideration. Let me say that while I respect public opinion, I would scorn to be guided in my official conduct solely or largely by it. Mr. Sutton was employed by the friends of the deceased to assist me and jointly we have concluded that the evidence will not justify us in holding the defendant to bail. I regret the homicide as much as any one, but I think that the interest of the state and county can best be subserved by discharging defendant for the present. We have had all the evidence that we shall probably ever be able to get. It shows that deceased gave the provocation, drew his revolver and gave defendant reason to fear he would be killed. Had this evidence all come from defendant's friends, I would ask that he be held; but coming from the warm friends of the deceased, from friends for years gone by, from Rutledge, Belt, Shanklin, and those men from Tennessee, I am bound to believe. I asked these men if defendant drew his pistol first, and none of them testified positively that he did. Masterson, Carrington, Robinson and others testify that St. Clair made no movement to draw his pistol until deceased had drawn his. On the testimony here brought out I do not believe that defendant can be convicted. Technically and from a strictly legal standpoint, he may be guilty of an offence, and in my judgment is, and the homicide is not justifiable. But I do not believe this evidence is sufficient to convict him before any jury. While I regret the homicide as much as any man, I still do not think as a citizen and as an officer that the defendant should be held to District Court. My associate, Mr. Sutton, is very positive in this matter, and the other attorneys of the town hold the same view. [17]

Whitelaw did attempt to prosecute Mysterious Dave Mather in a case he believed to be clear and uncomplicated, since he had on his side the sympathy of the community, favorable witnesses, a wounded bystander, Mather's statement that "I ought to have killed him six months ago," and Harry Gryden to assist him. Mather, however, was found not guilty. Whitelaw's old friend and partner, Sutton, was too much for Whitelaw in defending the former marshal. Juries, not evidence, make decisions, and Mysterious Dave went free to kill again. Within four months, he was back in Ford County's district court under a new murder charge.[18]

Whitelaw's record in the county attorney's office was at best a spotted one, comparable to Sutton's tenure only negatively. Happily, he served only two years. The citizenry and government officials apparently looked with more favor on his legal acumen than the record would have suggested. When the county was involved in a suit at Topeka during the following term of B. F. Milton, the county commissioners appointed Whitelaw to represent them.[19]

His return to private practice in 1885 was to bring him better times. In December he joined Colonel T. S. Jones in a partnership that established "the finest law office in the city" at the corner of First Avenue and Walnut Street. He continued his association with the Democratic party: served on the Ford County central committee, was nominated for the state senate, and attended the state party convention as an alternate delegate. He carried Ford County in the senatorial race by a safe margin (659 to 586) but failed to win the district. He also was elected county commissioner and served on the commission through the remainder of Dodge's cattletown days.[20]

Whitelaw managed to avoid most of the prohibitionists' squabbles. Frost, who kept careful book on such things, found him lukewarm, reporting that "although not a pronounced prohibitionist, he nevertheless brought with him from Barber county a strong [Governor John P.] St. John prohibitionist record." He could not escape entirely and was involved in the bizarre Wright-Sutton episode as counselor for Mike. But he apparently found the liquor situation more humorous than criminal. He reported to his friends in Medicine Lodge that the saloons in Dodge were all running in fine shape. The new drugstores, he wrote, have "a few bottles of drugs and plenty of foreign and domestic wines and liquors. The 'Long Branch' drug store, the 'Bon Ton' drug store, and so on."[21]

He continued his private practice, appearing in court frequently, and was admitted to practice before the Kansas Supreme Court, but like other lawyers before him, he became infatuated with the prospects of reaching a larger audience through the press. In 1883 he and Petillon, leader of the Democratic forces in Dodge, bought the equipment of the *Garden City Herald* and moved it to Dodge by boxcar. If they had completed their plans to publish, it would have been a strictly Democrat organ. However, both men were caught up in new ventures, and friction over the Luke Short affair developed between them. The press remained in packing crates until Whitelaw finished his term as county attorney and had time to put the project into operation by himself. The result was the *Dodge City Sun,* first published in April 1886. The editorial policy reflected some Democratic bias, but the *Sun* was more objective and impartial than any journal published in Dodge City at the time. Whitelaw had hopes of establishing a daily paper, but with three other strong papers in town, he had to settle for a weekly. He was both editor and publisher until January 1887, when Frank S. Whitelaw took over.[22]

Jimmie remained in private practice until 1894, when he moved to Silverton, Colorado, and he lived for a time in Creede; by then he had been remarried to Emma Warren of Dodge City. In Colorado he was elected to three terms as county attorney of San Juan County and served as a member of the state legislature. He returned to Dodge City in 1904, formed a law partnership with L. A. Madison, and practiced in Dodge until death by paralysis came on February 10, 1909. He was survived by his wife and two children, H. A. Whitelaw of Goldfield, Nevada, and Mrs. Harry Hubbard of Dodge City.[23]

Jimmie was one of Mike's most faithful disciples, but his legal and political influence never came to equal that of his mentor. Although he and Sutton remained close friends, even allies, Whitelaw established his own independence and was truly his own man. He was recognized as a sound practitioner and competent counselor. His success in Colorado clearly indicated that he could stand on his own. The newspaper venture proved a financial failure, but under his guidance it was the most objective recorder of news that Dodge City had during a crucial and transitional phase of development. In the end, the old town and its memories of triumphs and failures still held enough charm to lure him back to live out his life there. In hindsight, the threat posed by the Luke Short faction seems more apparent than real; at the time, however, it was perceived as a serious challenge. Whitelaw, in cleaving closely to his responsibilities as the elected champion of the law, had helped Dodge City move closer to a more stabilized social order. As a cowtown lawyer, officer of the law, and citizen, he made his mark a creative one.

### Frederick T. M. ("Fred") Wenie: 1882–1886

Fred Wenie was one of Sutton's home-grown lawyers, receiving his legal training in Mike's office and being admitted to the Kansas bar after completing his legal apprenticeship. He was born in Oneida County, New York, in 1859. His father remained in the army after the Civil War, and when he was transferred to Fort Dodge as quartermaster with the rank of captain, he brought his son along as a clerk. In April 1880, Fred moved to Dodge City and began clerking in Sutton's office. At the June 1882 term of court, he was admitted to the bar. That same year, Sutton took him on as a partner when J. T. Whitelaw withdrew from the firm to accept the position of county attorney.[24]

Wenie was judged to be a "bright young attorney" when he joined Sutton, and he never quite overcame the handicap of youth. In characterizing several Dodge attorneys, Nick Klaine described him thus: "Fred T. M. Wenie, he of the silky mustache, the only member of the bar who is known as a ladies' man. The ladies' pet, as it were." As the only bachelor attorney (except Gryden) in town at the time, it was a characterization easy to defend. It had not been always the case, though. When he arrived in Dodge, he was married and a father, but in June 1877 his wife, Doris, divorced him and received custody of the children.[25]

From the beginning, Wenie tended to concentrate on business cases. Gradually his dealings in real estate and selling insurance became more than supportive sidelines, eventually taking over most of his time, with legal work becoming a secondary concern. It

*Frederick T. M. Wenie was one of "Mike's Boys." He eventually left the practice of law and did well in the insurance business. Courtesy Kansas Heritage Center, Dodge City.*

is symbolic that he was first noticed in the press when he acted as business agent for Luke Short in establishing two Chinese men in the laundry business.[26] He did all the things a young attorney was expected to do, participating in the literary society ("with a shrill tuba voice . . . in Mr. Bennett's opera"), joining the Presbyterian Church, and becoming involved in politics. Politically, he followed his senior partner's lead, becoming an active member of the local People's-party central committee and the national Republican party. He remained the secretary of the People's party until he left Ford County and was serving in the same capacity for the county Republican central committee when he left. His political chores and his association with Sutton paid off when Mayor Larry Deger appointed him city attorney in April 1883.[27]

The city attorney's office was to be particularly busy for the next twelve months. There were the usual obligations—inquests, minor court cases, advice to the city council—and there were more unusual duties, such as accompanying the deputy sheriff to Trinidad, Colorado, to help return Eugene Stout, who had been convicted at the last term of the district court, jumped bail, and fled west. But, as was true of other Dodge City officials, Wenie spent most of his time dealing with the Luke Short affair. He was honored, if that is the proper word, by being the first to feel Luke's wrath.

When Short returned to his saloon late on the night of Saturday, April 28, 1883, and learned that his entertainers had been arrested, he headed for Wenie's house to secure bond and get them out of jail. He rousted Fred from bed and at gunpoint demanded and got the singers' release. From that first encounter until the end of the escapade, Wenie was committed to the anti-Short faction. He signed the early letter that informed Governor Glick that he had been misinformed about affairs in Dodge and the longer statement reprinted in the *Topeka Daily Capital* explaining the city officials' version of events. Dan Frost tried to create friction between the law partners by reporting the rumor that Sutton had dropped Wenie; it was a wasted effort. Wenie and Sutton remained on the same side in the Luke Short dispute and continued their partnership through 1883, even though Wenie was spending less time on strictly legal matters and more on his growing business interests.

When the partners moved to a new office at Wright, Beverley & Co. that year, Wenie was listed as "lawyer and financier." [28]

As long as he lived in Dodge, Wenie's interests remained oriented toward business. He became an agent for the Gilbert brothers in selling railroad lands, was the last agent of the original Dodge City Town Company, was a charter member and principal promoter of the speculation town of Rio Junction, and was the leading real estate agent for Dodge City property transactions. The *Times* reported in August 1884 that he had sold nine "lots on Saturday . . . a poor day for town lots at that." The following year, as befitted a town developer, one of the streets was named for him. His growing prominence as a businessman also was recognized in his election to the Dodge City Board of Trade. He added insurance and abstracts to his interest and acquired partners who specialized in these matters. Insurance was to become increasingly important to him, and the *Ford County Globe* labeled him the "gentlemanly and efficient insurance manipulator." One of his partners, L. W. Cherington, concentrated on real estate and used such modern ploys as organized excursions for prospective buyers to sites as far away as Lamar, Colorado. [29] In 1886 he liquidated his assets, selling his insurance business to Bayer and Hobble and his abstract firm to L. E. McGarry and Company. He was appointed special agent for Niagara Insurance Company, which had headquarters in Omaha, Nebraska, and was put in charge of a territory that included Nebraska, Wyoming, Utah, and Montana. Early in January 1887 he moved to Omaha to assume his new position. [30]

During the last few months in Dodge City while he was arranging his business affairs, he performed one last service for his mentor, Mike Sutton, and for a brief time returned to his earlier interest in legal affairs. Sutton had need for the temporary appointment of a sympathetic justice of the peace for Ford County when Dodge was declared a second-class city, its changed status invalidating the previous election. Wenie accepted the assignment when Governor John Martin made the appointment. Apparently, with this action, he considered all personal debts paid. He remained in the insurance business and did not return to the practice of law. In the early 1900s he moved to Kansas City, Missouri, as district manager of the Phillipsburg Insurance Company. He died unexpectedly on

April 15, 1914, at age fifty-four, being survived by his wife and one child. [31]

Wenie's legal career was brief, but it had given him the opportunity to develop new and more lucrative interests. Law proved to be a serviceable steppingstone to more and better opportunities, even if it had not been the direct path he first intended. Sutton's assistance to the young man was of considerable importance to Wenie because he became known as a partner of the leading attorney in Ford County. He shared many of Sutton's views and was supportive of Sutton's political manipulations. Their closeness grew when Wenie married Mrs. Sutton's sister, Jessie Clemmons. After he left Dodge, the two families remained in close contact. Although he did not pursue a legal career, the time spent as one of Mike's Boys was to shape Frederick Wenie's career and have a major influence on his life. The support he gave Sutton, in turn, helped Mike in his efforts to move Dodge City beyond what Sutton believed to be a limiting and vicious course as a cowtown.

## L. K. Soper: 1886

Sutton's last partner in cattle-town Dodge, but by no means his last law partner, was on the scene barely ten months. He came to Dodge City in late February 1886 from New York, where he had been in practice fifteen years. He made his first appearance before the district court in early March. It was an impressive beginning; both the *Times* and the *Democrat* judged him to be a "forceful speaker" and wrote of his "easy manner" and "untiring industry." [32]

Before the summer was over, he had become deeply involved in Sutton's attempt to discredit the antiprohibition forces through the disputed sheriff's election. He took the lead in the preliminary examination and shared the prosecution with Sutton when the trial moved to Topeka. As a result he incurred the wrath of Bat Masterson and admitted that he feared Bat would do him physical harm. The Dodge City community generally opposed Sutton in his efforts to prevent Pat Sughrue from being seated, and Soper encountered considerable hostility when he ran for county attorney in November 1887. He was soundly beaten by W. E. Hendricks. [33]

The defeat was not to be the last word on Soper's status in

Dodge City. He had chosen the correct side in the prohibition debates, since there was a growing shift in sentiment for prohibition. He was to remain in Dodge for several years, enjoying an expanded practice and a secure position in the social life of the community and figuring prominently in both the Prohibition and Republican parties.

### Robert E. ("Bobby") Burns: 1880–1884

Bobby Burns was Mike Sutton's protégé and his most faithful convert. He undoubtedly benefited from his association with Mike more than any of Sutton's partners. Although the tie with Sutton eventually led to public ridicule and an unflattering, if anonymous, niche in the folklore of the town, undoubtedly Bobby, and certainly Mrs. Burns, considered the humiliation well worth the redemption. His Dodge City story begins at the bleakest point in his career and ends with an upbeat drive toward improvement and respectability.

Harry Gryden was a drinker; Bobby Burns was a drunk. The difference was considerable, but then Bobby recovered and Harry did not. Both were caught in the bitter political squabbles of the day, and for Burns party strife was to spread his drinking problem and failings before the public. Gryden could give in retaliation as good as he got, and he held the platform that allowed him to respond. In the early years, Burns had neither the opportunity nor the wit to fight back. Consequently, most of what history records of him comes from the acid pen of his enemies. A political opponent makes a merciless biographer.

The story of Burns the drunk, which made him something of a legend, began in the intraparty squabbles of the Republican party. The Ford County Republican caucus in October 1884 was uncompromisingly split between two factions, one supporting Mike Sutton and the other backing Dan Frost. Frost was there as a proxy delegate, and the old-line Republicans took exception to him and certain other delegates as being unrepresentative of the approved Republican line. P. G. Reynolds, temporary chairman, tried to arrange a compromise between the feuding groups, but when George M. Hoover was made permanent chairman and the credentials committee, loaded with Sutton men, barred Frost and others as delegates, the caucus split wide open. The Frost faction, which included Bat Masterson and the remnants of the Gang, tried to counter the Sutton-dominated caucus with a meeting in Nelson Cary's Opera House Saloon, but the damage was complete and the Sutton forces controlled the official party ticket.[34]

During the heat of the squabble, someone, a bitter pro-Frost delegate, wrote a letter, signed "Coal House," that described several members of the Sutton faction who attended the convention in highly unflattering terms. Frost printed the letter October 21, 1884, and Klaine of the *Times* accused Bat Masterson of being its author. Bat's reply in the next issue of the *Globe Live Stock Journal* did not deny the charge but challenged anyone to find a false statement in it. Obviously, Bat wrote it: the letter is pure Masterson prose at his choleric best. Bobby Burns, who was presiding as police judge, was among those attacked most bitterly in the letter. He had taken a leading role in the ouster of Frost and had delivered such a violent attack on the Gang that "the 'crowd' sent forth hisses and cut him short." Masterson gave the police judge no quarter in the Coal House letter. The piece stands as Burns's fullest biography.[35]

Sutton had referred to Burns and others of his persuasion as good men during a speech before the caucus, so Bat made several sarcastic remarks about them and their qualifications for being so honored:

> Some years ago he [Burns] was sent to this city from Illinois on a pauper emigrant ticket; he landed among us without a penny; he has a wife and several children; he immediately became an object of charity, and the benevolent people of this community had his family to care for; the good women of this city, as well as many of those that are not so good, morally, carried provisions to this good(?) man's house and gave them to his wife and children to keep them from starving to death. All of this time this good man was laying around gambling tables, sponging drinks from the gamblers and steering the unsophisticated up against the different games. . . . his wife went among the neighboring women and endeavored to get them to aid her in cow-hiding him and giving him a coat of tar.[36]

The impecunious condition of the family of four children was a fact, and because of it the community did treat Burns and his family as a special charity case. Even his position as police judge, which

he held from 1882 through 1884, was on the order of British out-
door relief; a vote for Burns was considered a way of relieving
Dodge of a pauper's burden. As to gambling, Gryden's game above
the jail was one to which Burns must have steered "the unsophisticated," since he was dealer there. As for "laying around gambling
tables," Burns might have found his immortality in that posture,
enshrined as he was in a story Robert Wright told of the "Dodge
City Keeley Cure." Wright identified the victim as "Judge Burns"
and referred to a time when "there dwelt a lawyer in our midst,
who was quite badly crippled, but had a bright mind and was a good
lawyer." [37]

Wright's story has been repeated in most of the remembrances
and popular histories written about wild and woolly Dodge City.
Occasionally a name is attached by these writers, but it is never
Burns's. With his usual bluntness, Bat Masterson did name Burns
in his Coal House letter as the corpse on the table. For some reason, historians in their selective process have not reproduced that
letter; consequently, Bobby Burns has been denied his spot in cowtown lore alongside the likes of poker-playing Governor Thomas
Carney, Dirty Face Ed Jones, and Dr. Meredith, the bamboozled
physician of "private diseases." Masterson's version of the story
was brief and graphic:

The police had to carry him [Burns] home to his wife on several occasions
in a beastly state of intoxication, and on one occasion they laid him out on a
gambling table, painted him from head to foot, and placed about a dozen
lighted candles around him and called in everybody from the street to see
the dead Burns. [38]

Wright's version was longer and the one most old-timers remember, no doubt having their memory jogged by Wright's publication:

The fellows that decided to administer this dose of the "Dodge City
Keeley Cure" to the lawyer, waited until he was surcharged with booze,
which they knew would soon be accomplished. He attempted to leave the
bar, but fell in a drunken stupor. The boys then procured a coffin, attired
him in a conventional shroud, prepared him as carefully as though they
were preparing him for the long sleep, except embalming him, powdered
his features to give him the ghastly appearance of death, tied his jaws together, and then placed him in the coffin and placed the coffin on a table
between the two doors, where he lay "in state" and in view of passersby.

Many persons thought he was really dead and placarded him with these emotional and reverential lines:

> *Judge Burns is dead, that good old soul,*
> *We ne'er shall see him more,*
> *We never more shall see his face,*
> *Nor hear his gentle roar (in police court), saying,*
> *"Guilty, your Honor!"*

He remained in the coffin, in full view, for several hours before he awakened. He was a hideous sight, and, after looking in the mirror, he went home completely disgusted with himself, sobered up, and was never known to take a drink in Dodge City afterwards. He became one of our most respected citizens, and held several offices of honor and trust. This was a profitable lesson to him, and proved very beneficial to his family and the community.

The story is undated, so just when Burns became a recovered alcoholic is not clear, but certainly it was before he became the sober protégé of Deacon Klaine, Sutton, and the prohibitionist faction.[39]

Burns and his family arrived in Dodge in August 1881, coming from Naperville, Illinois. His first advertisement as an attorney appeared in late February the following year. Apparently he was elected police judge on the strength of his qualifications as an attorney, and apparently he did a good job; at least he was reported to have collected more fines than any other judge up to that time. He was the first police judge to make public the names of those fined and the amount. In the first week of March 1884 his records show that he collected $150 from saloons, $150 from gamblers, and $80 from prostitutes. Klaine's judgment was: "Judge Burns plunges the harpoon into all alike." Another Dodge Citian felt his sting when he "sent an insulting proposition to a married lady." She had him arrested and Judge Burns fined him $75 and costs. Deacon Klaine wrote in approval: "Judge Burns' court is becoming a terror and the evil ones may well stand in awe and dread, for in this court there is no leniency for a grave offense."[40]

Burns's practice of law in Dodge had been minimal when he was elected, and apparently it improved but little after he won office. Sutton had enough confidence in him, however, to allow him to serve as acting county attorney in minor cases when Mike was out of town on other business. Burns's health was poor, the result of wounds he suffered in the Civil War. A musket ball in the face had nearly cost him his eyesight. Evidently, his wounds were extensive and no doubt left him with some psychological impairment besides the physical handicap; at least he was unable to do manual labor or do justice to his profession. It was enough to drive a man to drink.[41]

In a March 1883 caucus to determine a slate for the city election, R. G. Cook, who had been justice of peace, aspired to the police judgeship. Several at the caucus supported him, but the decision went to Burns. The nominating committee's reasons for the choice were given in a recital of Burns's physical difficulties, the impoverished state of his wife and children, and the fact that Cook was able-bodied and already had a job. In short, kindness and charity recommended him over his opponent. Bat took that to be a great weakness and chided the voters for their action. In a poem published in *Vox Populi,* Masterson's one-issue venture into Dodge City journalism, Bat once again cruelly expounded on Burns's defects:

> *How poor was little Bobby Burns,*
> *That people paid his way?*
> *About as poor as he is vile*
> *That's what the people say.*
> *How come he got the votes*
> *That elected him one day?*
> *He limps and squints, and has sore eyes*
> *Upon election day.*

Regardless of Bat's opinion, Burns's nomination was a wise choice by the party. He won the contest with votes to spare.[42]

Burns's actions as judge bear all the marks of a repentant sinner. His fines were heavy, and he held to the strict letter of the law. He was known to give "moral lectures and Biblical quotations on the sin of blasphemy and indecent language [that] have so often caused the unfortunate listener to wish himself in hades for the same length of time." He also railed against booze and tobacco. As a now devoted member of the reform faction, he was entangled in the Luke Short affair. The arrested female entertainers from the Long Branch were brought before Burns's court and fined heavily. He joined the Twelve Apostles and Dodge City officials in publicly warning Governor Glick that if the legal representatives were not allowed to handle the Luke Short situation (that is, govern the city), there would be bloodshed and anarchy. These actions made Burns a tool of the opposition in the eyes of Short and Bat Masterson.[43]

In August 1883, Short swore out a complaint against Burns, charging him with misconduct in office and collection of illegal fees. It was one of many suits Luke initiated, including one against R. G. Cook, the man who challenged Burns in the city caucus. The county attorney reviewed the charges against Burns and dismissed them. All of the other suits eventually were dropped or settled out of court.[44]

Burns was not a candidate for police judge the next term. Aspiring to better pay, he ran for county attorney against B. F. Milton in November 1884, losing by a substantial margin. Shortly thereafter he moved to a homestead in the southeastern part of the county near the village of Bellefont. He was appointed justice of the peace there, which, according to Nick Klaine, made him the ranking official next to the governor because the township was at the moment unattached to any other political unit. But Burns found it hard to stay away from the action in Dodge City courtrooms. He continued his legal practice from his rural setting and on occasion defended certain unfortunate individuals charged with his own old indiscretions. It must have given him some comfort to win a case by appealing to the larger social evil. "The policeman," he told the judge, "should arrest the men who sold the liquor and not the men who drink it."[45]

In November 1886, Burns told Klaine he intended to move back to Dodge. The town was by then considerably quieter. The cattle-town atmosphere was changing rapidly, and Luke Short's friends had moved on to less-regulated communities. Perhaps Burns believed the time had come when a former veteran, former lawyer, former judge, and former drunk could feel safe in the town that had once treated him kindly. But he apparently did not move back, although he did continue his practice and appeared in district court occasionally until 1888. The last mention in Dodge of this strange member of Sutton's coterie was in November 1898 when a notice appeared in the Dodge papers reporting Burns running for and winning the probate-judge election in Payne County, Indian Territory.[46]

*Ezra D. ("Ed") Swan: 1883–1886*

Ed Swan claimed that he endured one of the West's least auspicious landings when he was "dropped on the prairie like a cat in a bag." He and a friend, W. V. Johnston, came from Chicago "along the line of the A.T. & S.F. R.R., prospecting." They had read in the railroad's promotional material glowing reports of new townsites in western Kansas and noted among them the townsite of Spearville, named for Alden Speare, a railroad director who was living in Newton, Massachusetts. On September 23, 1877, in the middle of the night, the conductor woke Swan and Johnston, indicating they had reached their destination. When daylight came and they could see the extent of the town, they discovered the railroad section house and one store; the rest was an unbroken stretch of prairie.

After a brief survey of the situation, they were satisfied that there was potential for growth and advancement, and so they returned to Chicago, where they began negotiations with Santa Fe officials to buy half the town lots. Swan and Johnston were joined by David Williams, and the new partnership completed the deal. Swan and family arrived in Spearville on December 9, 1877. When they arrived, there were only three houses; by spring forty-two houses had been built and the town, situated between Kinsley, twenty miles to the east, and Dodge, sixteen miles to the west, was booming.[47]

Swan was born in Ohio in 1839. He reported to the census enumerator that when the war came he enlisted in "Ohio Company W, Regiment 80, Infantry" and served throughout the war. After returning home he read law, was admitted to the bar in Illinois, and engaged in private practice until he decided to improve opportunities for his growing family by moving west. Even more than most of the early lawyers Swan proved to be an energetic jack-of-all-trades. Besides developing and boosting his adopted town, he homesteaded two miles west of Spearville, raised cattle, farmed, managed the land office in Dodge, served as station agent at Spearville, practiced law, acted as notary public, and edited the *Spearville Enterprise* from May 18, 1878, to August 24, 1878.[48]

During Swan's first years in Spearville, lawyering did not hold a high priority and only occasionally did he have a case before the district court. Editing the *Enterprise* in itself was a full-time job and one he filled with considerable success. Apparently, his wife's ill health forced him to leave the paper; in the last issue he edited, he apologized for the condition of the printing and indicated that sickness in the home had required him to spend much of his time away from the newspaper.[49]

From his farm near Spearville and his land office in Dodge, he continued to maintain a small legal practice. That might have been the extent of his contribution to the legal community in Dodge if his wife had not died in May 1883. Left with the care of his aging father and three children, the oldest of whom was fourteen, he moved to Dodge in September, established a law office in the Great Western Hotel, and advertised himself as "Attorney and Dodge City Collection Agency, Bills, Notes, Mortgages, Mechanics Liens." He continued his association with the land office but concentrated his efforts on developing a legal practice.[50]

Swan had been active in Ford County politics while in Spearville, and after moving to Dodge, he became even more involved with the Republican party. As was true of other lawyers, he made frequent bids for offices, attempting to be elected clerk of the district court, probate judge, and county attorney. He was successful in none of these efforts. He did not give up on the Republican party, however, but continued to fill minor party positions, doing many of the routine chores required of the organization. Not until prohibition became a burning issue did he achieve prominence in the Dodge City political battles. When he became closely associated with Mike Sutton, he found a cause that would give status with the Republicans and mark him as a special target by the opposition. He became a trusted companion of both Sutton and Dr. Galland in attending prohibition meetings and conventions and in planning political strategy. As Sutton's front man and errand boy, he assisted with Dr. Galland's quarrel with saloon owners Bond and Nixon and with inviting prohibition activists Governor John P. St. John, Albert Griffin, and A. B. Jetmore to bring their crusading zeal to Dodge City. For his pains he incurred the enmity of the likes of Robert Wright, W. F. Petillon, Bat Masterson, and the old status quo crowd on Front Street.[51]

Masterson made Swan one of the scapegoats in *Vox Populi*. If

Swan won in the upcoming election for probate judge, Bat wrote, it would be by the same method he won in Spearville, that is, "by misrepresentation." People ought to know, Bat continued, that Swan was unfit to be placed in charge of "poor widows and orphans of Ford County, after turning his aged and decrepit father out upon the streets to die of starvation." That charge against Swan was groundless; a year later, Saul Swan was still living in his son's home. However, Bat's vitriolic attack, which must have been read by every literate adult in Dodge City, may have influenced the voters: Swan lost the election. In spite of Bat's slander, Swan was to have reason to appreciate the sheriff, if ever so grudgingly, when a mob gathered around Galland's hotel, where Jetmore and Griffin were staying. Swan had been instrumental in bringing the two men to Dodge and felt responsible for their safety. In trying to defend the prohibitionists, Swan was "knocked down and trampled" and would have suffered even more if Bat had not intervened. [52]

For all his political shrewdness, Sutton occasionally misjudged a situation. Either through carelessness or the wrong assessment of certain individuals' convictions, Mike Sutton's minions had not prepared an 1885 city-election ticket that would ensure a dry administration. Fearing that Bat's latest ploy of closing down the saloons would result in even more saloon domination of law enforcement once the election was over, the prohibitionists decided quite late to contest the sheriff's spot. Under the direction of Sutton, Swan called a mass meeting to nominate a likely candidate on a new Independent-party ticket. Apparently, the masses met in Sutton's office and adopted a slate by acclamation. Swan testified that it was not just a Prohibitionist-party ticket, but admittedly it had a close connection: "The connection, as I understand it, between the Independent ticket and the Prohibitionist was . . . that everybody that supported the Independent ticket was not prohibitionist, but all the prohibitionists supported the Independent ticket." Swan also admitted that he was one of "the promulgators of the ticket, assisted and aided and advised and helped in the campaign." But when the election was held, he was so fearful of Masterson's threats that he hid out in Spearville and did not go near the Dodge City polls. He also denied that only a handful of men met in Sutton's back room to create the party and the candidates, but it was an unconvincing denial. Obviously, Sutton's hand was very much in all Independent-party maneuvers. It was a poor effort. The Independent ticket failed miserably, and Sutton's desire to prevent the victor, Pat Sughrue, from taking office because of election irregularities failed just as certainly, but not until Sutton pushed the issue all the way to the Kansas Supreme Court. Swan did receive some monetary compensation for his efforts in the trial, but more important for his career, he had remained loyal to Sutton and the prohibitionists in the face of threats and villification.[53]

Swan's support of Sutton came at a critical time when Mike could count on few faithful supporters. Because Swan's influence was so limited, his efforts seemed to contribute little to Mike's campaign and perhaps damaged Swan's standing in Dodge; however, the long run proved that Swan had backed the right issue, the right party, and the right leaders. His law practice was to prosper in the drier town. He had been counselor in only a few important cases before 1885, mainly the Dave Mather case and the Coolidge train-robbery case, but after the dry forces won control of local government and came to dominate the social life of the community, Swan profited from his early association, especially his contacts with Mike Sutton. In 1885 the *Times* noted that he had just returned from a business trip during which he had settled an estate worth a million dollars. He moved his office from the hotel room he had occupied when he came to Dodge to a suite over Mrs. Beadle's Millinery Store and then to one at Ham Bell's store on Front Street, where he maintained an "elegant and commodious suite of rooms." That same year, he was admitted to practice before the Kansas Supreme Court. He remained in Dodge only briefly after the cattle-town days before moving on to other law offices and other political battles.[54]

# 7. The Last of the Gang Lawyers

AFTER THE DEATH of Harry Gryden, there was no one of equal stature to support the Gang or its convictions, no one to match wits with Sutton in the courtroom or in the political arena. Of the three attorneys who did remain loyal to that way of life, none fitted Gryden's black-sheep mold; none was given over to the dissolute life of Front Street or was as intimately involved with the saloon and dance-hall crowd. At least two of the three came from more cultured backgrounds and had a better education than their opponents. While this might seem to have inclined them toward the "more high-minded citizens," the conditions of the quarrel had more to do with personal motivations and philosophical considerations than with personal lifestyles and tastes.

At the most basic level, the opponents of change simply did not like the opposition. They distrusted Sutton's political maneuvering, resented his courtroom success, and accused him of still tipping the bottle when given the opportunity. Even more offensive was the sanctimonious meddling of Deacon Klaine and his carping newspaper. As for Dr. Galland, who was responsible for bringing in outside prohibitionists to malign the town, he had been in court frequently over the years with petty moralizing cases and in one instance had been found guilty of striking a woman who owed him money. None of the reformers' hypocritical attitudes toward other citizens' morality would bear close scrutiny, Gang members believed. Such men offended their sense of pride and fair play while denigrating a lifestyle they believed to be acceptable, if not proper and preferable.

At the highest philosophical level the Gang saw the Sutton-Klaine-Galland reforming zeal as an attack on a free society through repudiation of the concept of inalienable individual rights to choose bad habits as well as good ones. The abolition of drink, the closing of dance halls, and the banishment of soiled doves placed unwarranted restraints on the citizens' right of choice as free agents in determining their own personal habits. It was not a matter of their own use or consumption, but, rather, the principle of who should determine what might or might not be chosen. Acquiescence, in the reformers' view of life and governmental authority, would place men and women who shared the Gang's own concepts under the guardianship of the likes of Sutton, Klaine, and Galland, a fate that would have caused Harry Gryden to toss restlessly in his grave. Control of personal values was at the bottom of the quarrel. Liquor consumption became a convenient rallying symbol for those favoring the status quo, just as it was an emotional issue for the forces of reform. "Live and let live" might well have been the Gang's motto, if one added "as long as it was legal."

Benjamin F. Milton, John H. Finlay, and Thomas S. Jones, whatever their motives, were to be the last of the Gang lawyers. Only Jones lived through the entire cattle-town decade; Milton knew Gryden for only a short time; and Finlay was there only for the final year, 1886. For Colonel Jones, the opposition's victory was his second bitter taste of defending a lost cause. By 1887 the reformers had won and cattle-town Dodge City was as dead as the Confederacy. And with it died that other symbol of a free spirit, the unfettered cowboy, whose demise was to be revered in later years as the price paid by a nation that had turned to dehumanizing machines, an industrial economy, and restrictive codes of conduct.

## Benjamin F. Milton: 1883–1886

Of the last Gang lawyers, Benjamin F. Milton was the most outspoken and was to delay the tides of change longer than any of his compatriots. Although something of a Johnny-come-lately in terms of the original members, he endorsed the principles of the early Dodge Citians and remained in Dodge long after the old-timers had passed on to whatever rewards they merited. When he arrived in Kansas in 1883, he was introduced to the likes of Harry Gryden and Robert Wright, who even then were fighting a rearguard action

*The portraits of Benjamin F. Milton (left) and John H. Finlay ap-*
*peared on the masthead of the* Western Kansas Advocate's *only issue*
*in April 1886 with this notation: "For the gratification of our enemies,*
*and the mortification of our friends, we hereby present cuts of the pro-*
*prietors of this paper." Courtesy Kansas Collection, Spencer Research*
*Library, University of Kansas.*

to preserve the status quo. He joined them in attempting to hold
back the tide of progress, prohibition, and purified morality; it was
a role he openly admitted. He was just as bluntly frank about the
people he favored as those he did not. While on the witness stand
in a case Sutton was using to expose the deplorable Dodge City
conditions that his faction was trying to eradicate, Milton un-
hesitatingly acknowledged that he had turned to the Gang elements for support:

Q. When you were elected county attorney, didn't you derive your support from the [Gang] element, the saloon keepers, gamblers, and that
class of people?
A. I suppose that they voted for me more than for my opponent.

When he was asked, "Wouldn't you help those who helped you?"
he again admitted he would, "if it were legal."

It was significant that Milton was county attorney through 1886, the last year Dodge clearly can be counted as an authentic cowtown. From that strategic position, he tried to delay the inevitable ending; he chose procrastination as his modus operandi and the law as his weapon.

Among the most distinguished citizens in early Dodge City were the brothers Dr. Charles A. and Benjamin F. Milton. After graduating from Rush Medical College in Chicago, Charles came to Dodge in 1882 to be associated with the town's pioneer physician, Dr. T. L. McCarty. A year later, Benjamin, usually referred to as B. F., followed his brother to Ford County. Both were born in Plymouth, Illinois, the sons of Eleanor and William Milton, who claimed descent from Revolutionary War stock.

B. F., the younger, was born August 13, 1855. When he was seven years old, his parents moved to Clinton, Missouri, where he completed his elementary-school education. In 1879 he was elected public administrator of Henry County, a position that gave him time to combine reading law with his public duties, and on his twenty-fifth birthday he was admitted to the bar. The following spring, he opened a law office in Clinton. As a firmly established professional, he was active in the social and political life of the community. On December 28, 1880, he married Harriet E. Rice of Wooster, Ohio.[1]

When the position of principal of the Dodge City school became vacant, Charles wrote B. F. suggesting he apply. Milton got the job, and in September 1883 he moved to Kansas. He spent the next nine months teaching and administering the school. When the term ended in the spring, he resigned and opened a law office. There was the usual slow start; his name does not appear as attorney of record for any case before the district court during 1884. His life, however, was busy and rewarding.[2]

Among other activities, B. F. was attracting considerable attention in the local Democratic party. As secretary of the party's county convention in September 1884, he was responsible for calling the meeting that was to select the slate for the upcoming election. In nominating their county attorney candidate, the delegates chose both Colonel Thomas S. Jones and Milton for the position. Jones graciously withdrew so that B. F. could receive the unanimous endorsement of the party. He could not have chosen a more opportune time to enter politics. The Republicans nominated Police Judge Bobby Burns as Milton's opponent. Burns had not redeemed himself in the eyes of many voters who still remembered the dead-drunk "corpse" stretched out on the barroom table. Although Milton was young and untested, at least he had a sober and successful year's experience as a teacher. He won the election handily and met with the county commissioners for the first time on January 14, 1885.[3]

Dodge City in 1885 was considerably subdued, showing signs of outgrowing the raucous days of Front Street license. In taking the post, the new county attorney did not anticipate dealing with the bloody confrontation of cowboys hurrahing the town and defending their honor with pistols. The winter term of the district court did in fact reflect the somewhat more settled climate: there were only eight criminal cases. The most time-consuming one saw a charge of attempted murder reduced to assault and battery of hack driver Andor Eliason of rural Pearlette.[4]

The guns had not been totally silent. The court session did have a murder trial that was in the best Front Street tradition, springing as it did from a quarrel between two Dodge City businessmen. Ed J. Julian ran a restaurant down the street from former police officer Benjamin F. ("Ben") Daniels's saloon, and there had been bad blood between them for some time. Julian's violent temper had brought him into conflict with the law on a number of occasions; in November 1884, for example, Marshal Bill Tilghman had arrested him for administering a beating to three cowboys who had refused to pay for a meal. The trouble between Julian and Daniels became a crisis when Julian attempted to obtain an injunction that would close Daniels's saloon. On the morning Daniels was notified of the legal action, Julian came out of his restaurant headed away from Daniels's bar. Daniels, standing in front of his saloon, opened fire. The first shot caught the restaurant owner in the back and was followed by three more at close range, the last two shots fired deliberately while Julian lay on the ground. Julian did not have a gun, had been shot in the back, and had not threatened or, for that matter, said anything to his assailant. Although Daniels immediately went to find the marshal to surrender, it appeared to be a clear-cut case of premeditated murder. An inquest was held before Justice of the Peace H. M. McGarry, who set Daniels's bail at five thousand dollars. As county attorney, Milton argued for and eventually got the bond increased to ten thousand.[5]

Trial was held in November 1886, with James T. Whitelaw and L. L. Ady of Newton as Daniels's attorneys. Their main defense lay in attempting to show that Julian appeared to be drawing a gun and Daniels fired in self-defense. Milton countered by citing the fact that Julian had no gun and was shot in the back, dying without knowing what had hit him. According to the press, Jones, who assisted Milton, had "made a stirring speech" when bond was increased, and the newspapers again were highly complimentary of the prosecution's work during the trial, noting that Milton "made one of the best speeches of his life . . . a brilliant effort . . . [in which] he acquitted himself with honor." All to no avail. Julian's pugnacious personality and past reputation were too widely known not to have affected the jury. The case took most of the week before "the twelve good men and true" began deliberations, and the jury stayed out until four o'clock in the morning debating the issue. Reportedly starting with half for conviction and half for acquittal, the jury saw each vote shift to acquittal. Daniels left the courtroom a free man.[6]

The local elections of 1884 and 1885 were fought mostly over the issue of prohibition. The Republicans split on the issue, and the Democrats, supported by W. F. Petillon's new paper, the *Democrat,* and backed by recently arrived German settlers, defeated the drys by a healthy margin. Milton, as a Democrat charged with the responsibility of upholding state as well as local laws, was criticized bitterly by the dry forces because of his sympathy for the saloon operators and cattle interests. Prohibition had become a symbol of progress for the drys, who hoped to create a more orderly life for Dodge; gentility, prosperity, progress, civilization, and prohibition were synonymous to them. With Robert Wright, a member of the original Gang who looked with favor on the cowtown days, in the mayor's office, Milton—even if he had wanted to—could have done little to force closure of the saloons. But in February 1885 the drys gained a new weapon when the legislature passed a bill providing that any citizen could seek an injunction against a saloon when a city or county attorney failed to act. This put heavy pressure on Milton to prosecute at least the more flagrant violators.

When the prohibitionists resorted to bringing whiskey dealers to court on their own, Milton, the elected official charged with the responsibility of initiating criminal action, was hardly supportive. Knowing the unfavorable climate of law enforcement in the county, the drys decided it was time for outside help. M. W. Sutton, Dr. Samuel Galland, Nick Klaine, and E. D. Swan invited Albert Griffin, the organizer for the Kansas Temperance Union, to come to Dodge to witness at first hand the flagrant flaunting of state laws. Griffin was pleasantly surprised by an enthusiastic, standing-room-only reception in Dodge's new Methodist church. Encouraged by the unexpected demonstration of support, he filed injunction papers against Dodge City's saloonkeepers. When Milton refused to prosecute, Griffin hurried back to Topeka to ask Attorney General Simeon Briggs Bradford to go in person to prod Milton into action or to act himself. The attorney general compromised by sending a representative from his office, A. B. Jetmore, to whip the town into compliance—a town busily preparing for the summer season of cowboys and cattlemen requiring entertainment and staggering quantities of liquor. The reception the two men received brought Bradford his first serious challenge to the new prohibition commitment of Governor John A. Martin. Undoubtedly aware that the ardent prohibitionists would be met by a belligerent body of men from Front Street determined to save their businesses, as well as their personal right to drink whatever was offered, Milton left town. Pat Sughrue also saw the wisdom of pursuing his business elsewhere.

Clearly, many Dodge Citians resented such outside interference, just as they had during the Saloon War. On June 29 a mob, obviously "well oiled" with illegal spirits, gathered outside Dr. Galland's hotel, where the two interlopers were staying, attacked Galland, and would have done violence to Griffin and Jetmore if Bat Masterson had not intervened. The town was in an ugly mood. Sam Prouty of the *Kansas Cowboy* urged moderation on all sides, pointing out that if the mob or the whiskey dealers were prosecuted, "hell would break loose and the devil would be to pay."

Milton agreed and refused to act. Griffin, now thoroughly shaken, advised the attorney general not to file charges until he had a force large enough to prevent a massacre. As in the bloodless Saloon War, outsiders urged the governor to send the militia to preserve law and order. Bradford was at least stirred to go see for himself how near to bloody anarchy the aging cowtown had come. His was an uneventful, even pleasant, visit, and when he reviewed Judge Strang's message urging patience, he reached the same conclusion. An uneasy truce prevailed, lasting for nearly a year.[7]

In one of his quixotic moods, or perhaps as a transparent bid for votes, Bat Masterson broke the truce in March 1886 by closing all saloons and filing the necessary complaints in Milton's office. As prosecuting attorney, Milton saw that the informations were written, warrants were sworn, and all who dispensed liquor, except the medical doctors, placed under arrest. Klaine and Sutton assumed that Bat's sudden conversion to strict law enforcement was a ruse to defeat prohibitionist A. B. Webster for mayor by making Robert Wright appear more attractive to voters not solidly committed to drying out the town. Sutton considered the arrests a form of blackmail supported by Milton, who was proceeding with the charges. Sutton believed that as soon as Wright won the election, all suits would be dropped and Dodge would be swimming in illegal liquor again. He wrote Attorney General S. B. Bradford about his fears:

The Co. Atty. [Milton] who would not prosecute when you urged him to—who would not do his duty when the Governor desired it—who would not entertain the complaints has upon the complaint of Masterson against the saloons decided to entertain it. The saloons are closed and prohibition reigns supreme. Now this break of Masterson is to force the saloon men to accept his man for mayor and drive Webster off the track. So soon as he accomplishes this feat he will withdraw the complaints. The Co. Atty. will consent and the affair will be ended. The game can only be defeated by your appearing on the field and informing the Co. Atty. that the cases must stand. The complaints must be pushed. [You] get to be an atty. of record, and let the courts know that the cases must not be dismissed. General, now is the opportunity. We pray you come next train.

As was frequently the case, Sutton signed the letter "Private and confidential."[8]

In a later suit, Milton testified under oath that Masterson was sincere in his prosecutions and was helpful in the trials—to the point of coaching Milton on who might be sympathetic jurors willing to convict violators. There was no subterfuge in Bat's or his own actions. The reason they failed to win favorable verdicts, Milton said, was that they "could not get twelve men that believed in conviction." Milton felt he had presented a good case and reminded his questioners that the judge told the jurymen that "they had perjured themselves that they didn't bring in a [guilty] verdict." The first jury had stayed out several days, and it was only after two more trials that proceedings were "adjourned by the court on his [the judge's] own motion, because he said, on the bench he was tired of the cases hanging there." After devoting most of his early term in office to shuffling papers and appearing in court over the whiskey cases, Milton won one conviction and another individual pleaded guilty. Obviously, neither Milton nor the community was committed to abolishing the consumption of liquor. Milton was by no means the only county attorney dragging his heels. The law was poorly written, and even when convictions were won the crime itself was only a misdemeanor. But Dodge City had been singled out for special consideration by the attorney general and Milton's stance required some finesse, if not courage. For Ford County, the do-nothing policy worked well.[9]

None of the worst fears of either the wet or dry forces was realized, at least not immediately. Webster won the election, but there was no wholesale closing of saloons. When the whiskey affair came before the courts, Milton could not find complaining witnesses. Since the Gang was thoroughly routed, Bat, the drys' worst enemy, left town for more congenial parts. Both the prohibitionists and the wets reduced the pressure on the issue as other serious matters demanded immediate attention. A series of fires destroyed much of the business district and distracted the more ardent prohibitionists and their foes. Time, however, was working against the Gang and for the dry forces. In the words of District Judge Jeremiah C. Strang:

The quarantine law passed last winter is quietly working out the salvation of Dodge City. The festive cowboy is already becoming conspicuous by his absence in Dodge, and ere long he will be seen & heard there, in his glory, no more forever. The cowboy gone the gamblers and prostitutes will find their occupations gone, and, from necessity, must follow. The bulk of the saloons will then die out because there will be no sufficient support left, and the temperance people can close the rest as easily as they could in any other city in Kansas.

Prohibition was to come gradually and without the blaze of any violent final fireworks.[10]

Milton's action, or lack of it, was well calculated to dampen the emotionalism that had built up on both sides. W. F. Petillon, albeit expressing a biased Democratic point of view, praised Milton and gave a rational explanation of the county attorney's position:

No county attorney anywhere in the state attends personally to a larger proportion of his cases. Mr. Milton is always accessible to those who have complaints under the criminal laws to make, and never denies a warrant unless he believes the case too trivial for attention, or unlikely to result in a conviction. Upon entering the office Mr. Milton determined to adopt the policy of treating all criminal statutes alike, and hence has been enabled, so to speak, to command the situation with respect to the particular statute which occupies so much of the public attention. That is, he has been willing at all times to listen to complaints for violations of the prohibitory law, and issue warrants for the arrest of the offenders, but has been unwilling to become detective and informer.[11]

More aggressive action by either side might well have touched off violence and more unfavorable publicity for Dodge. T. S. Jones had quashed fifteen whiskey suits in October 1884, an action that seemed to flaunt Dodge's promiscuous drinking habits in the face of the state's prohibition laws. His decision had aroused the dry elements and brought the outsiders into town. Milton avoided that pitfall. Concerned inaction was what Dodge needed; Milton carried it off with style and aplomb.

In 1886, B. F. made a bid to retain his office as county attorney, running in a four-man field. Although prohibition remained the major issue, the political parties were divided on the subject and the voters were considerably confused. The winner was R. N. Wicks, who campaigned under the Labor-party label.[12]

After his defeat, Milton continued his practice with John H. Finlay, who had joined him in 1885, and established an office at the corner of Bridge and Chestnut streets. The practice prospered, and in 1891, Milton was admitted to plea before the Kansas Supreme Court. In 1895 he was elected judge of the Southern District of the Special Court of Appeals and, from 1911 to 1913, he was a member of the state tax commission. Late in his career he formed a partnership with his son, W. C. Milton. He remained active in the Democratic party throughout his life: was an elector for the presidential election of 1888, ran for state representative in the Thirty-seventh District the same year, and was renominated in 1892. His wife preceded him in death, and he was living with his daughter, Mrs. R. H. Bennett, in Dodge City when he was stricken with his final illness. He became incapacitated in June 1914, suffering from cirrhosis of the liver, and died September 18, 1915.[13]

Milton's actions as county attorney were symbolic of the final days of Dodge's cowtown era. Like the town, his term of office was filled with the problems of prohibition; even the one spectacular murder case was the result of bitter emotions roused by an injunction to close a saloon. His role of peaceful procrastination also was in keeping with the community's ambivalence over liquor. Milton's record was not spectacular, but it was based on principles that were proper for Dodge at the time. He managed to hold back for two years the final alteration of the status quo. In the end, the Gang mentality was swept away in the tide of reform. Milton accepted the inevitable and remained in the town as a contributory member of the bar until his death.

## Thomas S. Jones: 1879–1881, 1884–1886

Colonel Thomas S. Jones was associated with Dodge City's legal community longer than any of the other attorneys except Mike Sutton. Jones was in Dodge at the beginning of the trail-herd business and remained to see its demise. He ran for most of the legal-related offices and fought those in the reform element who were hastening the decline of cattle-town ways. He defended the violent lawbreakers, knew personally the gunmen, and shared the excitement of the town's experience as an end-of-trail mecca. He never lost his enthusiasm for the freedom, fun, and magic those gaudy times afforded. For all his obvious delight with what Dodge City offered, the colonel was never fully accepted by the citizens of Dodge and was, in fact, a full-time resident for only part of the de-

cade. Ironically, not until progress, as understood by the reformers, had replaced the less restrained ways of cattlemen with more
cramped and controlled civilization did he and his family become
permanent members of the community. By then he was truly the
last of the Gang lawyers—the final embodiment of cattle-town
justice.

Jones was born in Pittsylvania County, Virginia, on August 14,
1845. He received a classical education at the University of Virginia
that led Kansans to admire his elegant dignity, his obvious erudition, and his affable manners. After graduating from Brockenborough's Law School at Lexington, Virginia, he was admitted to
the Virginia bar. He perhaps served briefly in the Confederate
Army, but the title of colonel was bestowed more as the mark of a
southern gentleman than of military distinction. After the war,
Jones practiced law in the eastern circuits of his native state and
married Mary G. West of Halifax, Virginia. Two children were born
in Virginia, Mary C., and Edgar W. [14]

As was true of many other young Virginians, Jones concluded
that greater opportunities lay in the West than in the Reconstruc-
tion South. His first stop on his migration was Chase County, Kansas. There he joined Augustin S. Howard in law practice in 1872
and the following year shifted to a partnership with Fenimore P.
Cochran. Jones was elected mayor of Cottonwood Falls in 1873 and
was re-elected the following year, when he was also nominated for
the position of state representative by the Republican party. In a
hard-fought campaign in which Jones was opposed by the granger
faction, he won a surprise victory over S. N. Wood, one of the
more prominent men in town. The colonel proved to be a diligent
legislator who succeeded in securing passage of several bills bene-
fiting Chase County, served on the prestigious Judiciary Committee, and, interestingly, in light of his later activities in Dodge City,
moved the "passage of a prohibitory law." He was defeated by
Wood in 1874 for state representative but was elected to the city
council. The colonel seemed well on his way to becoming one of
Cottonwood Falls's leading citizens. Perhaps there was something
in the settled character of the town, which had been a county seat
since 1862, and the bitterness of partisan politics that did not mesh
with Jones's vision of the West. On the other hand, his frequent

trips to Dodge City to attend Ninth District court sessions brought him into a milieu that was attractive and stimulating.[15]

Jones's introduction to Dodge had come when he was a young, unencumbered lawyer, miles away from home and family responsibilities, enjoying the freedom of boarding in one of Dodge's hotels. In such a setting there were sure to be some high times. He became an accepted member of the Gang and indulged in the rough horseplay that characterized that early camaraderie. The press, for instance, reported a fluid fishing expedition that ended with Jones's companions convincing him that he was experiencing the initial horrors of delirium tremens, complete with friendly, cuddly snakes. Like Bobby Burns, he swore off booze, at least in jug-size quantities and at least for that trip.[16]

The commuting also brought a contest of loyalties in his family that was to complicate the next ten years of his life. His personal desire was to move to Dodge, and he informed the *Ford County Globe* that he intended to locate there permanently, which caused the editor to comment that "he will make Rome howl when he gets fairly started." The problem was getting started. His wife did not want to move, and then there were other complications, including illness, a fire in the home, and his daughter's contract to teach in the Cottonwood Falls school. After several abortive attempts to get matters settled, Mrs. Jones did come in 1879 to look over the town from the safety of the Great Western hotel. Apparently persuaded that there was a reasonable degree of civilization, she reluctantly agreed to move. The colonel established a "spacious and handsome" office in the old railroad land office, his daughter secured a position in the Dodge City school, and all seemed settled into the new life.

No doubt one of the reasons he wanted to move to Dodge was the parsimonious attitude of the people in Cottonwood Falls toward the legal profession. Jones had been involved in a troublesome and time-consuming lawsuit against the Atchison, Topeka and Santa Fe Railroad with fellow attorney C. N. Sterry. The plaintiff settled out of court on her own and in doing so reduced the original claim from $10,000 to $750, leaving the pair of attorneys to split the $100 fee awarded by the court. Another case Jones pursued through appeal to the Kansas Supreme Court netted his client $33.25 and Jones little but experience. At about the same time, the editor of the *Chase County Leader* launched a campaign to reduce the annual salary of the county attorney from $400 to $25. After he moved to Dodge, Jones made a point of bragging about his new practice, knowing his boasts would be carried in the *Chase County Leader*. The reporter confided to his readers that Jones had told him he was "doing a heavy law practice and getting pay for it." [17]

Although the colonel's preference lay with Dodge, the allegiance of the colonel's lady remained in Cottonwood Falls. Her toleration of Dodge soon waned, and by December 1882 she was back in Chase County and the colonel was living the life of a traveling lawyer, with trips home to be with his family. Occasionally his son accompanied him, and the Dodge City papers carried frequent notices that Jones had just "returned from a trip down the road." Not until the spring of 1885 did the Joneses purchase a home in Dodge; L. K. McIntyre, the stage operator, sold them his place on First Avenue. Even then Jones frequently listed his official residence as Cottonwood Falls and apparently maintained a home and offices in both cities for much of the decade. In 1884 the *Dodge City Democrat* observed that Jones, "the irrepressible Tom of 'auld lang syne' . . . would come back and dwell with us, were it not that he is the only fighting lawyer in Cottonwood Falls, and they can't do without him." As late as March 15, 1885, he was still protesting his determination to make Dodge his home and was still commuting on the Santa Fe. Apparently, there was a marital dilemma that was never solved. His dual residence, however, did not prevent him from enjoying the cattle-town lifestyle, nor did it keep him from running for and briefly holding public office in Dodge City. [18]

Dodge Citians hardly could be expected to return the colonel's enthusiasm. He rarely won the offices he sought, although he was frequently appointed to fill unexpired terms, and he never had the number of clients needed to challenge either Gryden's or Sutton's dominance of the legal profession. His considerable abilities were recognized, but his erratic comings and goings undoubtedly made him appear undependable to potential clients. Still, there was no denying his presence. "The irrepressible Tom" was rated next to Gryden in oratorical powers: "truly able and eloquent." He also possessed elegance and southern dignity and the handsome good looks to match, a combination that impressed the frontier community. Even Deacon Klaine could find no demeaning description for him as he did for the other Democrats, but characterized Jones simply as "the handsome Tom with his bright democratic face." Democrats were more effusive. An account of him speaking before the Democratic county committee reported that "the old reliable speech maker came to the front as usual and made the best talk of the day. No matter when the Colonel is called on, he is able to wind off a two column talk with an ease and grace known only to himself." Another of his political speeches was said to "give the meaning of Democracy in its true sense." But it was Republican Dan Frost who paid him the highest compliment when he confessed that he was borrowing from Jones's "gentle and eloquent language" when he described the death of an old enemy with the phrase "the zephyrs are waving the daisies over his grave."[19]

Although his dual residence prevented Jones from building as large a practice as Gryden and Sutton, he certainly had more business in Dodge than he ever had in Cottonwood Falls. The number of cases he represented in the Dodge City district court varied with his availability: two in the January 1879 session, eight in June 1880, eleven in January 1881, and two in January 1884. As a friend of the more wayward citizens of the town, his cases involved some of the most notorious clients in Dodge, and considering the reputation many of them had, the judges' and juries' decisions were surprisingly favorable to them. Jones defended such notorious characters as Dutch Henry Borne, Johnny Gill, and James Allen, as well as lesser-known but equally lawless men, such as F. W. Bennett in the killing of Israel R. McGraw, cold-blooded murderer James Dempster, and the Coolidge train robbers.

Because of his early contacts with the Gang, Jones was a close friend of Bat Masterson, Dodge City's chronic troublemaker. His first public defense of Masterson came in a letter to a newspaper during the 1879 election when the first serious cracks appeared in the Gang's uncontested control of Dodge City politics. Robert Fry, editor of the *Spearville News,* published several statements designed to damage Bat's chances in the election for sheriff. Masterson lost the election to George Hinkle and blamed Fry, among others, for his defeat. Fry was aware of Bat's feelings but continued his abusive articles, reporting that Charles Roden, a Spearville resident, had told him, "Bat Masterson said he was going to whip every s— of a b—— that worked and voted against him in the county." A letter followed, signed by Roden, claiming that Bat accosted him in front of Jones's office, struck him several times, and stole his wallet. Jones came to Bat's defense in a letter that reflects Jones's character and style:

Editor Speareville News: In justice to myself, as well as to Mr. Masterson I wish to correct some erroneous impressions as to the difficulty which took place between Mr. Chas. Roden and Sheriff Masterson in my office a few days since, an incorrect report of which was given in the last Speareville NEWS signed by Roden containing statements untrue and unjust.

Mr. Roden and myself were engaged in a friendly conversation when Mr. Masterson entered my office, in response to an invitation extended to him during the early part of the afternoon, as I wished to see him in reference to a matter of business. Roden was standing up and in the act of leaving when Masterson came in, they met face to face and to all appearances the greeting between them was mutually friendly, soon after which a conversation commenced between them, in which Masterson accused Roden of using language against him before the election, which was untrue and which he had no right to do. Roden replying, that was alright.

They then assumed the attitude of belligerents, Roden putting his right hand in his rear pocket, evidently for the purpose of intimidating Masterson and making him believe he intended something more serious. Masterson immediately seizing him by the hand dealt him several severe blows, saying at the same time "pull it, if you can." Roden finally made an unceremonious exit from the scene of strife into the street and from thence into Mr. Mueller's shoe shop. Masterson was unarmed. While fighting is to be deprecated, frankness impels me to the belief, that in this instance, there was a merited rebuke visited upon the person of the wrong-doer. Yours

T. S. Jones

The above communication from Col. Thomas S. Jones of Dodge City puts a different feature on the case. The columns of the NEWS are always open for controversy in a courtroom manner.

Jones's letter cleared Bat of any wrongful act but did little to assuage his temper. The few Gang members, such as Robert Wright and Jones, who remained loyal could not persuade Bat to stay in

Dodge. Jones paid for his loyalty to the Gang at the polls. As one of five candidates for county attorney, he lost in the same election that prompted Bat to leave town.[20]

Apparently stirred by the Bat Masterson affair and his own loss at the polls, Jones became more active in politics than he had been in the early years. Among other changes in his life when he came to Dodge was his party affiliation. He had been a successful Republican in Chase County; now he returned to the party of southern preference. The shift disturbed editor Frost, but it was more in keeping with Jones's beliefs and sectional training. He worked with Gryden in attempting to lure the Greenback-party supporters to vote Democrat. He ran unsuccessfully against Mike Sutton in the county election of 1880 and supported the Gang in the city election that spring. Dog Kelley, the original leader of the Gang, won the mayor's seat once again, and Jones felt so encouraged by the voters' response that he ran for city attorney in April 1881. This time he was successful.[21]

Politics, however exciting, remained secondary to the job of lawyering. The 1880 year had been an active one for Jones's practice, resulting in several successes in spectacular criminal cases. Although he unsuccessfully defended Johnny Concho (John Gill), one of the town's favorite troublemakers, who received a sixteen-year sentence to Leavenworth, Dutch Henry Borne was acquitted. Jones also got F. W. Bennett freed from a murder charge through the testimony of the victim's wife and won acquittal for Frank Seeley, who was charged with larceny. His legal skills were evident when he persuaded Sutton to drop three other cases. In the face of Sutton's formidable presence, it was a better-than-average showing. The *Ford County Globe* noted that Jones was "building a successful practice" that included both civil and criminal suits. Mundane matters, such as drawing leases for sheepmen to let their flocks out on shares with farmers and disputes over preempted claims, occupied much of his time.[22]

But criminal cases, even minor ones, could hold a certain amount of interest and excitement. In March 1882, Jones was retained by Mrs. F. L. Pierce to defend her in the Dodge City JP court against the charge of assault with intent to kill. The case was tried with great tact and patience by Judge Rufus G. Cook and defended with total commitment by Mrs. Pierce, who employed N. A. Adams of Larned and R. W. Evans of Topeka to advise Jones. The *Ford County Globe*'s personal, moralizing coverage of the trial reflects the editor's belief in the trivial nature of the suit as well as his hackneyed understanding of sex roles. The court in comparison seems far more objective than the press, which professed to be a generator as well as a barometer of local attitudes:

There are two factions in the little society of Lakin, and the fight is rag-ing very bitterly. . . . The two factions had been engaged in a running skirmish for a year or two, gradually warming up as each faction gained new recruits, until about two weeks ago, when a hand-to-hand, square-open-and-shut fight between Captain Dillon and Mrs. Lieutenant Pierce was had. Dillon had been saying something tantalizing in the paper (which, by the way, he publicizes for amusement), which Mrs. Pierce at once ap-plied to herself, and it being more than her brave and haughty spirit could brook, she girded on her armor and bearded old man Dillon in his den with high tragedy in every feature of her countenance. Dillon received her with that dignity and military bearing which a great occasion demands, and in-formed her that he was ready for business, but added that the items in his paper did not refer to her. This latter remark was virtually a sympton of weakening on the part of Captain Dillon and gave courage to the enemy who at once made an effort to crowd him to his corner. A hand-to-hand fight ensued, which lasted nine seconds, the result of which is now, and may forever be, in doubt, as the only witness present was the handsome daughter of Mr. Dillon, who was so frightened that she will now attempt to give no accurate account of the second round. At any rate, Mr. Dillon, whether from a desire to shrink from the notoriety that the name of "champion lightweight of Lakin" would afford him, or from fear of getting worsted if the fight continued, called to some men for help; the assistance arrived and the lady was escorted away. As she retreated, however, she stopped in front of the office long enough to hurl a stone back at Mr. Dillon, which missile was brought down to Dodge as a witness against her. Mr. Dillon filed a complaint against Mrs. Pierce and she was arrested on a charge of assault with intent to kill. Mr. Dillon says at the time of the scuffle she had a pistol partly concealed in her belt, which she said would be used to settle his hash on certain conditions:
     The case was called for trial Wednesday morning. The state was repre-sented by Judge Burns, acting county attorney, Mr. Sutton being called east on important business. . . . When the time came for calling the case, the court decided that the prosecution should file a new complaint for as-sault and battery, which was done with neatness and dispatch by Judge

Burns, and the prisoner was arraigned. The defendant, Mrs. Pierce, who is as pleasant, intelligent and handsome a lady as ever Dodge City can boast, was very unanimously proven guilty. Judge Cook, with a dandy twirl of his silken mustache, gently placed the fine at five dollars and costs, and with a bewitching wave of his gold-headed cane, announced that court was adjourned. [23]

After the April 1881 election, Jones, as city attorney, was in the unfamiliar position of prosecutor of minor matters. Less than a year later he became responsible for more serious cases when Sutton resigned as county attorney in March 1882 and Judge J. C. Strang appointed Jones to fill the vacancy. Jones's term in office was relatively quiet, although he did have to contend with the emotional and bizarre Hardesty trial. One bit of clever detective work led to the identification of a skeleton, found on the prairie, that had lain exposed for about a year. Jones and Justice of the Peace Rufus G. Cook used the nails in the boots to identify the scattered bones as those of W. F. Reynolds, a freighter who became lost during a blizzard the previous winter. [24]

Jones missed much of the Luke Short affair, since he was back in Cottonwood Falls during 1883. He returned to the Dodge scene the following year in time to help the Democrats celebrate successful national, state, and local campaigns. He also was involved in his most unpopular trial that year when James Dempster was arrested and charged with murder. [25]

Dempster's wife was killed in their home at Coolidge, Kansas, by a single shot fired from a heavy pistol at close range. Dempster claimed his wife had been despondent over her continued ill health and had fired the shot herself. Neighbors who knew her testified that she was incapable of suicide, being so weak she could not feed herself, let alone crawl to the gun and hold the heavy pistol to her temple. Whitelaw, the prosecuting attorney, succeeded in the preliminary examination at Coolidge in having Dempster held without bail. The "excitement and indignation" against the prisoner was such that Jones offered no arguments or evidence but allowed his client to be brought to the Dodge City jail. However, when trial was held in late October 1884, Jones was prepared, and time had cooled somewhat the hostility toward Dempster. The first trial was a long one, interrupted by Judge Strang's leaving and a new judge's being brought in to preside; it ended with the jury unable to reach a verdict: "Eight for acquittal and four for hanging." A new jury was chosen, and Jones succeeded in getting a continuance. The contending attorneys in the case celebrated by forming a law partnership, or at least the firm of Whitelaw and Jones was established and hung out its shingle immediately after the trial. The third trial was concluded in October 1885 when Whitelaw "induced the accused to plead guilty, owing to the circumstantial character of the evidence and sentence made of murder in the second degree." Dempster received a twenty-five-year sentence.[26]

In August 1884, Jones was elected temporary chairman of the state Democratic senatorial convention and moved back into Dodge City politics as if he had never been absent, which in reality he had not been, because of his frequent appearances in the district court. When Harry Gryden died, Jones was appointed by the city council on August 6 to fill Gryden's unexpired term as city attorney. He ran for county attorney in November but lost.[27]

By 1884 prohibitionists stalked the town, intent on curbing rambunctious cowboys and drying out the entertainment joints. Jones's sympathies lay elsewhere. His attitude toward prohibition marked another Dodge City change in conviction, or at least a change from the public position he had held. As a Republican representative from Cottonwood Falls in the legislature in 1874, he had moved to pass a statewide liquor prohibitory law, but that was before he came under the influence of men like Gryden and Wright. Now, in 1885, his old friend Bat Masterson was back in town serving as deputy sheriff under Pat Sughrue, and Jones and the two law enforcers saw eye to eye on the prohibition issue. Jones's most controversial action during 1885 was to quash fifteen cases against liquor dealers that were being processed through his office. He ruled that the recent decision of the Kansas Supreme Court required that "the information against whiskey sellers must be made from actual knowledge of the violation of the law" and that such information had not been included with the charges presented to him. Dodge City did have one potentially explosive case on its hands, however, when Bing Choate was killed by Dave St. Clair. Choate was the son of a wealthy cattleman from Goliad, Texas, and St. Clair was an itinerant gambler. Jones escaped involvement when County Attorney Whitelaw assumed responsibility for not prosecuting the killer. Although doubtless unaware of the larger implications of not supporting a Texas cattleman's son, the courts and attorneys were witnessing a major change in public opinion that would alter the life of Dodge City significantly. No longer would the community favor cattlemen in their dealings and disputes, and certainly not in law-enforcement proceedings.[28]

In April 1885, Jones was reappointed city attorney by a new administration and landed in the thick of the liquor controversy. He and County Attorney B. F. Milton were of a like mind, and both were in agreement with Mayor Robert Wright. Jones came in for his share of abuse from the dry forces, which were still a year or two away from political victory. City officials undoubtedly were representing majority opinion in 1885 and were inclined to look the other way when the established saloons converted to drugstores, art galleries, and restaurants, complete with the appropriate signs, such as "Drug Store. Lager Beer on Ice, for Medical Purposes Only."[29] The liquor dealers were making the most of what was to be the Gang's last hurrah, and the Gang was extracting every legal leverage at its command to embarrass the opposition. Jones was no exception. In September he sued Nick Klaine to recover a four-hundred-dollar shortage he claimed to have discovered in the city treasurer's accounts; Masterson had done the same thing earlier in harassing Dan Frost. Klaine denied the charge and no guilt was found.[30]

For the moment, old-time Dodge Citians clearly had the government offices under their control, but the future belonged to the reformers. Jones was nominated in 1886 as the Democrats' state-representative candidate and lost in a four-man race. He lowered his ambitions in the April city elections, accepting the nomination for police judge in an open meeting; this time he won. By now, all parties were espousing reform, and the *Dodge City Democrat* boasted that in putting A. B. Webster, a Democrat, in the mayor's office, "Gang Rule is Forever at an End in Dodge City." Jones's close association with the Gang apparently was ignored, but he had not changed his convictions or loyalties to the cattle-town interests.[31]

When Jones became county attorney in 1882, he had turned some of his cases over to younger lawyers, including John H. Finlay. However, he and Finlay merely joined forces and worked well together; they did not form a partnership. Ironically, the good times came as the cattlemen's domination was ending and the forces of change and reform that Jones had distrusted were triumphing. During the next few years Jones's legal practice grew, as did his reputation. In the March 1886 session of district court, the *Dodge City Democrat* lamented that "a greater portion of time was spent on cases with no convictions" because of the work of Jones and Finlay. Jones was by then something of a patriarch who could administer a verbal spanking to young upstart lawyers appearing in court. When Jones met young W. E. Hendricks, who had recently defeated him in the county attorney's race, he could not help showing his resentment. The *Dodge City Sun* reported that Jones "waxed a little wrathful as well as eloquent," declaring that Hendricks "knew very little law, that he had been a lawyer so short a time he was as yet hardly dry behind the ears."[32]

As the land rush swelled in western Kansas, Jones, like most of the other attorneys in town, found an increasing amount of business coming from real estate. In late 1886 he formed a partnership with L. L. Dysert under the designation of "law and land office." He continued his law practice and served for a while as police judge.[33]

Jones remained in Dodge through the town's trail-herd years. With divided loyalties forced upon him, he did not have as successful a career as his beginnings in either Cottonwood Falls or Dodge City would have indicated. In fact, Jones appears to be almost two persons: the Republican prohibitionist legislator of Chase County and the last of the Gang Democratic lawyers in Ford County. His contributions to Dodge City were considerable, but they could not prevent the inevitable changes he had hoped to thwart. Like Cottonwood Falls, Dodge became a rural county seat with only memories of more troubled and more stimulating times. Jones apparently found frontier towns more to his tastes than settled communities. When the Oklahoma territories offered new opportunities, he moved to Guthrie to spend his last years.

*This drawing of John H. Finlay's home appeared in* Hand-Book of Ford County, Kansas. *Finlay became Benjamin F. Milton's partner in 1884—the last of the Gang lawyers. Courtesy Kansas State Historical Society.*

### John H. Finlay: 1884–1886

John H. Finlay joined B. F. Milton when Milton was elected county attorney. Although Finlay was several years older and had far broader experience in the West than the senior partner in the firm, Milton deserved the lead position, in spite of Finlay's advantages, because of his knowledge of the Dodge City legal environment and his political position. The partnership arrangement was a happy one.

John Finlay was born in Ashland County, Ohio, in 1834. While he was a boy, his parents moved the family to Stark County, Illinois, where he acquired his early education. In 1853, at age nineteen, Finlay joined the gold rush to California and spent the next ten years there. As the Civil War progressed without resolution, he decided to enlist and joined Company L, Second Massachusetts Cavalry, as a private. He saw considerable fighting, was taken prisoner at Taneytown, Maryland, and was confined in the prison at Danville, Virginia, for a few months. He managed to escape and made his way back to the Union lines, reaching the Union troops on November 10, 1864, at New Bern, North Carolina. Discharged July 20, 1865, with the rank of first lieutenant, he returned to Illinois. As an attorney, he was given the honorary title of "Captain" rather than the customary "Judge" as a mark of respect for his military service.

In Galva, Illinois, he married Rebecca Rickle on December 28, 1865, raised five children, and engaged in a mercantile business. At some time during the twenty years he spent as a merchant, he studied law and was admitted to the Illinois bar. In 1883 he moved to Warren, Illinois, then to Kiowa, Kansas, for a short time, and finally, in 1884, to a farm northwest of Dodge City. In August 1885 he joined Milton as an attorney specializing in real estate and general loans. Finlay's experience with cattle-town Dodge was brief and relatively calm. He was described as being "one of the most companionable of men" and proved it by steering clear of the major political squabbles. During his first year he remained inconspicuous, dealing in minor suits and doing routine legal work.[34]

During Dodge's last year as a bona fide cattle town, Finlay moved beyond the apprentice stage to become attorney of record in a number of important criminal suits. He and T. S. Jones successfully defended some of the highly publicized whiskey cases. Although he was still relatively new to Dodge, he and J. T. Whitelaw were hired to defend Pat Sughrue in the contested sheriff's election of November 1885. There was more at stake in that contest than the determination of who should wear the sheriff's badge. Sughrue was backed by Robert Wright and the remnants of the Gang. Sutton and the prohibitionists had realized too late that neither of the announced candidates for sheriff was sympathetic to their cause, and in a very tardy gesture they persuaded R. W. Tarbox, a former Panhandle rancher, to enter the race. Under different conditions Tarbox would have given the popular incumbent a serious challenge, and even with a late start he made a creditable showing, although he did not receive the most votes. Sutton was unwilling to leave the decision alone, and he backed Tarbox in his challenge of the Dodge City precinct returns.[35]

Disputed elections were fairly frequent on the Kansas frontier, generating heated debates and occasionally violence. Ford County had had its share of such challenges, but they were always settled locally. Only the year before, in the November 1884 election, Sutton disciple R. E. Burns had challenged the returns of Clark City in Klaine Precinct. Burns had the best of grounds for contesting that vote: the polling books had been stolen while they were being transported to the county clerk's office. The fiasco caused a furor with resultant charges, countercharges, and a number of sessions of the county commissioners to discuss the matter, but it was reconciled at the county level.[36]

Sutton was unwilling to see this latest defeat buried in the commissioners' debate. Among other things, he planned to use the investigation to expose the worst of his opponents' public and private lives and to paint a picture of the sorry state of Dodge Citians' morals and law enforcement under the old administration. The result was a contesting of the precinct votes that was carried to the Kansas Supreme Court to determine "the title of the parties to the office of sheriff as well as certain other proceedings in the nature of *quo warranto.*"[37]

In the general election of November 1885 three tickets sponsored sheriff candidates. The canvass of the county commission declared Pat Sughrue of the People's party the winner by a vote of 1,052 to Independent candidate R. W. Tarbox's 926 and Democrat T. J. Tate's 189. Tarbox petitioned to have the office vacated and awarded to him because he had received the most *legal* votes. He further charged that People's-party members had intimidated voters, connived with the election judges to count ineligible and double votes, and blocked the polls when all else failed.

In testimony given to the commissioners in Dodge City, beginning June 15, 1886, Sutton and L. K. Soper stood for Tarbox, and S. B. Smith and T. S. Jones represented Sughrue. Nearly all the attorneys in town—Frost, Milton, Swan, Wenie, and Whitelaw— were involved through their testimony if not their legal services. The hearing was a free-wheeling affair. Sutton tried to impugn the character of Sughrue's supporters to illustrate the debased morals of Dodge and the shoddy law enforcement that was being tolerated, and he tried to expose every political squabble of the past ten years to illustrate the instability of Dodge under the influence of the Gang. Bat Masterson was singled out as a leader of the Sughrue faction and as a particularly dangerous man. Under questioning, Bat admitted to killing two or three men in Dodge, including the cowboy who had shot his brother Ed. Much time was spent on the nature of Bat's threats before the election and on an incident at the polls, where it was alleged he had struck a man trying to vote for Tarbox. Sutton claimed that many of those voting were not recognized as local citizens and charged that rumors of mass importation of illegal voters and charges of double voting were widely believed. Sutton and Soper had various witnesses try to identify by name men whom they had seen at the polls and compared this list with that in the tally book. The defense countered by demonstrating the difficulty of any one man's knowing and recognizing all voters because of the rapid population growth in the precinct. Between March 1, 1885, and March 1, 1886, six hundred to seven hundred heads of families had located on public lands in one precinct, and the population of Dodge City had doubled between 1884 and 1885; consequently, the defense claimed that no one person could recognize all the names appearing on the rolls.

When the case went to the Kansas Supreme Court, Finlay joined Whitelaw on the defense team. Their presentation was thorough, amply documented, and clearly presented. As a result, they won on all points except their questioning of the court's jurisdiction in the matter. The court accepted the defense's description of Masterson's "blow" as a backhanded shove to keep a man from crowding in ahead of him. All the personal quarrels Sutton had brought before the county commissioners were negated as cause for invalidating the election. The court agreed that those who feared Masterson, including Sutton's partner Soper, undoubtedly had a right to be fearful, but the incidents were unrelated to the outcome of the election. No evidence of collusion between election judges and Sughrue's supporters was proved. The final judgment was in favor of Pat Sughrue, with only one dissenting vote.

Finlay was relatively unknown at the beginning of the contest, but by the end he had proved his ability as an attorney by defeating Sutton, a mark of unusual distinction no doubt noted by prospective clients in his hometown. Sutton, on the other hand, could not have been disappointed. He had been able to get Masterson labeled as a "dangerous man" and to bring to public attention the continuing evils of drink and the consequences of bad administration. If he lost the case, he most certainly won his prime objective of discrediting the status quo.

Finlay's most publicized legal appearance in the district court occurred while the disputed election was moving to the Kansas Supreme Court. As an associate of T. S. Jones, Finlay became prosecutor in one of the last Front Street killings. Ben Daniels, saloonkeeper and former deputy marshal, shot and killed Ed Julian, a restaurant owner and something of a town bully, over the issue of serving liquor. The community's sympathy rested with Daniels, and the trial was given extensive coverage. The *Globe Live Stock Journal* printed District Judge R. G. Cook's complete charge to the jury and carefully summarized the attorneys' final statements. The defense, under Whitelaw's lead, was given high praise, but so was the prosecution:

Col. T. S. Jones followed the county attorney for the prosecution, after which James T. Whitelaw acquitted himself with honors. The heavy weights in this case were to make the closing argument, Capt. J. H. Finlay for the state and Joe Ady, the great criminal lawyer, for the defence. Mr. Ady was the last to speak for the defence, and when he got fairly wound up to the subject it was thought that the state might as well agree to an acquittal of the defendant, but the battle was not so easily won. There was one yet to speak whose power as a criminal lawyer had not yet been fully appreciated in Dodge City, from the fact that never before had an opportunity presented itself when he could make himself known. But here was the time and the occasion and Capt. Finlay was not slow in embracing the opportunity in the concluding argument in the Ben Daniels case. The Captain made a stronger case by adhearing to the strong points. The question of assault or the relative positions of the parties when the first shot was fired, there was the whole case, and as the evidence both for and against was so equally divided upon this point the attorneys each concluded that it favored their side of the case. The Captain adheared strongly to his point. He briefly dispatched Joe Ady in his argument for the defence by saying that Ady's speech was not a correct presentation of the law of self defence, but on the contrary was inflammatory, inciting bad men to riot and blood shed, and that all such teachings tended to anarchy and barbarism. He claimed there was no justification for the crime that was committed; that the defendant had gone beyond the power of the law of justification and hence was guilty of the crime as charged.

But the jury, after due deliberation, said no, and acquitted Benjamin

Daniels, but not until a number of ballots had been taken in the case, the first being six for conviction and six for acquittal, a tie, which was reduced ballot after ballot until all cast their vote for acquittal. There never was a case in this county where both sides were so ably handled. Public sentiment was divided as to the innocense or guilt of the party charged with this killing. This the jury had to settle and they did it in favor of the defendant.[38]

Daniels's exoneration was not the last time there would be a doubtful tilt of Justice's balance in Dodge City, but it was to be the end of the kind of Front Street violence that had given Dodge City its unsavory reputation. Daniels had been a popular peace officer, and he represented the lawman's role in the minds of many citizens. Sheriffs, marshals, and policemen were upholders of the right, right being interpreted as what was best for the community as a whole. Lawmen were killed and maimed in the streets of the cattle town as part of their job. By the same standards, law enforcers "in the line of duty" killed more individuals than any other western type. They were understood to be men who had to make quick and fatal judgments and consequently could be forgiven a certain amount of bloodletting indiscretion. In the courts of law they stood as people's champions. In defense of former Marshal Daniels, Whitelaw only had to show that Daniels had stood in danger of assault. Julian's past record made that a likely circumstance, and Finlay was unable to overcome community prejudices. With predictable certainty, Finlay lost and Daniels went free. It was an anachronistic decision deserving to be called the last of cattle-town justice.[39]

After the cattle-town days, Finlay remained in Dodge City as a practicing attorney and served two terms as probate judge. A son, Gordon L. Finlay, became an attorney and moved to Los Angeles, California, where he served as district judge. In his declining years, Captain Finlay spent considerable time in Los Angeles at his son's home, but his residence remained in Dodge City. He died at his home in Dodge on June 28, 1916, at the age of eighty-two.[40]

John Finlay was older than most attorneys when he entered the profession, and from his first appearance he was considered an able lawyer. Although he missed the more exciting days in Dodge, he figured prominently in the final stages of the Gang's demise. The courts in which he was to spend most of his career were no longer guided by sentiments favoring the cattlemen or the solution of personal quarrels with violence. Sobriety (at least official prohibition), peaceful advisory suits, and a calmer civilization marked the Dodge City he was to know.

# 8. Editors and Real-Estate Men

LAWYERS IN THE UNITED STATES have never considered themselves as having an iron-clad lifetime commitment to their profession; leaving practice to accept some new opportunity has been fairly common. In the late nineteenth century, when formal legal education was not required and it was still relatively easy to pass the bar examination, changing jobs or occupations was an obvious option. Particularly in the West, where all of society seemed in a state of flux, abandoning law for some other means of making a living was not considered unusual or a waste of previous training. Even today less than 60 percent of law-school graduates go directly into private practice, and about 11 percent choose a nonlegal position in business. The Dodge City lawyers of the 1870s and 1880s frequently left practice, and even more frequently they tested new ventures while still keeping their shingles nailed to law-office doors. Although they attempted most of the routes to wealth that were available on the frontier—ranching, mining, insurance, farming, even education—the two occupations they turned to most frequently were newspaper editing and dealing in real estate.

Newspapers seemed to hold special fascination for Dodge attorneys. Dan Frost, W. C. Shinn, W. N. Morphy, J. T. Whitelaw, M. W. Sutton, and Ed Swan tried with varying degrees of success and diligence to be editors and publishers. Only Shinn came to Dodge with journalistic experience; fascination with publishing seemed to come with the western Kansas territory. What could there have been in the Dodge City milieu to entice competent attorneys to attempt to please the reading and advertising public in weekly print?

189

Certainly there could have been no sense of filling a community need. Walter Shinn and his brother might have used that as an excuse, since Dodge City's first newspaper, the *Messenger*, suspended publication in the spring of 1875, leaving a void for nearly a year until the Shinns brought out the *Times* in May 1876. After 1877, however, there were always two, sometimes three or four, papers available to the transient cowboys as well as permanent settlers. Hence Dodge was, throughout its cattle-town days, amply furnished with newspapers, as was most of frontier Kansas. "Newspapers in western Kansas are more numerous than frogs in Egypt," the Coolidge editor observed in 1886. "They are making their advent at about the rate of three to each county per week. There is supposed to be a great big bonanza in land office legals, and everyone wants to get rich and carry a gold-headed cane right away." The requirement that official homestead claim notices had to appear in both Republican and Democratic papers did much to subsidize the early western press and to saturate the state with short-lived newspapers.[1]

Even with government support, editors and publishers did not make much money. On the other hand, competition among attorneys was fierce, and business tended to be dominated by a few old hands, that is, men who had been on the scene for more than a year. At least newspaper work was steady and generally afforded a modest living. As an alternative to scrambling for the few elected positions and the few paying clients, perhaps editing did have a certain monetary appeal, but there seems to have been something more compelling than the economic motivation at work here. Perhaps it was that newspapers presented a broader, more sustained opportunity for the same kind of adversarial confrontation found in the formal and restrictive courts. Freed of the controlled environment of due process, editors could be unrestrainedly frank, emotionally argumentative, and entertainingly partisan. Editors could be absolutely candid. They did not need just to call a spade a spade but could refer to it as "a damned bad instrument for moving other people's dirt." Any lawyer, especially a frontier attorney of the 1870s and 1880s, would have enjoyed the freedom of uninhibited expression the frontier allowed, even demanded.

While it is true that the communication medium of the lawyer changed with the printed word, the goal was still the same as that of the courtroom. Words—their use, interpretation, and emphasis—were the tools of editor and lawyer alike. Vocal as they were, frontier lawyers had to be proficient writers; none could depend on oral communication alone. Consequently, journalism was a natural second vocational choice. Many who did not go all the way to printer's ink and the clanking presses found writing newspaper copy an acceptable alternative to what they had been doing. Harry Gryden could spread his purple-tinged prose in the newspaper with as fine a hand as he exhibited before the sinners in night court or the farmers and townspeople in the jury box. All lawyers were wordsmiths—creators of images, choppers of logic, and artists of persuasion through the use of the King's English, or what passed for it on the frontier. Their success depended to a large degree on how articulate they were. The written phrase and the oral statement had the same roots; he who enjoyed the one was likely to appreciate the other.

Lawyers undoubtedly found motivation for redirecting their talents in their love of a political contest. All of them sampled a bit of political strife early in their careers when they bid for local office. That small taste stimulated a steady diet. Newspapers provided larger audiences and allowed, even required, the editors to pursue partisan ends the year round: no more waiting for annual elections. Frontier papers carried on the political fight under the guise of news and public service in nearly every issue. Even when lawyers had no paper of their own, if they were politically involved, they were suspected of being a subversive force. Before he became a publisher, Mike Sutton was accused repeatedly of controlling one or another of the Dodge papers; he was even charged with writing copy. The result was that some lawyers with a passion for politics, and well acquainted with the work habits of editors, may have felt that the demands of putting out a weekly paper were not all that burdensome and the opportunity such a public forum afforded was well worth the price. Thus, for varied and understandable reasons, lawyers in Dodge City turned, if not instinctively at least happily, to the role of editor. Still, that more than 22 percent of the practicing lawyers smudged their fingers with printer's ink is a remarkable and significant fact. Life in Dodge City and historians' knowledge of that life would have been the poorer if the lawyers, for whatever reason, had not been lured to the press to present their side of the case to the larger audience.

The three attorneys most serious about the obligation of editing—serious in the sense that they did not view publishing a weekly paper as a sideline, hobby, or mere political forum—were Daniel Frost, Walter C. Shinn, and William N. Morphy. The other three may have found the newspaper business fascinating or of political value, but they never considered it an alternate way of life. They remained lawyers first, editors only incidentally. Sutton backed the publication of a purely partisan paper for exclusively political reasons; for Swan, the press served both to boost his hometown and as a medium of political expression; Whitelaw found it a diverting hobby about which he could be politically objective. The discussion of the brief journalistic ventures of these three men is found elsewhere.

None of the six was to pour his life and convictions into his publication as Dan Frost did. His rivalry with Nicholas Klaine was a running battle that has left a fairly complete record of both sides of public opinion on nearly every issue. Without Frost's contribution, it would be difficult to recapture an authentic history of cattle-town Dodge City.

### Daniel Montague ("D.M." or "Dan") Frost: 1874–1886

Daniel Frost was born in Pennsylvania in 1843. His parents moved to Illinois when he was quite young, and he was raised in DuPage and Will counties. He came to Kansas in 1868 and worked as a clerk in a general store at Sheridan, then at end-of-line for the Kansas Pacific Railroad. In 1869 he moved to Elizabethtown, New Mexico, to try mining in the Morino mines; by fall he had experienced enough of that way to wealth to cause him to return to Sheridan. In the spring of 1870 he followed the construction crews of the Kansas Pacific to the line's new terminus, where he was appointed deputy postmaster under Major J. A. Soward at Kit Carson, Colorado. There he also taught one term of school and became Soward's

*Daniel M. Frost and Alma Hagaman were married at Ivory Station in St. Louis on January 30, 1879. Lawyer Dan found his niche in Dodge City as editor of the* Ford County Globe *and a critic of government. Courtesy Kansas Heritage Center, Dodge City.*

partner in a mercantile house. The new firm, D. M. Frost & Company, and the post office were destroyed in a fire that caused total loss of its assets. There was a brief stay in Dodge City in 1872 before Frost moved to Sergeant on the western boundary of Kansas. That same year, he was appointed postmaster there and again started a modest mercantile operation that brought him equally small returns. In 1874 he returned to Dodge City while it was still basically a buffalo station. Sometime before the town began catering to Texas cattlemen, he was admitted to the Kansas bar.[2]

As was true of other early-day attorneys in Dodge, Frost had to scratch to make ends meet. He advertised himself as a lawyer, notary public, and real-estate agent. Paying clients needing any of the three services before 1875 were few, since laws and legal interpretations were not much in demand and land was dirt cheap. Old-timers remember the buffalo days of Dodge City as a time when

"there was no law, no organized law in existence," and, consequently, little demand for legal advice. With the incorporation of
the town as a city of the third class on November 2, 1875, the legal
structure—city, township, county, district, and state—was complete, and with it came new law-related jobs. The first election
after the reorganization was held on December 1, 1875. Even at
that date there were more than enough lawyers to fill the assign-
ments, especially when most of the new jobs, such as probate
judge, police judge, JP, clerk of the court, and even the city and
county attorneys, did not require certification by the bar. Frost
managed to snare only the position of justice of the peace, the job
with the least financial return. As for the rest of his livelihood, a
contemporary recorder of the lives of important persons willing to
provide copy and pay for the privilege indicated that Frost "was
engaged in several avocations," probably meaning his was a precarious day-to-day existence.[3]

By the time he settled in Dodge permanently, Frost had five
years of frontier experience behind him and thus had no difficulty
adjusting to the rough pace of the community. As a bachelor until
1879, he engaged in the sporting life and rude humor of Front
Street and was an accepted member of the Gang. His close and
easy associations with the voting citizens of Dodge led to his election as representative to the state legislature from the 103d District; he served through the 1875–76 sessions. By then there
were six active lawyers in the town of less than six hundred residents—people, incidentally, who had devised means other than
litigation to solve most of their problems. Frost's absence while in
Topeka, even though the legislative sessions were brief, must have
been welcomed by the lawyers who remained behind to pick up his
few clients.

The year after his election, the 103d District was reorganized as
the 122d and Frost lost his seat to Robert Wright, who held it until
1883. The city council that year, 1877, declared all nonelective
offices vacant except that of marshal, and Mike Sutton was appointed both city clerk and city attorney. With few paying political
positions available, Frost ran hard for police judge and won. At
least the *Ford County Globe,* Frost's paper, judged him to have performed his duties well. "During the turbulent time of '77, he pre-

sided . . . and his decisions were a terror to evil-doers." The prompt and efficient action of the new police force, comprised of Ed Masterson, Joe Mason, and Larry Deger, and the restlessness of the cowboys in one of Dodge's biggest trail-herd seasons, made for a busy court.[4]

Frost presided with vigor, and the fines were indeed stiff. He controlled the court with an even hand, threatening at one point to fine both Gryden and Sutton, the local giants of the legal fraternity, for contempt of court. At least one evildoer, Bat Masterson, however, was not struck with fear when appearing before Judge Frost; the feeling apparently was more akin to outrage. Masterson was usually on the right side of the law, but in June he found himself in the Dodge City jail and then before the judge. The cause of his troubles was his loyalty to an old friend, a personality trait that, over the years, was to cause him and Dodge City a great deal of grief. Bobby Gill (Gilmore), drunk and humorously orating as usual, was collared by Marshal Deger. Bat came to the aid of his inebriated friend. Even though Deger had the law and his own three hundred pounds on his side, he had to call on a half-dozen bystanders to handle Bat. After considerable tussling, Bat was dragged off to jail and then hauled before Judge Frost. Frost heard the charges and with little hesitation fined him twenty-five dollars and costs. Gill, with his usual gift of disarming blarney, had gotten off with a small lecture and a five-dollar fine after reminding the judge that Jesus Christ had died on the cross for just such sinners as himself. This incident was the beginning of Masterson's bitter grudge against Deger, and the decision against him was remembered by Bat among the many wrongs he had suffered and would suffer again at Frost's hands. Only their mutual dislike of Mike Sutton and Nick Klaine kept Bat and Frost on speaking terms most of the time. There were breaks, however, even in that cold courtesy.[5]

One such breach forced Frost to apply his legal acumen in his own behalf. He, Sutton, and Klaine were held responsible by Bat for Bat's defeat in the November 1879 election. Shortly after the voting, Bat, acting in his capacity as deputy U.S. marshal, arrested Frost on charges of buying stolen "Government property." Frost was accused of knowingly purchasing stolen goods—building materials and stationery—worth about $127 from Sergeant Joe Evarts, the Fort Elliott quartermaster. The U.S. commissioner, acting on Bat's complaint, set a $5,000 bond and Frost was indicted by a grand jury. A petition signed by twenty-four prominent Dodge Citians urging the Kansas attorney general to dismiss the case had the desired effect. The trial first was continued, then, like many others, dropped from further consideration. At the time of his arrest by Masterson, Frost's paper played the story with a light touch:

> The affair is liable to cause Mr. Frost considerable trouble and expense, but his vast fortune will be poured out like water from the clouds to secure his vindication. But if, on the other hand, it shall be proved that he has been systematically plundering the government of the United States and wearing government socks purchased from one of the brave defenders of his country, then we shall be tempted to place our right hand upon our left breast and swear a mighty oath that the human race has lost its virtue, the devil is a saint, and "things are not what they seem."

Frost did not forget the incident. Three years later he printed the petition from his fellow townsmen in a supplement to his regular edition when Frederick C. Zimmermann, a Dodge merchant, raised the question of Frost's honesty in a letter to the *Times* reminding voters of Frost's previous arrest. Frost vehemently denied the charge and used the letter of endorsement as part of the proof of innocence. Although the affair did not affect Frost unduly as editor or politician, it was embarrassing. Most people had not taken the claims seriously, since Dodge Citians were becoming accustomed to the erratic actions caused by Masterson's bad temper. This incident seemed only one more of Bat's peevish overreactions.[6]

While Judge Frost weighed the legal sins of Dodge citizens, he continued to maintain a private law practice. It could not have occupied much of his time, but he did manage two rare victories over County Attorney Sutton: in the first, John Tyler was acquitted of the charge of murder when the case was tried in Larned; in the other, Frost was working with Harry Gryden when Bill Tilghman escaped Sutton's prosecution on a horse-stealing charge. Frost continued to be listed as attorney of record in a few cases each session of the district court, and items in the papers and gazetteers dealing with lawsuits and advertisements related to his practice continued to appear for the next few years, but the actual cases he tried were infrequent. His legal work consisted mainly of minor civil affairs or routine filings. In the January 1879 term, for example, when some forty cases were on the docket, Frost was counselor for only two clients, while Gryden represented fifteen. It was apparent that Frost was not to make his mark on history as a trial lawyer. He was never admitted to practice before the Kansas Supreme Court, and it is doubtful that after 1882 he had any intention of pursuing a career as an attorney. In 1878 he had made a strong bid for county attorney, being nominated on the "People's County ticket." He failed to oust incumbent Sutton but continued the campaign against him in the newspaper, criticizing many of Sutton's actions during the next two years. Frost was not one to forget old grudges, and he was not easily discouraged. He tried twice more, in 1880 and 1882, to replace Mike and was beaten both times. His role as attorney ended with the last defeat.[7]

In December 1877, Frost finally found his niche in cattle-town history when he and William N. Morphy, a fellow attorney, established the *Ford County Globe*. Frederick Zimmermann lent the pair two hundred dollars to buy equipment. They paid the money back with advertising space in the paper. Later, when Zimmermann found Frost's politics distasteful, he called it a bad deal. Frost, however, had discovered his true avocation as editor and critic of governments, a role that was to last him a lifetime. The *Globe* appeared under various banners over the years and Frost acquired other partners, but throughout the changes his voice, as reflected in his papers, remained a powerful one—nearly always in opposition.[8]

He began as a hard-line opponent of the Gang and moved to a position favoring (but never quite espousing) Republicanism, although a paper he published later was called the *Globe-Republican*. But if he was not a solidly faithful follower of the Republican line, he was consistently anti-Democrat. To have become a dedicated Republican, he would have had to deny, frequently, his favorite role of critic, and that was a fate he apparently could not tolerate. His political loyalties were often hard to distinguish by reading his newspaper, since they were usually in opposition to the ins. In fact, during much of his time in Dodge, he appeared to favor the Democrats when the Republicans were in office, but they in turn became the targets of his caustic pen when they were victorious.

The problem Frost had with political affiliation lay in his devotion to the cattle interests and the kind of social and economic climate in Dodge City that catered to their wishes. As the old Dodge City ways and policies came under increasingly heavy attack by the local Republican leadership, Frost became even more adamant in his support of the status quo. When his paper became the official organ of the Western Kansas Cattle Growers' Association, he changed the name to the *Globe Live Stock Journal,* of which the first edition appeared on July 15, 1884. Frost was at last editing and publishing under his true colors, which were neither Republican nor Democrat. Even before the masthead change, his readership lay primarily among the cattlemen of the region. Since his circulation in 1883 was approximately seven hundred, his following did represent a substantial block of voters in a town with scarcely twice that population. Rarely, however, did his endorsements of policy receive majority-party support, although until 1884 he probably represented the sentiments of a majority of the townspeople. Politically, he was invariably the voice of dissent. And in aiming at various targets, he opposed none with the steady consistency of his differences with and antagonisms toward Mike Sutton and Nicholas Klaine of the *Times.* Whomever or whatever Old Nick, as he frequently referred to Klaine, supported sooner or later suffered Frost's scathing scrutiny. It was more than journalistic rivalry, it was journalistic warfare: bitter, emotional, and mutually shared.

Frost was an amiable companion under normal circumstances, better liked than his rival, the more pious Deacon Klaine, but he was a difficult business associate because he opposed the establishment in harsh, uncompromising terms. Partner Morphy lasted barely nine months before he withdrew, ostensibly for health reasons and the need for a "change of climate." However, Morphy did not leave town immediately, and a year later he was still practicing law. Frost carried on as editor and publisher until Lloyd Shinn, founder of the *Times,* who had sold out to Klaine, joined the *Globe* in January 1879. Within three years Shinn also found "ill health" a reason to withdraw from the partnership, but not from the town. After that Frost operated alone until 1892.[9]

The newspaper business was at best a precarious one, and Frost did not accumulate great wealth. Life as an editor, however, was far better than that afforded by following settlements to end-of-track or sweating in a New Mexico mine. Besides enduring the normal risks of the business, Frost seemed to have inordinately bad luck. In 1885, for the second time in his life, his business burned to the ground. The whole block from Robert Wright's store at the west end to Dog Kelley's Opera House at the east end was leveled. Equipment for his paper was minimal, but the loss was reckoned at more than five hundred dollars. Colonel Samuel S. Prouty's *Kansas Cowboy* office also burned, and he was unable to rebuild, but Frost kept his paper alive and in regular publication.[10]

If journalism was Frost's chosen vocation, politics was his passion. As editor and lawyer, he was a frequent candidate for office, especially if it was known that Sutton supported someone else. As a man in opposition, Dan flirted with every political faction that came along, but he never completely left the Republican fold. He was a diligent worker in the party, serving throughout the period on the Ford County central committee and acting as its secretary for several years. He ran for the county attorney's office three times on the Republican ticket and in 1884 made a bid for state senatorship, succeeding in gaining the support of the Larned Republican convention.

For Republican-party members in Dodge City, Frost's success was unacceptable, and they fought hard at the Larned convention to prevent his nomination. The fight carried through 159 ballots, indicating the extent of the split in the party. When Frost was finally nominated, the losers immediately called for a new convention to be held in Garden City with Frost's bitter enemy, Klaine, in charge. Although Frost did not give up without a stiff fight, the controlled delegates there defeated him and submitted the name of J. W. Rush as their nominee. The conflicting returns from Larned and Garden City were forwarded to the GOP's state central committee, which chose Rush over Frost. Klaine explained in the *Times* that Frost had "tried to foist himself upon the people as a candidate [and] . . . was taken down by the State Central Committee. Frost is a candidate for office every year, and for no other reason than to be bought off. In this instance, his political tricks did not win. . . . His election would have been a disgrace to an intelligent community." Actually, Frost was not officially ousted by the party, as Klaine reported, but withdrew in the name of party unity

when the senatorial committee appeared to be approaching a dead-
lock. It was a grand gesture toward harmony and one of the few
such concessions he was guilty of during his long association with
the Republican party.[11]

Frost's difficulty with the GOP was bound to continue as long as
he endorsed the old Dodge City practices and cowtown commitments. The local Republican ranks were filled with men envisioning
quite a different future. Two years before the Larned nominating
convention, Frost had signed his name to a resolution that revealed
his true feelings. The other signatures represented some of the
oldest residents of Dodge, including Gryden, R. J. Hardesty, Bob
Wright, Chalk Beeson, A. J. Anthony, Ab Webster, R. W. Evans,
and John Towers, who, like Frost, saw an era slipping away and
tried to forestall it. Purporting to represent "the best element" in
Dodge, they tried to reassure the Texas cattlemen that things had
not changed:

> Dodge City and Western Kansas send their heartiest greetings to their
> many friends of the Lone Star state, and tender their green prairies and
> hearty welcome to the stockmen of Texas, who have always been our best
> and beneficial friends. Hoping that a national trail will in its meanderings,
> extend to our state and through it and should it touch Dodge City, we
> tender it a hearty welcome—only regretting that we cannot, one and all,
> share your friendly hand and be with you in Austin.

Some of the signers were to have second thoughts on the national-
trail issue, but the statement truly represented Frost's sentiments.
This was clearly understood by the Sutton faction, as well as anyone who followed Frost's editorial policy. The Garden City convention in effect read Frost out of the local party and clearly stated its
reasons for doing so. Although couched in highly pejorative terms,
the emphasis was correct in assuming that Frost preferred the old
Dodge to a newer, tamer one, a position that was not in keeping
with the Ford County party leaders' policies:

> Resolve, that D. M. Frost, the nominee of that convention [Larned], by
> his corrupt bargain that if elected he would use his influence to remove
> men from official position solely for the reason that they do not support
> him; by his support of gambling, whiskey selling, prostitution, and kindred
> vices and crimes, is a man wholly unfit to receive the votes of this sena-
> torial district, and his nomination is an insult to every man who desires to
> see good society and pure homes.[12]

If there were any direct payoffs in Frost's interest in politics, they came early in his career. The one term as state representative in 1875–76 and his appointment as enumerator in Ford County for the census of 1880 seem to have been the only tangible fruits. The recommendation for the latter post came from Lloyd Shinn, who was Frost's co-editor and publisher at the time. Senator Preston Plumb, Republican, made the appointment for Ford County on the strength of Shinn's recommendations, which included Shinn's brother, Walter, and J. H. Dewees, G. W. Potter, and H. P. Myton, all Republicans. Nick Klaine, a fellow Republican, ran a front-page editorial criticizing Lloyd Shinn, but not Senator Plumb, for the appointment of relatives and cronies. Letters appeared in the rival papers supporting or condemning the action on either political or personal grounds. None questioned the qualifications or ability of the men. The job Frost did was as accurate as could be expected, although, like many nose counters, he forgot to count himself.[13]

After 1882, Frost was, for all practical purposes, no longer an attorney, although he was still called Judge on occasion in deference to his profession or in tribute to his time on the JP bench. From time to time in his capacity as editor or politician, he did lend a hand in activities that affected the legal life of Dodge. He worked to get a new judicial district established in 1884 and succeeded in calling a meeting that endorsed the idea. He may have acted as his own attorney in a civil property dispute that developed among him, Fred Wenie, and F. W. Boyd, owner of the Dodge House. The contest centered on whether the original filing on a plot of land had been made properly with the land office. The amount of land in dispute was eighty-nine acres; Frost won title to the lion's share of eighty-six acres.[14]

Frost's tenacious support of cattle-town ways is not as easily explained as that of other Dodge Citians who clung to the past. For a man like Bat Masterson, preference for the glory days came naturally. The saloon operators had a vested interest, but even some of them, notably Henry Sturm, were won over to the new vision. Some merchants, A. J. Anthony, for example, could understandably have championed old customers and the certainty of trail-herd profits. But in terms of self-interest, Frost's position seems counterproductive. Since he was a man with a growing family, it would appear that it was in his best interests to see a tamer, more settled town. At times he even worked for that goal.

In 1879, Frost married Alma H. Hagaman, sister of A. J. Anthony's wife and daughter of Abraham Hagaman, a Presbyterian minister in St. Louis. As a concerned parent with four children, Frost was a member of the Dodge City school board and was chairman of the committee that designed the new school building and selected its site. Certainly, as the town developed, Frost reaped the advantages of modernization and the expansion of business. He invested in property, built a three-story hotel, and became a member of the board of directors of the telephone franchise for Ford and surrounding counties (Southwestern Telephone and Telegraph Company). He was also one of fifteen directors of Dodge City's board of trade. What did he have to gain by holding on to the old ways? The answer appears to be purely personal preference.[15]

Like Robert Wright, he seemed to remember with particular fondness the early days and the early companions. There was also the intransigent rivalry with Mike Sutton, Deacon Klaine, and the *Times*. These and the rebuffs he had received from the Republican party may explain his resistance to change, at least change that coincided with Klaine's desires. Whatever the explanation, Frost remained true to the spirit of the early days when he was establishing himself as an attorney and a successful politician. He was known in cattle-town Dodge and is remembered by historians today as an editor, but his philosophical convictions had been fixed when he was a rising attorney. He apparently retained a preference for the rough pioneer life to the end. After leaving Dodge, he served for a brief time as register of the Garden City land office. He ended his professional life far from an editor's desk as superintendent of irrigation on the Ute Indian Reservation in Utah.[16]

## Walter C. Shinn: 1876–1881, 1885–1886

The first editor-lawyer—that is, the first editor to turn lawyer—was Walter C. Shinn. He and his brother, Lloyd, established the second newspaper in Dodge City, the *Times,* after the first suspended operations in the spring of 1875. Neither of the Shinn brothers ever forgot that experience, although both turned to

*Walter, Eva, and Lloyd Shinn. The brothers were editors of the* Dodge City Times, *and Eva taught school. Courtesy Boot Hill Museum, Dodge City.*

other opportunities when the newspaper failed to prosper. Walter tried lawyering, and when that proved to be scarcely more profitable than selling newsprint, he shifted to real estate. In the booming 1880s he finally found what his previous ventures had missed: enough clients and customers to make him a rich man. In 1887 the *Dodge City Times* ran a special section boasting of the local men who had made a financial success of their lives in Dodge; Walter C. Shinn was one of those listed. He came, the editor reported, "a poor boy . . . with a wheelbarrow full of type given him by the publisher of the paper on which he was last employed, the Leavenworth *Times.*" His press, he claimed, was an equally inexpensive item, being rescued from a cheese factory that had gone bankrupt. In slack time, the story continued, Shinn met the grocery bills by putting up hay in the Arkansas River Valley. If not the literal truth, the stories of the early shoestring operation were close to the mark. The returns from sales and advertisements barely justified even these investments, and he was forced to sell his interest in the *Times* to Nick Klaine before the first year was out. Lloyd, who remained as Klaine's partner, lasted only until 1878, when he, too, sold his share to Klaine. Walter took over a road ranch, and Lloyd accepted a job managing a buffalo-tanning establishment in Dodge City. But it was not to be the end of their publishing careers.[17]

Walter was born in 1854 in Iowa and on reaching manhood drifted west, looking for a favorable location. He had received a good education and was blessed with a willingness to work and little else. He learned the journalistic trade in Leavenworth, Kansas. There was a brief and unprofitable venture at Sterling, in Rice County, where the brothers were left in debt even after they had put their press in hock. Lloyd claimed they sold their equipment at auction for $6.85. Looking for greener pastures, they saw in the bustling cattle town of Dodge City a possible site for a new paper. The town continued to prosper; the paper did not. After he sold his share of the *Times,* Walter built a road ranch on the old Camp Supply Trail at Red Hole, some four miles south of present-day Ashland, Kansas. It was a poor choice of location, lying between Deep Hole and John ("Red") Clarke's Boss Ranch, both of which had already been designated way stations for the stagecoach line. There was not enough travel on the trail to warrant another way station, so the experiment lasted only briefly. Walter returned to Dodge to live with his brother and served for a while as clerk of the district court, where he developed an interest in the law. In the summer of 1879 he went to Ann Arbor, Michigan, where he attended law lectures for six months at the University of Michigan Law School. He returned to Dodge in March 1880 and on the recommendation of his brother was appointed as one of the enumerators for the Ford County census. Shinn was responsible for canvassing residents within the city limits, beginning June 1 and finishing June 28.[18]

Having passed the bar examination sometime after his Ann Arbor experience, Walter hung out his shingle and began practicing law, with emphasis on real-estate transactions. Among the projects that he and his brother promoted was the sale of lots in what became known as the Shinn Addition south of the Arkansas River across from the standpipe. (Later there was to be another Shinn Addition north of Division Street between Sixth Avenue and Avenue A.) Although his legal practice remained minimal, it was perhaps useful in advancing the addition. For example, he did secure a "perpetual injunction" to prevent collection of city taxes on the new development, which gave the Shinns considerable advantage in competing for sales, and he successfully defended himself against one of Dr. Galland's many lawsuits by proving to the court's satisfaction that Galland had agreed to take lots in the Shinn Addition as payment for the fifty dollars owed him.[19]

Since Dodge City in 1881 was blessed with an overabundance of lawyers, publishers, and real-estate agents, Shinn was obliged to look elsewhere for employment, first in Washington, D.C., then St. Elmo, Colorado. He eventually purchased the *St. Elmo Mountaineer* and combined publishing with mining interests and work as an attorney. When he returned to Dodge City in 1884, he did not take up the practice of law again but devoted all his energies to business and real estate. For a time he and a sister, Eva Shinn, made their home together while she taught school in Dodge City and later in nearby Spearville. In October 1885 he married Christianna A. Newcomer of Freeport, Illinois.[20]

Shinn's second venture in Dodge was far more successful than the first. Little of his new success, however, was directly related to the legal business. After he returned to Dodge, he listed his oc-

cupation variously as investor, real-estate agent, or merchant,
never as attorney. He was to hold several prominent positions in
the community: secretary of the new Merchants State Bank, director on the board of Soule College, chairman of the library association, and member of the city council. Shinn Addition grew, and part
of it was set aside for the settlement of blacks, an area some called
Shinn's New Africa. It was at the height of this period that the
*Times* estimated his personal worth at a hundred thousand dollars. [21]

When the land boom went bust, Shinn joined with partners
D. W. Moffett and Ed Madison in purchasing the *Globe-Republican.*
He retained his connections with the paper until February 1895,
serving as editor from January 21, 1892, until the paper was sold.
Undoubtedly he lost heavily in the panic years because he not only
had invested in real estate but had actively sponsored the Rock
Island, Dodge City & Denver Railroad Company and the Dodge
City & South Dodge Railway Company. Neither survived the
1890s.

As was true of most of the other lawyers turned newspaper editors, Shinn made little use of his legal knowledge. It is doubtful that
the law even served as a steppingstone for him. His contributions
in Dodge were made in business, real-estate development, and
speculation. Still, he was for a time an attorney in cattle-town
Dodge and bore the honorary title of "Judge" throughout the rest
of his life. It was a prideful symbol that he had once served the
bench and the bar.

### William N. Morphy: 1876–1879

Dan Frost's cofounder of the *Ford County Globe,* William N. Morphy, was also an attorney. When and where he passed the bar is
not recorded, nor, for that matter, are any of the particulars of
his life before he arrived or after he left Dodge City. Many of the
cowtown lawyers appear as shadowy figures with the details of
their lives lost in the obscurity of time, but only one was considered a man of mystery, the subject of legends, during his lifetime.
William N. Morphy was a youngster, just out of law school, suffering from tuberculosis when he came to Dodge City. According to
the remembrances of old-time printers in Dodge City, "he was

found apparently dying, near a pile of ties along the railroad in the east end of Dodge City. . . . He was cared for and improved greatly and joined the partnership with Mr. Frost which began the *Ford County Globe* on that Christmas day in 1877." Even his name attracted legends: some said he deliberately misspelled the original Murphy to conceal his past, while others thought he changed it because of a crime his brother had committed.[22]

He apparently arrived in Dodge early in 1876, and after recovering from the illness that had nearly cost him his life, he joined Harry Gryden as a partner in law. He was just the sort of homeless stray Gryden tended to pick up to revive. The first notice of Morphy in official records (spelled Murphy) was on September 20, 1876, when the Ford County commissioners employed him and Gryden to recover school funds belonging to Ford County but held by the probate judge of Ellis County. After Morphy joined Frost in publishing the *Globe,* he continued serving legal clients, advertising his availability in the paper as long as he remained in Dodge. By 1877 he had acquired a fairly substantial practice, at least in terms of clients. In the January 1877 term of the district court, he was attorney of record in thirteen of forty-two cases; in the June session, he was responsible for seven of twenty-eight. In most of the cases, he was working with Gryden, and most of them were not successfully prosecuted. In none of the suits could there have been more than a very modest fee.[23]

Even if his business was not profitable, Morphy at least had interesting clients. They included Sallie Frazier, the strong-willed and litigious matriarch of Dodge City's minority community; Miss Carrie Pembleton, who had been assaulted by Monroe Henderson and was herself charged with carrying a concealed weapon; Mattie, the "Maid of Athens," who "loved wisely but too well"; and the cowboys jailed as accessories in the killing of Ed Masterson. The kinds of people Morphy and Gryden served were not likely to be found innocent once charged. It was a poor way of building a reputation that would attract better-paying clients. So Morphy was obliged to make his living by other means and he joined the partnership with Frost.[24]

Objectivity might be essential for a prospering attorney, but it held no priority in a frontier journalist's success. Morphy and Frost were openly tendentious and liberally mixed their bias into their news stories. They and their rival editor at the *Times* did much to stimulate political hostilities, as well as personal grudges, in and around town.

Morphy's pen was nearly as caustic as Bat Masterson's, and occasionally it got him into serious trouble. At one point, according to Robert Wright,

> he abused [Wright] so maliciously and scandalously and lied so about him . . . , that the latter [Wright] whipped him on the street; for which Morphy sued [Wright] . . . for ten thousand dollars. The jury awarded a damage of four dollars and a half, for the plaintiff's doctor bill, and they hung out for a long time against giving anything, until the judge instructed them they must render a verdict for the amount, as Mr. Morphy had clearly proven he had paid the doctor four dollars and a half, as a result of the whipping.

The quarrel stemmed from the *Globe*'s efforts to unseat the Gang in 1877, and the beating Morphy took was more than the mild whipping Wright had casually mentioned. Apparently, Wright struck Morphy with a pistol, knocking him senseless, and then kicked and stomped him. Wright's memory also boosted the amount of the suit to ten thousand dollars from the actual request for three thousand, but both figures were large for that day. Both Frost and Morphy had undeniable talent for stirring up personal and, particularly, political animosities.[25]

When the first rift in the Gang's solidarity occurred with the sheriff's election in 1877, Morphy and the *Globe* played a major role in it. As a supporter of Larry Deger, Morphy had been a sharp critic of Bat Masterson. As the election approached, the *Globe*'s criticism concentrated on Masterson's toleration of a growing number of confidence men preying on strangers in town. When two of the "notorious and well-known confidence men, Bill Bell and 'the Handsome Kid,'" were allowed to escape after being jailed, a protest meeting was called at the schoolhouse. At the meeting Morphy was one of the main critics, along with merchants F. C. Zimmermann and Morris Collar. He charged that "the officers [meaning Masterson] could stop the nuisance if they desired to do so." The *Globe* story of the meeting read like an editorial, indicting Masterson for malfeasance, and ended with a plea for reform at the next election: "What Ford County needs is a complete change in judicial office and the ballot box is the place to get it. Remember this, voters of Ford County, and vote against any and every man who has not done his duty in driving out the confidence curse from our midst." Later, when the mass meeting was held in the Lady Gay to nominate county-office candidates, Morphy and Frost worked hard to get Larry Deger to replace Bat and with Gryden gave seconding speeches in favor of Deger. The *Globe*'s campaign nearly succeeded: Deger lost by only three votes. The power of the press, even a defeated press, did seem to have some positive value. The close call at the polls stimulated Bat to become more active in enforcing the law.[26]

Apparently, the hostility between Bat and Morphy was eventually smoothed out. Frost, of course, never forgave and rarely let up on his harassment of Masterson. Shortly before the election, Morphy sold his interest in the paper, pleading ill health and the need to find a more agreeable climate. In the issue announcing his departure, Morphy explained his policy in editing a newspaper: "In conducting the *Globe* we have found it necessary to use cream, vinegar and vitriol, and if at any time, our vinegar and vitriol were harsh, we do not think that the supply or quality any more than equalled the demand." It was an apology of sorts for the bitter partisanship of the editors.[27]

Morphy did not leave town immediately but stayed on as an attorney for another year. During that time there appeared to be a reconciliation as he, Sutton, and Masterson electioneered together, and he even accompanied Bat and Charles Bassett to Leavenworth to deliver prisoners to the penitentiary.[28]

Morphy had ended his connection with the paper because of poor health and had indicated at the time that he would seek a more salubrious climate. Apparently, he was suffering from tuberculosis, and since there was no improvement during the winter of 1879, he left for Arizona. It was the end of his career in Dodge, and within a year a rumor drifted back that he had died.[29]

Morphy's time as a lawyer in Dodge was a brief one, but it did include the roughest period of Dodge as a cowtown—rough in the sense of the accepted Hollywood tradition. His major role, however, was not as an attorney, where he made little impact on the courts or his clients, but as an editor who helped shape the first public criticism of the lax law enforcement that had characterized Dodge and helped to create factional antagonism on Front Street.

When a lawyer left practice to become an editor, rarely did he believe he had found a new and easy way to wealth. Fascination with their own words in print, expectation of molding public opinion, or anticipation of providing an influential political voice were strong idealistic motives affecting men to various degrees. None expected to get rich. Real estate, on the other hand, could make a man wealthy overnight, or at least quickly. Idealism had little to do with shifting from law to dealing in land. When the market was booming, the prospect of making it big was all any lawyer needed to justify abandoning his profession.

Businessmen in Dodge City in the mid-1880s were in an expansive mood. Robert Wright wrote that these "early Dodge City boomers never cut the cloth scant when fitting the garment for general utility. They had no narrow vision of prospect, and the perspective appeared the same width at both ends." In 1884 business was never better and the goods on store shelves moved with pleasing and profitable speed. As for the future, who could guess the extent of the boom? "History," the editor of the *Dodge City Times* wrote in 1883, "furnishes us with the rise and fall of nations. Cities, countries and individuals come under this natural order. . . . Nature follows a course definitely and immutably. . . . There is no backward step." Two years later the editor of the *Times* still felt the rising optimism: "There are many su[r]mises regarding the future of Dodge City and the surrounding country, but there is one generally accepted opinion, which places the city and country in the line of continued prosperity." There was nothing on the economic or political horizon that anyone could see to cause doubt.[30]

What was fueling the boom and the extravagant optimism was an influx of new settlers. Dodge City's population had made a steady advance from about six hundred in 1876 to around twelve hundred in 1880 to more than two thousand in 1886, when Dodge moved from third-class-city status to second class. For the newcomers, the lure was land: free or, if it was improved or a town lot, at least cheap. Each year, however, the cheap lots and acres increased in value and good free land became more difficult to find. Still the seekers came, comparing favorably western Kansas costs and productivity with the crowded lands and lots "back East." Some of the homesteaded land was reaching the stage of final proof of claim, which meant that even more land would be placed on the market. Property was changing hands; there was good money to be made assisting people who had land to sell or a desire to buy real estate.[31]

Lawyers who were finding the legal crumbs few and far between while they bucked the reputation of a limited number of established colleagues, and who were attuned to the drift of community affairs, saw the possibilities of cashing in on the growing demands of the recent arrivals. When the census was taken in 1880, only two men listed themselves as real-estate agents, and only one real-estate dealer was advertised in the Dodge papers that year. In a town with six physicians and nine lawyers, the number of real-estate agents seemed disproportionately small. Obviously, more people were handling property transactions than these sources would indicate. Lawyers and a few merchants had for some time handled land transactions as a limited sideline to their major commitment, but by the mid-1880s real-estate activity on its own had become a profitable business. Eventually, five attorneys left the active pursuit of civil and criminal law to concentrate on land transactions and town development, and one real-estate agent acquired the status of attorney without becoming an active practicing attorney.

Nearly all lawyers, at any rate all who had money or could get their hands on credit, invested in town lots, railroad schemes, new town speculation, or farmland, and nearly all were to rue the day they strayed from the practice of law to gamble on the future. A few made money early and got out before the collapse came. Walter C. Shinn was one of those who did make money in Dodge City by developing Shinn Addition, then leaving town, but even he was lured back when news of the land boom in Kansas reached him in Colorado. Most were caught, within four years after the end of the Texas cattle trade, in the sharp economic depression that hung on for a dozen years. Land prices plummeted, settlers stopped coming, and established homesteaders abandoned their claims to return "to the wife's folks back east."

Besides Shinn, four attorneys became involved in real estate to

the near or total exclusion of their law practices: H. M. McGarry,
E. H. Borton, J. F. Frankey, and R. G. Pendleton. One entrepre-
neur, Martin S. Culver, read law and was admitted to the bar to
buttress his real-estate schemes.

### H. M. ("Harry") McGarry: 1885–1886

Although he was one of the earlier Dodge Citians, H. M. McGarry
came late to the practice of law. He was born in 1852 in Wisconsin,
and his family moved shortly after to Noble County, Ohio, where
his father, Samuel McGarry, was one of the principal organizers of
the county and served as probate judge. In the fall of 1863, the
McGarrys then moved to a farm in Jefferson County, Illinois,
where they remained until 1876. The next move west carried them
to Missouri. In 1879 they made the last of their westering treks to
Foote County (now Gray County), Kansas. H. M. McGarry had
received a contract as principal of the Dodge City school, and the
family apparently used that as an excuse for one more western
venture, this time homesteading in the county adjoining the one
where their son held a steady job.[32]

During McGarry's two-year term as teacher-principal, the town
built and dedicated, with considerable ceremony, a two-room
schoolhouse; student enrollment reached two hundred. As principal, H. M. was fairly active in the community's social life and assumed a minor role in the Republican party. At the end of his second year he left Dodge City, undoubtedly to go east to prepare to
become an attorney.[33]

By 1884, McGarry had located in McPherson, Kansas, as a practicing lawyer. His younger brother, L. E., left the Foote County
homestead to become clerk of the district court in Dodge City.
Since clerking for the court did not absorb all of his time, he also
engaged in the real-estate business. In July 1885, H. M. returned
to Dodge to join in establishing the firm of H. M. McGarry, D. F.
Owens, and L. E. McGarry, advertised as a "Law, Loan, Real Estate, Collection, and Insurance Agency." H. M. was the legal officer, and the other two handled the insurance and property business. The firm caught the land rush on the rise and soon was
prospering with the western Kansas economy. The volume of busi-

ness within two years was such that the firm required another person with legal training, and J. F. Frankey was employed. For the next half-dozen years the business prospered, but in the 1890s, when the bottom dropped out of the real-estate market, the company disbanded. McGarry had started the breakup in January 1888 when he and Frankey left the firm and set up legal practice on their own.[34]

During his brief period as a cowtown lawyer, McGarry concentrated on the legal work of the firm. It was not until the boom began to wane and after Dodge was no longer a cattle town that he and Frankey joined in a general-practice partnership. There is no indication that the real-estate firm lost large amounts of money, but the depression and the panic of 1893 made it unprofitable to concentrate on land. Fortunately for McGarry, he had the profession of lawyer to carry him through a rough time. During the depression years of the 1890s, he had the good fortune to become Mike Sutton's partner. Theirs was the only legal firm in Dodge City having enough business to warrant an occasional advertising box in the papers. Although McGarry had some influence on early Dodge City, it was not primarily as a lawyer.

## E. H. Borton: 1880–1886

From the beginning, E. H. Borton emphasized the real-estate aspects of law. Ironically, he left Dodge just as the land boom was reaching its height. He did not leave the business, however, but merely shifted his base of operations farther west.

Borton was born in Iowa City, Iowa, and came to Dodge in 1880 after graduating from Iowa University Law School. For a time he shared an office with Colonel T. S. Jones, then moved into his own office in the *Globe* building. Although he did not limit his practice to land matters, he did strongly emphasize that aspect of his work, as is indicated in an advertisement in the *Ford County Globe:*

E. H. BORTON
ATTORNEY AT LAW
DODGE CITY, KANSAS

Government land business done for all counties and west of Dodge City. Maps and plats for inspection. Pension claims promptly looked after. Office at Globe office.[35]

From the first, Borton, as a college-trained lawyer, impressed the community with his erudition. His knowledge of the finer points of law, or at least his ability to uncover them, was reinforced by his own extensive library of "two hundred volumes . . . , valuable, rich and rare in legal lore." Furthermore, his scholarship was not limited to legal tomes, and the community was properly impressed and entertained when he presented to the Ford County teachers association "a well written paper on orthography." When the 1883 Fourth of July celebration was scheduled, Borton was not on the program, but he was repeatedly "called for" by the audience and he eventually obliged with an extemporaneous presentation that convinced the *Globe* reporter that Borton was "a brilliant young orator and able thinker." As one of the more eligible bachelors about town, he also impressed the community as "gay and fascinating." His availability was misleading; he had already met Clara Bill, who lived at Sidney in Ness County, and in October 1882 they were married.[36]

Borton's association with the Bill family led to a shift in his legal practice and introduced him to a new group of clients. E. M. Bill, Clara's father, came from a prominent Iowa family boasting an ancestry that could be traced back to the court of Henry VIII. Bill was an Iowa politician of some note who had been attracted to the West by the prospects of free homestead land. Once in Kansas, his interests quickly changed to livestock and he acquired substantial holdings in Ness County. He was one of the organizers of the Western Kansas Stock Growers' Association, which was established on May 8, 1883, in Sidney and sponsored its own newspaper there. As a member of the executive committee, Bill invited Borton to attend the organizational meeting, where the young attorney was elected the official attorney for the association. This position put him in contact with clients having totally different concerns from those he had served in Dodge City. When the Hebrew Immigration Society of Cincinnati needed someone in western Kansas to supervise the sale of its cattle at auction, the official association attorney was selected. Such leads were not always a blessing. A company lawyer was like a country doctor: he went wherever and whenever he was called.[37]

A case in point was a trial held in the Crooked Creek post office some twenty-five miles southwest of Dodge City. Borton's client, Frank Davis of the Smokey Hill Cattlepool, and two friendly witnesses rode in a wagon, but Borton and Chalk Beeson made the trip on horseback, protected only by the slickers they wore. When they started their trip from Dodge, it was a cold, raw day that quickly changed to an even colder one, aggravated by heavy rain. The case, presented before the justice of the peace, concerned a cow purchased by Andrew McCauley, a Crooked Creek farmer. Davis claimed the cow had been stolen from him or had strayed. McCauley had purchased the cow from a third person, and the identity of the cow, not the criminality of McCauley, was in question. The case finally was determined, in the best cowtown tradition, by examining the animal's brand. A letter from one of the spectators in attendance explained:

Although the plaintiff tried to make it appear that the brand on the right hip was a heart brand, the plaintiff's attorney had some little trouble in his arrangements there. Mr. Hungate [an old-time cattleman who served as an expert witness] said there was a spade and a triangle, but after shaving the hair off the cow, which the court subpoenaed there, it was seen to be a plain triangle. So Mr. Davis was awarded the cow and yearling calf.

Borton had won the day for his client, but there was a long ride home in the rain. The following issue of the *Kansas Cowboy* carried an understandable notice that Borton was "very sick and confined to his bed."[38]

There was to be a time of sickness for the Bill and Borton families. Typhoid fever, which E. H. may have contracted at the Crooked Creek trial, struck both families: his father-in-law, E. M. Bill, and his brother-in-law, G. F. Bill, died, and Mrs. Borton was near death for several weeks. Her troubles were not over when she did recover; that summer she was injured severely in a storm that blew down several houses. The only positive note the entire summer, so far as Borton was concerned, came with notice of a substantial inheritance from E. M. Bill's estate.[39]

Borton returned to the comparative safety of his old practice, which by 1884 was secure and almost exclusively based on his recognized knowledge of real-estate law. All of his court appearances that year were civil suits involving property. He was, however, called upon by the court to clarify a point of law in a divorce case. Borton was consulted not because he was in any sense a divorce lawyer, but because his reputation and resources for research were respected. The logic and evidence he marshaled in this instance must have been extraordinary because he persuaded the court "that a judgment, after the statutes of limitation had run out, could . . . be opened again."[40]

As was true of the other cowtown lawyers, he dabbled in politics. Although his role was minor and he had no long-term commitment, he took it seriously. After he returned from his chilling ride to Crooked Creek, the *Globe* reported that he got out of his sick bed to go to the polls and vote for his favored candidate for sheriff, Pat Sughrue. Sometime before that election, a political quarrel had led to charges of disorderly conduct and disturbing the peace against Borton before Judge R. E. Burns's police court. Borton was found guilty by Burns, but on appeal to district court the verdict was changed to not guilty.[41]

Eventually, administering the family holdings in Ness County called Borton away from Dodge for such long intervals that he and his family moved to Ness City, where he established a law office. When the land boom swept over western Kansas, he, like many of his colleagues, diverted his energies into real-estate development. He ran large advertisements in the *Ness City Times* boosting the "metropolis of Sidney," which was fated to become a ghost town soon. Although he had a long association with Dodge, he never achieved the prominence of men who had a broader practice. His interest in Ness County also divided his loyalties. Then, too, he did not seek political office, which would have put his name before the public. His real-estate business was fairly lucrative from the start, and after the death of his father-in-law, Borton did not feel the economic pinch that had forced many other attorneys into politics. He did not abandon law as other successful real-estate agents had done, but he did concentrate on the real-estate aspects of it and made the most of the opportunity that came his way.[42]

## J. F. Frankey: 1886

J. F. Frankey was another late arrival, so late that for most purposes he missed the cattle-town era. As the population explosion of new settlers hit western Kansas, the McGarry brothers' real estate boomed and the firm needed another attorney. Frankey was employed in October 1886. He came from Colorado, where he had spent the previous six years; he had a total of fifteen years' practice as an attorney before coming to Dodge.[43] His work was generally confined to real-estate transactions, but he and H. M. McGarry did serve the three party plaintiffs (Democrat, Republican, and Labor) in contesting the November 1886 election in South Dodge Precinct. Later he and McGarry formed a partnership in the general practice of law.[44]

Few attorneys attracted by the land rush of the mid-1880s were able to predict its sudden decline or have the opportunity to leave. Frankey had obtained the position of assistant attorney general in 1888, and apparently he saw what was happening in western Kansas before the bottom dropped out, because in 1890 he left Dodge. His contributions to the cattle-town legal community were very late and quite limited.[45]

## R. G. Pendleton: 1885–1886

Another of the late-arriving lawyers attracted by the booming land business was R. G. Pendleton. He was born in Kentucky in 1856 and moved to Missouri after finishing his legal education. He married, and four children were born before he moved on to Nevada, Wisconsin. When R. G. Cook's land agency in Dodge City began expanding in 1885, Cook brought in Pendleton to handle legal matters. Cook had been closely associated with the legal system in Dodge as justice of the peace, county clerk, and U.S. commissioner, but he had not passed the bar. Pendleton's stay in Dodge was brief; he departed before the end of 1886.[46]

## Martin S. Culver: 1885

During the February 1885 term of district court, John Groendyke entertained members of the court with an "oyster feed" at the Wright House. The occasion was in honor of the two "new limb[s] of the law" who on that day had been admitted to the bar by the district court: Martin S. Culver, who was an industrious backer of several Dodge business enterprises, and Groendyke himself, who was the school superintendent seeking reelection. The oysters were "cooked and served in an artistic manner," congratulations were extended, and everyone had a jolly time. If the Dodge City district court was ever guilty of a quick fix through an easy examination of uninformed cronies, this was it. The two men posed no competitive threat to the other attorneys, since neither expected to practice law. Both, however, could profit by and use the prestige and image that the title *Attorney at Law* would give.[47]

Martin Culver was a former Texas rancher, reputedly of considerable importance, from near Corpus Christi. In Dodge City the Texas cattleman joined Casimero Romero, former Texas sheepman and freighter, in the saloon business. When George Hoover moved his wholesale liquor store in 1884, the partners converted the Front Street building into a saloon and billiard parlor. Culver was part of the anti–Luke Short faction in the bloodless saloon war and held the position of chairman of the Democratic county committee. He had been useful in reaching Democrat Governor Glick and reversing the governor's support of the Luke Short–Bat Masterson crowd. After the furor died down, he joined R. G. Cook, the United States land commissioner, in a real-estate firm.[48]

Culver's combined interest in cattle and real estate led him into a new area of development, one in which the title of attorney as well as the knowledge of land law was to be important. He was a member of both the Texas Livestock Association and the Western Central Kansas Stockmen's Association. From that vantage point he carefully monitored the progress of the Kansas effort to keep Texas cattle out of the state. With the movement for a national trail gathering momentum, he went to Washington to persuade federal officials to set aside a three- to six-mile strip for the trail along Colorado's eastern border. He also arranged with Atchison, Topeka and Santa Fe Railroad officials in Topeka to collect two cents a head for cattle passing under the Santa Fe railroad bridge. With these assurances in hand, Culver laid out the town of Trail City in the summer of 1885. Investors in the Trail City Town and Improvement Company had visions of a new Dodge City–type town flourishing as the Texas cattle drives moved west to meet the Santa Fe in Colorado. Lots in the new town sold for $100 or $150 apiece. Soon Cook and Culver were, as the *Kansas Cowboy* put it, "up to their elbows" in sales. H. P. Myton and Bennett & Smith Realtors of Garden City were also cashing in on the new boom town.[49]

Culver was designated "Mayor of Trail City" and led in developing the townsite with a large limestone hotel and a saddlery and harness store with five full-time leather workers kept busy meeting the trail-herd cowboys' demands. The allurement of a revived cattle trade led other Dodge Citians, including Henry Beverley, Robert Wright, Print Olive, and others, to build frame stores and invest in lots.

Culver's family remained in Dodge for a while, since booming and roaring Trail City was no place for a respectable family to live. Culver, however, spent nearly all of his time and energy developing the town some 125 miles west of Dodge. There is no indication that he used his new status as attorney in any capacity other than as realtor, and he was that mainly, if not exclusively, in the Trail City project. There is no doubt that the title, if not the knowledge of the law, was well worth whatever effort had gone into its acquisition.

# 9. Attorneys of Record

AS WOULD BE EXPECTED of a community with a highly mobile population on the cutting edge of the frontier, some lawyers following the westward migration to Dodge City did not remain long enough or were not professionally prominent enough to leave much of a mark on the town. A few of the also-cames made the marks they did because of something besides legal activities or because of one dramatic episode. Others were little noticed and soon forgotten and are included here only because at some point they appeared as attorney of record. Of the eight lawyers in this category, two or three were so inconsequential that it is difficult a hundred years later to know whether they were indeed attorneys or even residents of Dodge. Two made their biggest impression on the town by standing in the prisoner's dock, burdened with heavy charges. Two came so late to law offices in Dodge that they nearly missed the cattle-town period, and two were more closely associated with the Dodge City of buffalo days and their brief incursion into the cattle-town period had little or no influence. All were minor actors. Still, for however brief and unspectacular a moment, they were performers on the legal stage and deserve at least a mention as being bit-part actors in the role of attorney of record.

Three men have such dubious claims to cowtown-lawyer status that they are not included with the twenty-seven attorneys listed in summary or statistical statements. William S. Tremaine was admitted to the bar in Dodge's district court but never practiced there. W. A. Frush probably did not live in Dodge, at least on a permanent basis, and Tom Masterson did not practice law there, although he listed his occupation as that of attorney. They are included in Appendix B only because there is a remote possibility that their claims might be valid.

## Jesse F. Wyckoff: 1876

The first county attorney in cattle-town Dodge was Jesse F. Wyckoff, who is truly representative of the attorney-of-record category. If his name had not appeared on certain official documents, he would have left no trace of his work. As county attorney before 1876, he had been busy in district court representing the state in twelve cases. But on May 22, 1876, just as the trail herds began arriving, the county commissioners declared the position vacant because "of the absence of the late County Attorney Jesse F. Wyckoff from the County and change of residence." Apparently, he left town without giving notice. He was still listed as prosecuting attorney in cases brought to the June term of district court, but he did not appear in court. No further mention of him appears in Dodge City documents or papers.[1]

## D. M. Sells: 1876

Wyckoff's successor, D. M. Sells, is an equally shadowy figure who served from June to October in 1876. Sells was in office long enough to bring several civil suits and five criminal cases to the district court; two were against the notorious Dutch Henry Borne. The only hint of his ability came from the biased pen of Dan Frost. In attempting to defend Mike Sutton's failure to convict in the case of Kansas vs. John Tyler, Frost claimed that Tyler was released because of a "defect of information" drawn by Sells. He disappeared from the scene without leaving a trace.[2]

## George A. Kellogg: 1876, 1879–1880

One of the most active of the short-term attorneys was George A. Kellogg. Apparently, he first came to Dodge City in 1876 from Nevada, Iowa. The difficulty of breaking into the legal business, which most newcomers experienced, was to hold for Kellogg also. Business was limited, and during his first year only three of his cases reached district court: two divorce suits and a small damage claim against the Atchison, Topeka and Santa Fe Railroad. Before the next session of court, he left Dodge, undoubtedly to return to Iowa. Sometime during the winter of 1878–79, he came back to

Ford County and opened an office with Police Judge R. G. Cook. In March 1879, his wife, Maude, and his children joined him, and within a month he began the construction of "a very neat and substantial house."[3]

The second time in Dodge, he made a better start of it by working in the community and taking part in one of the local political organizations (both activities seem to have been considered essential for successful law practice). He was elected chairman of a Republican precinct committee, spoke to the initial Spearville Republican organization meeting, and was elected to the Ford County executive committee. His efforts were rewarded with the position of police judge and party support in the county attorney race in 1880.[4]

His legal business did pick up as he and his family became active and accepted members of the community. As Harry Gryden's associate, Kellogg defended one or two important clients in district court, including the successful defense, after a "long and tedious hearing," of Charles Trask, who was charged with stealing government mules. When Trask was rearrested and taken before the U.S. commissioner in Topeka, the evidence that the defense had presented earlier prevailed. But if business improved for Kellogg, it was still hardly enough to support a family. In the January 1880 district-court term he was associated with only four cases on a docket of thirty-seven, while among the established lawyers Harry Gryden had twenty and E. F. Colborn had fifteen. Kellogg even tried to attract clients by advertising with more than just the usual box in the paper, suggesting that "all persons having claims for losses occasioned by the Indian raid of 1878 will do well to call on me."[5]

Before his good works and his enhanced reputation could pay off, Kellogg and a dozen other Dodge Citians were struck with gold fever. He joined Colborn as the rush to Colorado gathered momentum in the spring of 1880. Editor Frost believed that if Kellogg had remained in Dodge, he would have won the county attorney's office; instead, he had stayed just long enough to acquire the impressive nickname *Senator* and then moved on. He opened an office in Gunnison when gold fever subsided and continued his career as an attorney there. He apparently did not miss his lost opportunity in Kansas.[6]

## George U. Holcomb: 1877

One of the briefest and most unfortunate attempts at lawyering in Dodge was made by a Cimarron, Kansas, youth, George U. Holcomb. His father, Colonel James Holcomb, was a substantial cattleman in Foote (Gray) County and was well known in Dodge City. George was admitted to the bar in the summer of 1877 and for a brief time practiced in Dodge City. He then moved to nearby Cimarron, where he found the legal pickings embarrassingly slim.

In December 1877, Holcomb and George A. Watkins stole seventy to one hundred head of cattle from a neighboring ranch, drove them to Ottawa County, and were arrested there. Bat Masterson brought Holcomb back to the Dodge City jail, and District Judge Samuel R. Peters set his bail at one thousand dollars. Sutton, the county attorney, filed "a certain information" with the district court, and on order of the court Masterson jailed Holcomb for failure to make bail. Because of his past unblemished reputation and the status of his family, Holcomb was given fairly free range in the building housing the jail. He took advantage of the leniency to escape. Masterson pursued him to Pueblo and brought him back to stand trial. His attorney up to this point had been Harry Gryden, who sought a writ of habeas corpus for him, an action that eventually moved the case to the Kansas Supreme Court. The major legal point to be decided there was the constitutionality of the act attaching the unorganized western counties to the Dodge City judicial district. Nelson Adams of Larned and A. A. Hurd of Great Bend, Gryden's frequent partner, took over the defense of Holcomb, and Ford County Attorney Sutton and a Topeka lawyer, "Gen." H. B. Johnson, acting with Attorney General Willard Davis, stood for the state. The decision of the court was handed down in April 1879; it denied Holcomb's entitlement of discharge and remanded him to the custody of the Ford County sheriff.[7]

In May, Holcomb attempted another escape, this time using a case knife to carve through the wooden planks of the jail, but he was caught before he could finish the job. A week later he was released on bond approved by Gryden, his former defense counselor, who was now acting county attorney. The case by then had missed the June session of the district court, and sometime be-

fore the next session Holcomb dropped between the cracks of the
Kansas justice system, although he was only twenty-five miles
away on his father's ranch, the colonel having secured his release
on bail. That seemed to end his careers as criminal and lawyer.[8]

It is doubtful that any of Holcomb's legal training was of much
value in the various maneuvers brought to his defense. Apparently,
he relied more on his ingenuity and persistence in escaping Dodge's
flimsy jail to put distance between himself and the long arm of the
law. He was not the only cowtown lawyer to stand trial on serious
charges, but he was the only one not to be exonerated of the
crime.

### Edward F. ("Ed") Hardesty: 1878–1880

Among the other Dodge City lawyers to see justice from both sides
of the bar was Edward F. Hardesty, and his record as defendant
was far more successful than that as defender. Hardesty came to
Dodge City in 1878 or early 1879 from Colorado, where he had
been admitted to the bar. Born and raised in Kentucky, he was
twenty-seven years old when he arrived on Front Street, married,
and shortly thereafter became a father. He advertised as "Attorney at Law and Collecting Agent." In June 1879 he and Harry
Gryden formed a partnership that lasted only through the summer,
when Hardesty hung his own shingle at new quarters just west of
the post office. Clients calling for assistance were few, as the established attorneys handled most cases. One barometer of success
for any attorney was the number of cases he represented in district
court. Hardesty's name rarely appears: the one case he presented
in the January session was his own suit to recover a fee owed by a
client. In April 1880 he ran for police judge and came in a distant
third. Later the same year he was no more successful in his bid, as
an independent candidate, for the position of county attorney. With
four other candidates running, all better known, he made a poor
showing. At that point he apparently realized that Dodge had more
lawyers than it needed and decided to leave the profession.[9]

Relatives of Hardesty had moved to Hamilton County earlier in
the decade, and John F. Hardesty had taken over the Holly Ranch,
which straddled the state line, with the ranch house located on the

present site of Holly, Colorado. The ranch consisted of a large acreage along the Arkansas River that extended well into Kansas. By 1880 the settlement at Syracuse, the town nearest the ranch, had seen better days, and the range was wide open, with few settlers or barbed-wire enclosures in the area. The Hardestys had managed to preserve friendly relations with the Indians, occasionally at considerable cost in time, patience, and money, and the ranch was expanding. Young Ed was invited to become a part of the operation. He did and reported back to the folks in Dodge that things were progressing just fine. The Dodge City press wished the former lawyer the best of luck and the town promptly forgot about him. In December 1881, however, he was back in the news: on trial in district court.[10]

On a bitterly cold day in December 1881, Harry Gryden, Ed's old partner, now city attorney, was summoned with Sheriff George T. Hinkle to Coolidge, Kansas, to investigate the slaying of Barney Elliott, a hired hand working for Ed Hardesty. Elliott had been at the ranch for only a short time, had a good reputation, and was, as Deacon Klaine put it, "a temperance man." Elliott was about the same height and build as his boss and had "about the same physical appearance," a fact that was to have much influence on his destiny.[11]

One night when Hardesty was expected to return late or perhaps even be away all night, someone "crept into his wife's bed." She assumed it to be her husband. The next morning when Hardesty did appear, Mrs. Hardesty became hysterical. She was pregnant at the time and within a few weeks of delivery. When he had heard his wife's story, Hardesty strapped on his two six-guns and went looking for his hired hand. Other members of the ranch crew joined him. When located and confronted with the accusation, Elliott remained mute, neither denying nor confirming his involvement. At that point, in the presence of witnesses, Hardesty turned prosecutor, judge, and executioner and sent eleven bullets into Elliott's body. Apparently, one shot missed.[12]

Hardesty and some of the men who had accompanied him were arrested and charged with murder. In the legal maneuvering that followed, Hardesty waived a preliminary hearing and Gryden, now out of office, joined T. S. Jones and John Martin of Topeka in defense. Hardesty gave bond in the amount of ten thousand dollars, as did Thomas Brown, one of the men accused as an accessory. The other accused man, Joseph Davis, could not raise bail and was lodged in the Dodge City jail. The case went to the June 1882 session of district court in Dodge. The roles of the various attorneys now were reversed, and Jones, now county attorney, led the prosecution; Whitelaw and Sutton assumed the defense. Davis and Brown soon were released because there was no concrete evidence linking them to the actual shooting. Whitelaw, making his first appearance before the district court, was said to have been "masterly and able" in stating the defense's version of what happened. In summary, Sutton spoke for more than two hours and, with his usual "solid, logical . . . cool . . . and dispassionate manner," won the jury. The trial had attracted much attention and "a full court room." Mrs. Hardesty stayed through it all and "was greatly affected" by the proceedings.[13]

No one was surprised when the jury found Hardesty not guilty. It had been a physically difficult as well as nerve-shattering and embarrassing time for Mrs. Hardesty. Her presence in the courtroom and her obvious discomfort while she was there were thought to have influenced the jury. As the outraged husband, Ed carried the sympathy of both Coolidge and Dodge City. Justice, as far as the citizens were concerned, had triumphed; the cad, Barney Elliott, had got what he deserved. There were repercussions, however, when the Hardestys returned to Hamilton County. Even at the time of the trial speculation and rumors as to the circumstance of Elliott's death were rife. The *Caldwell Commercial* informed its readers that "Mrs. Hardesty told the ravishing story to shield her husband." Within a year, Mrs. Hardesty was back in district court seeking a divorce. The decree was granted in the June 1883 session, and custody of the one child was given to the plaintiff; it was to be the last appearance of either Hardesty in the courts of Dodge City. Undoubtedly, much of the mystery of the tragedy would be dispelled if the grounds for granting the divorce were known. Without the record, the Hardesty affair remains an elusive and enigmatic episode. Ed returned for a visit in 1886 and was at that time living in Wells, Nevada. It was reported that he died in Denver, Colorado, on May 23, 1898, leaving a wife and six children.[14]

## Vine DePui: 1886

On the surface, Vine DePui might appear to be one of Dodge City's earliest attorneys with one of the longest tenures, but information on him is so sketchy that it is hard to know much about his youth, when he became an attorney, or where he ended his days. He spent at least three years, probably between 1879 and 1882, in Garden City, working as a clerk in the federal land office, and there may have been other times when DePui was not a resident of Dodge City.

By his own testimony he came to Dodge in September 1877 and was employed for a number of years as "clerk, bookkeeper, and that kind of work." Not until the last days of the cattle-town era did he advertise himself as an attorney. In April 1883 he was serving as deputy county clerk, a position certainly in the category of clerk and bookkeeper. Later that year, he ran on the People's-party ticket for register of deeds, winning with a comfortable plurality of fifty-three votes.[15]

At a special meeting of the county commissioners on March 3, 1884, a Dodge City businessman, Morris Collar, called for DePui's resignation because "of insufficient bondsmen on his bond, and his conduct being unbecoming an officer of Ford County, Kansas." On motion, the county clerk was instructed to deliver the following notice to DePui:

By petition of your bondsman, M. Collar, you are requested to furnish additional responsible security on your bond, and if not successful, he and the County Commissioners request you to resign your office as Registrar of Deeds, as your conduct since your election to office is unbecoming an officer of Ford County, Kansas.

Whatever the offense, other than not having a sufficient bond, DePui did not resist ouster, and on May 20, 1884, the commissioners accepted his resignation.[16]

A later, cryptic note in a neighboring town's newspaper does little to clarify the mystery, but does suggest that DePui's lifestyle conformed more to Front Street rowdyism than to the responsible decorum of a public official. Addison Bennett, the editor of the *Garden City Irrigator,* who spent considerable time in Dodge, reported that DePui was "slowly recovering from wounds inflicted by Clarence Wentworth" and would not press charges against his assailant.

In September 1884, DePui opened an office in conjunction with attorney B. F. Milton but seemingly limited his activities to real-estate business only: "Homestead, Pre-emption and Timber Culture entries made, and First Proofs written, Deeds, Mortgages, and other instruments drawn with neatness, dispatch and accuracy." It does not appear that he was acting as an attorney at that time. However, in the summer of 1886 he placed a running advertisement in the *Globe Live Stock Journal* indicating that he was a "U.S. Land Attorney," and he apparently had established his own law office. In the late 1890s he joined Grant Pettyjohn as a full-time attorney. In 1900 he married Grant's widowed sister, Mrs. Maud Mabel Pettyjohn Scott. He sought the Republican nomination for county attorney in 1898, but W. W. Jackson was named instead. [17]

DePui remains an elusive figure who may have been a practicing attorney but probably was not until late in Dodge City's cattle-town days. However, he was involved in matters closely related to the courts and the business of lawyers through much of the period, and he ended his career in Dodge as an attorney. Whatever his official position, he was a minor figure in the legal community, and his influence on the courts of law was meager.

## E. N. Wicks: 1886

One of the handful of lawyers who were marginal in their interest and residence in Dodge City was E. N. Wicks. From the limited information that is available, it is difficult to know whether Wicks was more than an occasional visitor, merely a partner of a Dodge attorney while living in a neighboring town. If Wicks was one of the attorneys of record as a bona fide resident of Dodge, it was for only a few weeks in 1886.

He ran for county attorney in 1886 as a Labor-party candidate against two of the better-known and well-established attorneys, B. F. Milton and Colonel T. S. Jones. To the surprise of the local politicians, if not the voters, Wicks won by a margin of more than two hundred votes. Up to that point, he was not a resident of Dodge City, but with the obligations of his position, he was required to establish an office in the Ford County Courthouse. For approximately two months, he was a Dodge City lawyer during the cattle-town era.[18]

E. N. Wicks was born in La Salle County, Illinois, on May 11, 1856. At age fourteen he began attending the academy at East Paw Paw, Illinois, and in the fall of 1874 he "entered upon a select course of study at Northwestern College of Naperville, Ills. where he attended for three years." He then transferred to Oberlin College and graduated with honors in 1878. In the fall of the following year, he entered the first law class of Valparaiso Law School. After a year of formal study, he left Valparaiso to read law in Frankfort, Indiana, and was admitted to the Indiana bar in the spring of 1881. He established a practice in Fowler, Indiana, where he remained until he moved to Cimarron, Kansas, in January 1885.

Wicks retained his office in the Cimarron Bank Building and maintained his association with C. B. Riley, his law partner, while serving as Ford County attorney. When he completed his term, the partnership was dissolved and Wicks moved the twenty miles from Cimarron to Dodge City. But by then the old cattle town had entered a new phase and his career in Dodge reflected the new order of things.[19]

*John Groendyke: 1886*

Among the latecomers to legal practice who remained in the ranks for only a short time was John Groendyke. In the summer of 1886 an advertising box began appearing in Frost's *Globe Live Stock Journal* listing Groendyke as an "Attorney at Law." It was a new role for him. He had come to Dodge in August 1881 as principal of the school, had moved to Spearville in the same capacity in 1883, and had returned to Dodge in 1884 to hold the office of superintendent of schools.

Groendyke was an Indiana native who grew up on a farm near Independence. He taught in a country school for a while, then entered National Normal School in Lebanon, Ohio, before returning to teaching. He continued in that profession until he announced his availability as an attorney. The move may have been a politician's ploy in preparation for the 1886 school election.

Groendyke had been warmly received in Dodge, was active socially, and had filled minor roles in local politics. Apparently, his first venture in the legal arena came earlier in 1883 when he became a part of Mike Sutton's scheme to get a sympathetic justice of the peace appointed by Governor John A. Martin. Groendyke agreed to serve as JP, and that endeavor seems to have been his major—perhaps only—feat in the legal community. He won the November 1883 school election handily and returned to the full-time duties of superintendent of schools. Although he maintained an office as an attorney through 1887, his return to the position of superintendent apparently occupied most of his time if it did not in fact end his active legal career. At the completion of his term, he moved on to other teaching jobs at Bunker Hill and Russell, Kansas. If he was a cowtown lawyer, it was for only a brief time and he apparently made little impact on the legal community.[20]

# 10. The Legacy

TO EASTERN TOURISTS passing through western Kansas, Dodge City's legacy might seem to be the row of slick restorations in the place where Boot Hill used to be, the changed street names of Wyatt Earp Boulevard and Gunsmoke Avenue, and the annual ten- to fifteen-million-dollar tourist trade the city enjoys today. Its notorious past has kept the image of Dodge fresh in the minds not only of Americans but of all people who read for pleasure or attend movies for recreation. Over the years, old Dodge City has been a fertile ground for writers of western fiction and the producers of Hollywood movies and television serials. The Saturday matinees of B westerns, the oaters, found magic in the name of Dodge City, no matter whether the action was filmed in the mountains, on the desert, or at the lakeshore. *Gunsmoke,* first on radio and then on television, relied for twenty years on the Dodge City reputation and myth for plots and characters. Hugh O'Brian, as the star of the *Wyatt Earp* television series, also discovered that the town's past evoked mood and expectation that surpassed reality. And before them, Errol Flynn, Ann Sheridan, and company made Dodge City, as the title of a spectacular movie, a worldwide household word in the 1940s.

These perpetuations of cowtown Dodge may have borne little resemblance to the Dodge City of 1876 to 1886, but they did keep the town on the map, put dollars in its residents' pockets, and undoubtedly contributed to its growth and prosperity. Yet, despite its notoriety and its recognition, Dodge has never, or as the true Dodge Citian would say, has not yet reached metropolitan status. In fact, only Wichita of the Kansas cattle towns rose to big-city grandeur. Dodge settled for second place with a 1986 population of

231

*Dodge City in 1882. The county seat of Ford County had a population of twelve hundred at the time. Courtesy Kansas State Historical Society.*

20,873, well over twice the size of third-place Abilene. The Front Street legend continued from year to year to be an important and lucrative legacy.

As monetarily important as the legend is and has been, cowtown Dodge and the attorneys who practiced there left another and perhaps more important patrimony. None of the cowtown lawyers contributed great new interpretations of American criminal or civil law, achieved high political office, or left a fortune to their families. Still, their contributions to the foundation on which the community was to build were considerable.

In a period of adjustment after the cattlemen's dominance, the town doubted that it had received positive benefits from its association with cowboys and their camp followers. Many citizens felt only gratitude that the town was no longer dependent on trail herds and wondered why they had been so nearsighted in clinging to that dependency. They were lucky, they believed, to be well out of the business and luckier still to have found new and better opportunities.

One citizen who would have endorsed such sentiments was Carrie Rath, the divorced wife of one of the cattle town's leading entre-

preneurs, Charles Rath. Her years in Dodge had netted her little
but trouble, and she could hardly believe the news given by a
neighbor that the government had unexpectedly thrown open the
Fort Dodge reservation land for settlement. Carrie did not wait for
details or additional confirmation but hurried home, yelled for her
son to hitch up the horse while she dressed the youngest child, and
all three piled into the buggy. She whipped the horse into a lather
on her way out of town and managed to beat much of the rush
down Military Road. A mile north of the fort, she found an un-
claimed quarter section, staked her claim, and squatted on the land
to make certain no one preempted her 160 acres. Later she had a
sod house built, with a fence and a plowed fireguard around it. She
brought her family out every week and spent the night in the soddy
so that she could demonstrate that she had proved up the place and
lived there.

It seemed to her almost too good to be true: free land close to
home at a time when the rush to western Kansas had seen the
good farmland in Ford County taken by settlers pouring in by train,
stage, horseback, and covered wagon. Good luck had returned to
Dodge City, and May 1886 was to be her lucky spring. Nor was
she the only one who felt the thrill of unexpected ownership. Before twelve o'clock the next day, when the land grab was said to
have ended officially, more than a hundred claims had been staked.
Carrie knew it was not like the big deals Charles Rath had made
when they were first married, but she took great satisfaction in
knowing that she had got into the land business, no matter how
small her catch, on her own without Charlie's aid or blessing.
Things had not gone well for her of late, not since the divorce.
Now, just when life looked bleakest, she had received this unexpected windfall. Charlie could have Mobeetie—and he did own
most of it; Carrie was for the moment happy to be part of the
booming town of Dodge City.[1]

Mrs. Rath's plight and subsequent good fortune were remarkably similar to those of Dodge City in general. At a time when
Dodge had ceased to serve the Texas trail-herd trade and Front
Street merchants had been separated from the lucrative source of
funds, symbolically their breadwinner, the unsettled land had attracted a new source of support from the homesteaders who were

*A page from the Dodge City court records, which range from crumbling sheets that are unusable to clean pages of neat handwriting. Courtesy Kansas State Historical Society.*

fueling an unprecedented rush to the West. The earlier trickle of German settlers changed to a flood of newcomers from nearly ever state in the Union. It was easy for Dodge City to forget the summer loss of the Texas cowboy and his rowdy ways when the year-round trade in goods and services brought by the stable granger families more than equaled the trail-herd profits.

Women like Carrie with families to raise and merchants like Wright, Zimmermann, and Collar with goods to sell were grateful to Sutton, the meddlesome deacons, and Mike's Boys, who had won the battle with the old-time holdouts: Gryden, Masterson, and the Gang. There were good economic reasons to praise the new progress and godliness that had triumphed over saloons and the minions of evil. As Deacon Klaine informed his readers, "developing and building up moral and material interest of the city" was a combination that paid handsomely. In the new Dodge City a woman had no fear in walking the streets alone, summer or winter, and at the same time her husband was doing well selling to respectable folks in from the country. God was in his heaven; all was right with Dodge City.[2]

Carrie's achievement stood as a symbol for other developments in the town as well. For her, there had been the divorce, then Charlie had remarried, and the monthly payments he had promised stopped coming. Even the initial cash settlement had not been secured without a struggle: in the end, Carrie had been forced to sue to get the last $650. Little setbacks like the children's illnesses and unexpected household expenses seemed to plague her. Luck—good luck, that is—seemed to have deserted her along with her husband. The town was in a similar situation and mood. The year 1885 had seen three fires sweep through the central business district. A January fire destroyed the west half of the block between Second and Third avenues and a number of warehouses south of the railroad tracks. The first November blaze took the whole block on Front Street between First and Second avenues. Ten days later a fire that began in the room of a soiled dove known as Sawed-off destroyed even more business buildings and several residences. Winter brought the awesome Blizzard of '86 with several deaths and much suffering. Open-range ranching for all of the High Plains

died in the storm when ranchers' losses ran as high as 50 to
90 percent of their herds. The long-sought railroads to the south
that cut through the Dodge City freighting trails destroyed the
wagon-road economy that had bolstered Dodge's prosperity since
the early 1870s. Shutting off the Texas trail herds was only one of a
series of financial troubles Dodge was to suffer in 1885–86. Like
Carrie, townsfolk were beset by problems and personal losses.

Despair, however, was not in Carrie's nature or the town's.
Robert Wright had contracted for the replacement of his building
before the fire died down and was back in business five days later in
a temporary structure; James Kelley rebuilt his Opera House as a
brick building finer than the old one; George Reighard, just south
of town, concluded that ranching as he had known it was gone, converted to farming, and prospered in his new enterprise. The old
enthusiasm returned and was to be justified in the years immediately following the cowtown era. "There will be an ebb to the
flow," editor Klaine wrote. "We believe Dodge City is emerging
from the thralldom of vice—that demon which has so long throttled
her precious life." Dodge, without the evils of saloons, clear of the
rousting cowboys, and populated by peaceable, God-fearing families, was destined for better times. Klaine concluded:

A board of trade, a telephone line company, a telegraph line company,
electric lights, water works, more bridges across angry streams, better
society, better business, more facilities for trade. These are demanded,
and are receiving that attention due an enlightened and progressive
people.[3]

Mike Sutton and his boys could look with pride on battered but
reviving Dodge City and know that all their hard work, their humiliation at the hands of Bat Masterson, and their behind-the-scenes
maneuvering had achieved the desired public and private good.
Even the old stalwarts, such as Colonel Jones and Bob Wright,
agreed that Dodge had weathered its second economic transition
with success. The loss of the cattle-trail business had not been the
disaster many had predicted. Even Samuel Prouty, the last editorial champion of Dodge City as a cattlemen's town, conceded that
the farmers had brought with them "success and prosperity" for
the town and all of western Kansas, which was "blooming and
booming."[4]

Then, just as predicted, the bonanza came: for Carrie Rath, a free quarter section of land; for Dodge, a land rush of unprecedented proportions. In 1887, Klaine's paper carried banner headlines:

CAUGHT ON.

DODGE CITY AWAKENED

TO THE IMPORTANCE OF

MAKING THE DIRT FLY!

THE PEOPLE THOROUGHLY
AROUSED!!

A Well Defined Case of Boom
FEVER DEVELOPED

The Great Southwest, Dodge no more than dozens of other towns, plunged into the heady speculation of a full-blown land boom with equally full conviction that it would last a lifetime. By 1888 the McGarry brothers were running a quarter-page ad with inch-high type announcing they had a half-million dollars to lend for the purchase of land and that they had available sixty farms in Ford County, 8,000 acres in Gray County, and 82,000 acres in Finney and Hamilton counties. Walter Shinn matched the McGarry brothers with a full-page ad urging investment at home in "South Side property," where Shinn Addition held 280 acres. Land agents flocked to Dodge City, Garden City, and southwest Kansas in rising numbers. Lawyers joined the ranks, since most of their legal business now revolved around land. Dan Frost warned strangers not to throw objects at the dogs in the streets, not because of his sympathy for dogs but because the thrower was "liable to hit three or four land agents."[5]

The city council took Klaine's enthusiasm as gospel when he wrote that Dodge was "no longer a border town with frontier characteristics," that it had "entered the arena of metropolis" and would soon take its place in "the constellation of great cities." Extensive waterworks, electric power, and street improvements begun in 1886 were followed the next year by a natural-gas works and a system of sewage disposal for the business district. An envious neighboring editor wrote: "Dodge is rapidly assuming metropolitan airs. In addition to electric lights . . . posts have been placed at street corners, on which are nailed boards bearing names of the streets and avenues." Even the press in the state capital noticed that there were "silent but irresistible forces at work to regenerate Dodge City." For three years Dodge was to indulge herself in the euphoria of a boomtown economy.[6]

Then came reality. For Carrie Rath, reality was the chilling news that the run for reservation land had not been warranted: the government had not opened the land for settlement. The affair had been the result of false rumor and idle gossip passed from one neighbor to another. The one hundred squatters were just that: squatters with no more legal right than squatters had ever held. For Carrie, prosperity was not to return with the windfall of free land. And so it was to be for Dodge. The land-rush bubble burst in 1889. The three years of unparalleled boom evaporated overnight. By 1892, Klaine's headlines revealed the difference when he wrote of the "Calamity Craze."[7]

As drought dried up the crops and jobs in town disappeared, the people in western Kansas began moving back east. In 1888, Ford County had an estimated population of 7,249, with Dodge City claiming 2,705 residents. Not until 1904 were there to be comparable figures after the population hit a low mark in 1891 of 4,992 in the county and 1,860 in the town. Meade County, adjacent to Ford on the south and a fair representative of surrounding counties, lost more than 70 percent of its population between 1888 and 1895. Order-of-sale notices spread through the newspapers, replacing the previous notices of final proof of claim. In reporting the closing of the Merchants State Bank, the *Dodge City Times* observed that "the collapse of the boom period and the stringency left the borrowers unable to meet their obligations." Among those who could not honor debts was the Dodge City municipal government. The extensive utility and street improvements begun in 1886 added to the crisis; by 1891 the town could not meet its scrip obligations in either interest or principal payments. Before the dreary decade was over, city officials had refused to acknowledge their own scrip and had admitted that they did not know the total amount of Dodge City's indebtedness.[8]

Obviously, the end of the Texas cattle trade was not responsible for the hard times of the 1890s. In fact, the end of the cattle-town economy coincided with a burst of prosperity. It would be equally wrong to suggest, as Klaine contended, that the acceptance of prohibition and the exit of the gunmen, prostitutes, and gamblers brought on the boom period; land had been responsible for both prosperity and depression. What cattle-town Dodge could claim responsibility for was the sound base of business activity that had grown between 1876 and 1886, which put sufficient capital in the hands of merchants to weather the fluctuations in the economy. Dodge Citians A. J. Anthony, George Hoover, and Robert Wright were stung by the depressed times but remained solvent and quickly recouped their losses once prosperity returned. A few lucky ones were able to capitalize on other people's misfortunes and by 1907 emerged stronger than they were when they were caught on the financial roller coaster. Dodge retained its preeminence as a supplier and market, and above all else it retained its advantage as an established transportation center. The Santa Fe Railroad retrenched after 1888 but was available for immediate increases in services when settlers began returning to the area. Cowtown Dodge had prospered and established a broad-enough base so that recovery from the depression of the 1890s and the Panic of 1893 was possible. Undoubtedly, Dodge City as a cattle town made its best contribution and left its best legacy simply by existing.

The attorneys experienced the same whirlwind boom-and-bust ride as the other Dodge Citians. The town saw many new attorneys arrive as the boom gathered momentum: fourteen practicing attorneys in 1886 as compared with six at the beginning of the era. In 1887 the *Dodge City Times* alone carried advertisements for nine lawyers and, significantly, thirteen real-estate firms. Five years later, only the Sutton and McGarry partnership occasionally ran a box, and no real-estate agents could afford the tab. Many of the lawyers joined other discouraged Dodge Citians in leaving for other opportunities. Still, some remained, tightened their belts, and rode out the storm. Like Wright's emporium and Dr. McCarty's City Drug Store, the attorneys who stayed were available when business and litigation prospered once again. It was not the least of the cattle town's legacy.

The attorneys who were still practicing in 1907 would not have accepted such a low assessment of their contribution to the revived and flourishing town. It would be understandable if Sutton looked back with a certain amount of gloating pride on his triumphs over Gryden and the Gang as the turning point in the history of Dodge City, and it would have been a misplaced if understandable interpretation of the lawyer's role in determining the prosperity and morality of the town.

Walter Prescott Webb contended that the West, the frontier West, was lawless by necessity. "The lawlessness," he wrote, "grew [in part] out of the social situation in the early days. Other forms of lawlessness arose because the law was wholly inapplicable and unsuited to the West." The people, he contended, "worked out an extra-legal code or custom by which they guided their actions." When Dodge City was dominated by the buffalo hunters, the town was in that state of lawlessness. The code of the buffalo men was unsophisticated and, to the uninitiated, appeared inconsistent and erratic, but it was useful. A hunter could leave a hundred hides unattended on the open prairie with no fear of theft, and he could be expected to shoot without question a man caught stealing a mule worth far less in dollars and cents than the stinking hides.[9]

By the time Mike Sutton arrived with his mismatched boot and shoe and began his spectacular career as county attorney, the code was already changing and the kind of lawlessness tolerated by Dodge as a cow town was of a different order. Business transactions were negotiated by established entrepreneurs who required a safer and more orderly business climate. At the same time, the young, restless cowboys in town after their long, tense, and arduous adventure needed to let off steam in a manner considered shocking by more settled society. Drinking, gambling, whoring, and the generally boisterous skylarking were not only tolerated but encouraged. Mike had seen Dodge first as a town that would not tolerate murder or larceny, crimes that would have had a chilling effect on the cattlemen's trade, but would allow a rough, immoral lifestyle to be flaunted as a condition necessary to attract that same cattle trade.

The law of any community comes to represent just about what society considers convenient, proper, or profitable at the moment. Just as the lawlessness under the buffalo hunters' code had been expedient, law and order—loosely interpreted—became a necessity under the cattlemen's domination. The major role of the local court system was to determine just where the community was in accepting standards established in more normal communities. Within the framework of formal legal procedures, the attorneys and judges interpreted and verified the community's position. Since people's attitudes do not advance as a monolithic force, the adversarial confrontations of the cowtown lawyers clarified the concessions. Justice Oliver Wendell Holmes recognized this expediency and observed:

Every important principle which is developed by litigation is in fact and at bottom the result of more or less definitely understood views of public policy; most generally, to be sure, under our practices and traditions, the unconscious result of instinctive preferences and inarticulate convictions, but none the less traceable to views of public policy in the last analysis.[10]

In the Dodge City real-life morality play, in which Gryden and Sutton played leading roles, the final scene was not dependent exclusively on the talents or convictions of either man. In the end, Sutton was destined to win, not because of the adroitness of his court appearances or the cleverness of his behind-the-scenes maneuvers. The shift in population, the new economic developments—not only in Dodge but south of the Kansas border—and the changed attitude toward liquor in Kansas and the nation had doomed the old way of life just as surely as early changes had eliminated the old buffalo hunters' code and lifestyle. Harry Gryden, who had been so thoroughly in tune with the community conscience in the early days of the cattle town, gradually fell behind the new standards established by a changing social and economic order. The *Atchison Daily Champion* referred to Harry as "the celebrated romantic." It was a remarkable insight into his character. In defending the old cowtown ways, he was tilting against windmills like Don Quixote. He fought for the romanticized image of the cowboy as a self-contained, free-spirited hero in harmony with the great outdoors, and the image of the equally fictitious caring prostitute with a heart of gold. Sadder still, he may have been living out his own fantasized version of a Sydney Carton–type lawyer transferred from the Bastille of Paris to the plains of Kansas.[11]

Leadership falls into the hands of those who can best articulate
and act on a community's moods. Sutton possessed the tools: a
sharp, orderly mind, a glib tongue, and an unerring sense of community preferences. He became a leader, frequently in advance of
other political figures but always within easy range of the majority
consensus. If the larger currents of frontier history in the nineteenth century were moving Dodge City into the mainstream of
American moral and social concepts, Sutton and his boys were at
least influential in timing and detail. In a sense, Sutton found himself in the position of most leaders, best expressed by the French
revolutionary: "There go the people. I must hurry. I am their
leader." A case in point was Mike Sutton's behavior as county attorney. He was obviously convinced of the evils of drink and the
need to rid Dodge of its influence, but he could not lead his fellow
Dodge Citians to such a goal through a head-on confrontation. His
leadership was far more subtle, and his true feelings did not become apparent until he saw the certainty of success. While in public office, he tolerated the mores of the community, accepting
leadership somewhere back in the pack. Eventually he plunged
ahead, even when it was personally dangerous to do so, but he and
his boys knew which direction society was headed. Such political
agility did not cause the public to like him, but, as Robert Wright
reminded his readers, Sutton did retain "the respect and esteem of
his community" and deserved his role as leader. Leadership did not
necessarily belong to the lawyers. Ministers, editors, politicians,
and lawmen of whatever stripe might have assumed the spokesman's role, and in fact an editor and a physician-businessman did
aid, abet, and occasionally lead Sutton. Yet the results of Sutton's
leadership, regardless of how they were achieved or what his contemporaries thought of him, were positive legacies from the cattle-
town days.[12]

For the rank and file of cowtown lawyers, their legacy, like that
of the town itself, was being there. In performing their assigned
duties as counselors, barristers, and court functionaries, they kept
as a clear goal the vision and reality of the justice system as a bul-
wark of fairness, order, and community conscience—a goal well
within the grasp of the frontier settlement. Deviation was never
uncontested, perfect alignment rarely achieved. But there was al-

ways within the court system, the most rational governmental structure in town, an ongoing testing of what pragmatically the community would tolerate.

In the end, the cowtown lawyer's most significant legacy was his presence and his adherence to the canons of his own profession. The twenty-seven lawyers who served Dodge City between 1876 and 1886—wayward, flawed, brilliant, likable, hated, gullible, romantic, and human as they were—contributed an essential element in the maturing of Dodge City and its environs. Through their actions as attorneys in the privacy of their offices and before the bar of justice, they performed, with varying degrees of understanding and success, an essential service in advancing an orderly, democratic way of life. Being a cowtown lawyer was, to quote Mr. Dooley, "a grand profissyon." [13]

# Appendix A
# Ford County Officials, 1876–1886

## District Judges Presiding in Dodge City

Samuel R. Peters, Newton, Ninth District, 1875–1882
Jeremiah C. Strang, Larned, Sixteenth District, 1881–1890

## Ford County Probate Judges

Herman Fringer, elected November 1876
Nicholas Klaine, elected November 1878
Lloyd Shinn, elected November 1880
Ezra D. Swan, elected November 1882
August Crumbaugh, elected November 1884
T. J. Vanderslice, elected November 1886

## County Attorneys of Ford County

Jesse F. Wyckoff, December 1875–May 1876
D. M. Sills, June 1876–October 1876
M. W. Sutton, October 1876–December 1876
M. W. Sutton, January 1877–December 1879
M. W. Sutton, January 1880–February 1882
T. S. Jones, March 1882–December 1882
J. T. Whitelaw, January 1883–December 1884
B. F. Milton, January 1885–December 1886
R. N. Wicks, January 1887–December 1888

245

## Sheriffs of Ford County

Charles E. Bassett, 1873–1878
William B. Masterson, 1878–1880
George T. Hinkle, 1880–1884
Patrick F. Sughrue, 1884–1888

# Appendix B
# Doubtful Claimants to
# Cowtown-Lawyer Status

### W. A. Frush: 1883[?]

One of the men who possibly was a Dodge City attorney but whose record there was so scant that verification is impossible was W. A. Frush. In 1880 he was listed as the law partner of J. S. Haun of Jetmore in Hodgeman County, and in 1882–83 he was county treasurer there. In the 1883 spring election of municipal officials for Dodge City, he was listed as Gryden's partner while running against Bobby Burns for police judge. When he lost by a large margin, he dropped out of the picture. It would appear that his stay in Dodge, if indeed he lived there at all, was brief, temporary, and probably as Gryden's guest. Once his bid for political office failed, Frush returned to Jetmore.[1]

### Thomas Masterson, Jr.: 1885[?]

The best-known and one of the most doubtful of the self-proclaimed lawyers had a name that evoked sharp responses from most Dodge Citians. Thomas Masterson Jr., the youngest of the four Masterson brothers, apparently was in Dodge City looking for employment when he was interviewed by the census enumerator in 1885. The enumerator listed Masterson's occupation as "attorney." There is no record of his legal training or practice.[2]

According to his obituary and death certificate, Tom was born in Fairbury (Fairfield), Illinois, on August 11, 1858. The Masterson family was in the middle of a slow westward trek that was to take them to many temporary farmsteads. In 1871 they settled in Sedgwick County, Kansas. Tom remained on the farm when his older brothers left and was twenty-six when he reached Dodge City. There would have been time in his life up to that point for him to have read law, but there is no record of his having done so.[3]

One thing was certain: in Dodge, at least, the name *Masterson* meant trouble, and trouble meant lawsuits. Tom was not long in finding both. But times had paled in the few months since brother Bat had dominated Front Street, so that Tom's troubles were dim images of his brother's escapades. Bat's involvement in the election of 1885 was carried to the Kansas Supreme Court. In a bit of déjà vu, Tom found himself in the middle of an election protest in November 1886. The three local parties on the ballot— Republican, Democrat, and Labor—jointly signed a protest because of irregularities in voting procedures in South Dodge Precinct. Among the discrepancies was the fact that Masterson and Thomas F. McGeary had presided over the election when neither was a resident of the precinct. An array of Dodge City attorneys was engaged by the plaintiffs, including Colonel Jones, J. H. Finlay, J. F. Frankey, and H. M. McGarry, while W. E. Hendricks and J. T. Whitelaw came to the defense of the precinct. After considerable debate, it was determined that only one of the offices being contested, the clerk of the district court, was in jeopardy, and since the Kansas Supreme Court had undoubtedly heard enough of Dodge City election troubles, the protest was dropped.[4]

Tom also was involved in a contest, which was not settled until 1887, over land in the Fort Dodge reservation. He was to step, at least partway, into his brother's boots when he was appointed deputy sheriff of Gray County; it appears to be the extent of his association with the justice system in Kansas. In 1894 he moved to Fort Scott, where he served as county assessor until he moved to Wichita, where he died November 8, 1941.[5]

### William S. Tremaine: 1879 [?]

During the June 1879 term of district court, Mike Sutton sponsored W. S. Tremaine's application for admission to practice law. Dr. Tremaine was widely known and respected in southwestern Kansas and the Oklahoma and Texas panhandle for his work as post surgeon at Fort Dodge. He not only treated military personnel but had performed surgery on many civilians who sought him out because of his experience and reputation.

Tremaine was born on Prince Edward Island in 1838. During the Civil War he served in the Twenty-fourth Massachusetts Volunteers and the Thirty-first U.S. Colored Troops. He continued on in the army after the war, eventually being assigned to Fort Dodge. There he was known for his efforts to improve the sorry medical facilities as well as the general living conditions of the enlisted men. He was one of the signers of the Dodge City Town Company charter, and he and Mrs. Tremaine were active in the social life of Dodge City and the military post.

Mrs. Tremaine died in 1878, and Dr. Tremaine considered giving up his military career. To help relieve the sense of loss and depression he felt, and because occasionally he had been called to serve as counselor or judge advocate in courts-martial, he read law under Sutton's guidance and even started to build an office in Dodge City. However, before his plans to change careers could be completed, he received a year's furlough, moved to Kansas City, and was appointed professor of surgery at Kansas City Medical College. At the end of his leave, he was transferred to New York. He served part time as a professor at Niagara University Medical College, organized the emergency hospital, and served as consulting surgeon at other regional hospitals. He remained in the army and had been promoted to major surgeon when he resigned in 1891. He died in Buffalo, New York, on January 13, 1898. There is no evidence that he ever practiced law in Dodge City.[6]

# Notes

The Kansas State Historical Society at Topeka is indicated as KSHS. All court cases are listed in the notes by title only.

## Preface

1. Robert R. Dykstra, *The Cattle Towns.*
2. Lawrence M. Friedman, *A History of American Law,* p. 9; Francis H. Heller, "Lawyers and Judges in Early Kansas: A Prospectus for Research," *Kansas Law Review* 22 (1974): 220, 223.

## Chapter 1: Dodge City: The Venue

1. *Dodge City Ford County Globe,* July 9, 1878; Fredrick R. Young, *Dodge City: Up Through a Century in Story and Pictures,* pp. 39–41; *Washington Evening Star,* quoted in the *Ford County Globe,* January 1, 1878; *Wilburn Argus,* April 16, 1886.
2. *Hays Sentinel* quoted in Young, *Dodge City,* p. 39; Dykstra, *Cattle Towns,* p. 58.
3. Frank H. Mayer and Charles B. Roth, *The Buffalo Harvest,* p. 87; David A. Dary, *The Buffalo Book: The Saga of an American Symbol,* p. 97; "Interview of George M. Hoover," *Dodge City Democrat,* June 19, 1903; Gary L. Roberts, "From Tin Star to Hanging Tree: The Short Career and Violent Times of Billy Brooks," *The Prairie Scout* 3 (1975): 20. Roberts estimates that, using the present method of computing homicide statistics, Dodge's rate would have been 10,000 per 100,000 population as compared with an average rate of 9.3 per 100,000 in the United States in 1973; "From Mrs. Anthony's Diary," *Dodge City Globe-Republican,* June 30, 1898.
4. Dykstra, *Cattle Towns,* pp. 60, 144–46; Jimmy M. Skaggs, *The Cattle-Trailing Industry Between Supply and Demand, 1866–1890,* p. 92.

5. *Dodge City Times,* October 6, 1881.

6. *Dodge City Ford County Globe,* May 7, 1878, July 1, 1879.

7. *Dodge City Times,* January 4, 1883.

8. For the extent and influence of freighting on Dodge City, see C. Robert Haywood, *Trails South: The Wagon Road Economy in the Dodge City–Panhandle Region; Dodge City Ford County Globe,* January 1, 1884.

9. Testimony of Dodge's growth given during examination of the disputed precinct election of 1886. See Tarbox vs. Sughrue.

10. Robert M. Wright, *Dodge City: The Cowboy Capital and the Great Southwest,* p. 262; *Second Biennial Report of the Kansas State Board of Agriculture,* p. 519; *Dodge City Ford County Globe,* September 2, 1879.

11. Dykstra, *Cattle Towns,* pp. 107–11, 246–53.

12. The analysis of the U.S. Census for Dodge City in 1880 appeared in a different form in C. Robert Haywood, "The Dodge City Census of 1880: Historians' Tool or Stumbling Block?" *Kansas History* 8 (Summer 1985): 95–109.

13. *Dodge City Times,* August 17, 1878.

14. *Second Biennial Report of the Kansas State Board of Agriculture,* p. 285; Leo E. Oliva, *Fort Larned,* p. 62.

15. The number of accidents on the railroad reported in the papers would seem to indicate that railroading was as dangerous as any Dodge City occupation. Violent death came as frequently on the tracks as on the sidewalks of Front Street. The coroner's records of deaths investigated before 1900 show only two fewer deaths caused by railroad accidents than were recorded as the result of being "shot" or "killed feloniously." Ford County Coroner's Records; *Dodge City Ford County Globe,* August 30, 1883; C. Robert Haywood, "The Dodge City War," *Kansas Territorial* 3 (May–June 1983): 14–20.

16. *Dodge City Times,* September 1, 1881; *Dodge City Ford County Globe,* January 1, 1884.

17. Klaine's preface to Wright, *Dodge City,* p. 3.

18. Using twentieth-century occupational classifications established by the Bureau of the Census, Dykstra found a "relatively large craftsman-foreman group." Undoubtedly, he reached his conclusion by including railroad-related craftsmen and foremen in his sample. Remove the railroad men and the skilled group appears rather normal. See *Cattle Towns,* p. 110.

19. *Dodge City Times,* August 17, 1878; *Dodge City Ford County Globe,* May 17, 1878.

20. John Phillip Reid, *Law for the Elephant: Property and Social Behavior on the Overland Trail,* pp. 362–64.

## Chapter 2: The Courts

1. My article "Cowtown Courts: Dodge City Courts, 1876–1886" in the Spring 1988 issue of *Kansas History* covers much of the same material that is in this chapter.

2. Paul Trachtman, *The Gunfighters,* p. 141.

3. Philip H. Lewis, "The Changing Practice of Law, 1882–1982," in Robert W. Richmond, ed., *Requisite Learning and Good Moral Character,* p. 89.

4. T. J. Philipin et al. vs. Thomas L. McCarty, County Superintendent, etc.

5. *Dodge City Ford County Globe,* December 25, 1877; *Dodge City Times,* April 1, 1886.

6. Frank Richard Prassel, *The Western Peace Officer: A Legacy of Law and Order,* p. 236; information from the Kansas Judicial Administration Office in Topeka; Glenn Shirley, *Law West of Fort Smith,* p. 198; *Dodge City Ford County Globe,* July 2, 1878, January 25, 1881; *Dodge City Times,* January 11, February 1, 1879.

7. Dempster, who killed his wife, received a harsh penalty in spite of his guilty plea: he was sentenced to twenty-five years in the penitentiary. *Dodge City Times,* October 30, 1884, February 12, 1885.

8. *Dodge City Ford County Globe,* February 21, 1882. For the same process at the district-court level, see report on State vs. J. W. Choulton in *Dodge City Times,* June 30, 1877.

9. *Dodge City Ford County Globe,* January 15, 1878; Young, *Dodge City,* pp. 62, 80, 91, 108.

10. Prassel, *Western Peace Officer,* pp. 235–36; Joseph W. Snell, *Painted Ladies of the Cowtown Frontier; Dodge City Times,* August 10, 1878.

11. Adams Express Company vs. David Rudabaugh; Joseph Briggs vs. William Witkins; Beeman vs. Perea.

12. Mix vs. Hoover. At least one type of civil suit was given more careful review than such cases receive today. Because of social attitudes in that period, divorce was considered a serious breach of community mores. It is difficult to determine how many divorce cases were processed in Dodge City. A report by federal agencies indicated eighty-seven divorces granted between 1867 and 1886, and the District Judge's Journal indicated about three a year from 1878 to 1883. Department of Commerce and Labor and Bureau of the Census, *Special Report: Marriage and Divorce, 1867–1906,* II, p. 758; Judge's Journal A, passim.

13. "Official Roster of Kansas, 1854–1925," *Collections of the Kansas State Historical Society, 1923–1925,* 16 (1925): 667–68; Session Laws of Kansas, 1876, pp. 120–21; 1881, pp. 199–200.

14. *Dodge City Ford County Globe,* December 25, 1877.

15. General Statutes of Kansas, 1876, passim. When Myton's decision was appealed, the district court upheld him. Civil Appearance Docket A.

16. Anne M. Butler, *Daughters of Joy, Sisters of Misery,* pp. 100–102.

17. *Dodge City Times,* August 11, 1877; Nyle H. Miller and Joseph W. Snell, *Great Gunfighters of the Kansas Cowtowns, 1867–1886,* p. 171; City of Dodge City vs. Monroe Henderson.

18. *Dodge City Times,* May 26, 1877, April 10, 1880; Wright, *Dodge City,* p. 187; *Dodge City Ford County Globe,* February 15, 1881, April 13, 1880.

19. Cook vs. Ford County Commissioners; City of Dodge City vs. Hattie Mauzy. The earnings of a Dodge City prostitute are difficult to determine. An 1887 grand jury in Wichita investigated three hundred women in the trade and found the typical fee to be five to seven dollars a night, but living expenses tended to deplete all earnings. Sedgwick County Grand Jury Records, 1877–1878.

20. *Compiled Laws of Kansas, 1879,* p. 440.

21. Tarbox vs. Sughrue; *Dodge City Ford County Globe,* November 18, 1879; *Dodge City Times,* November 22, 1879.

22. *Kinsley Graphic,* May 18, 1878.

23. *Dodge City Ford County Globe,* January 14, 1879; Frost's coverage of the courts was fuller than that of any other journalist, except for the few reports made by John Speer.

24. *Dodge City Times,* February 22, 1883.

25. Ibid.

26. *Dodge City Ford County Globe,* February 12, 1884.

27. *Dodge City Kansas Cowboy,* August 2, 23, 1884; *Dodge City Times,* January 8, 1884; *Dodge City Globe Live Stock Journal,* August 5, 1884; A. T. Andreas, ed., *History of the State of Kansas,* I, p. 344.

28. *Dodge City Times,* June 12, 1884.

29. Ibid.; *Dodge City Democrat,* March 27, 1886.

30. *Dodge City Journal,* September 25, 1948.

31. *Dodge City Times,* September 4, 11, 1880; *Dodge City Ford County Globe,* September 7, 1880, January 25, 1881. Events were to prove Allen correct, but only after considerable inconvenience and doubt. At one point he was convicted of third-degree murder, but Gryden strung out the process to the advantage of his client.

32. Butler, *Sisters of Joy,* pp. 112–15.

## Chapter 3: The Bar

1. Edward J. Bander, *Mr. Dooley on the Choice of Law,* p. 34.

2. *Compiled Laws of Kansas, 1879,* p. 113.

3. T. A. McNeal, *When Kansas Was Young,* pp. 115–16.

4. Glenn Shirley, *Temple Houston: Lawyer with a Gun,* pp. 51–53.

5. *Dodge City Ford County Globe,* March 2, 1880, September 10, 1881; *Dodge City Times,* February 7, 1880.

6. Alexis de Tocqueville, *The Republic of the United States of America and Its Political Institutions, Reviewed and Examined,* I, pp. 299, 305.

7. Andreas, *History of the State of Kansas,* II, p. 1561; Wright, *Dodge City,* p. 307. Wright's reference to making a senator undoubtedly referred to the election of 1895, when Lucien Baker defeated J. R. Burton. According to the *Kansas City Star* of June 13, 1918, Sutton "was one of the men who fought Burton and made Baker's election possible. Baker appointed Sutton internal revenue collector, which place he lost in 1901 when Burton defeated Baker." Commissioners' Journal Briefings, Ford County, Vol. A (1873–1885), p. 269.

8. *Dodge City Times,* January 29, 1881.

9. Ibid., April 28, 1877; *Dodge City Ford County Globe,* August 31, 1880.

10. Shirley, *Temple Houston,* p. 88; Prassel, *Western Peace Officer,* p. 14.

11. *Hays City Ellis County Star,* June 22, 1876.

12. City of Dodge City vs. Alice Chambers, City of Dodge City vs. Monroe Henderson, and City of Dodge City vs. Sallie Doke.

13. Wright, *Dodge City,* pp. 183–84.

14. *Dodge City Times,* September 1, 1877, July 5, 1879.

15. General Statutes of Kansas, 1876, pp. 599–600. The Ford County population was listed as 3,122 in 1880 and did not exceed 4,000 by the end of 1886. *Second Biennial Report of the Kansas State Board of Agriculture,* p. 519; Young, *Dodge City,* p. 175.

16. Session Laws of Kansas, 1876, p. 248; *Dodge City Ford County Globe,* January 25, 1881, July 8, 1879.

17. *Dodge City Times,* August 30, 1879. See also a trip to Garden City with officer William Duffy to arrest L. T. Walker, who was involved in a stabbing, in ibid., May 3, 1879; *Dodge City Ford County Globe,* August 27, 1878; *Dodge City Times,* April 20, 1878, December 22, 1881; *Dodge City Ford County Globe,* October 9, 1883, October 21, 1879; *Dodge City Times,* September 3, 1879.

18. Session Laws of Kansas, 1876, p. 249, 1881, p. 297; *Dodge City Ford County Globe,* October 29, 1878; *Dodge City Times,* August 7, 1880; W. A. Johnson to Frank P. Kellogg, March 15, 1881.

19. *Dodge City Ford County Globe,* February 13, 1883.

20. *Kansas State Gazetteer and Business Directory, 1886–1887,* 5: 271. For an example of Gryden's news stories, see the *Kansas City Times,* reprinted in the *Dodge City Ford County Globe,* July 1, 1880.

21. *Dodge City Ford County Globe,* May 14, June 18, 1878, January 14, 1879; *Dodge City Times,* January 17, 1880.

22. *Dodge City Times,* June 16, 1877, June 29, 1878, December 4, 1883; *Dodge City Democrat,* February 16, 1884.

23. *Dodge City Democrat,* June 30, 1877; John Blake vs. City of Dodge City.

24. *Dodge City Ford County Globe,* October 9, 1883, February 16, 1884.

25. *Dodge City Messenger,* February 26, 1874; *Dodge City Times,* June 30, 1877; Jim Herron, *Fifty Years on the Owl Hoot Trail,* p. 134.

26. *Dodge City Ford County Globe,* October 23, 1883.

27. Ibid., October 2, 30, November 27, 1883; June 17, July 8, 1884; *Proceedings of the Convention of the Western Kansas Cattle Growers Association,* pp. 18–20; Miller and Snell, *Great Gunfighters,* pp. 328–29.

28. Ex parte George M. [U.] Holcomb; *Dodge City Ford County Globe,* October 2, 1883.

29. For an example, see *Dodge City Times,* June 16, 1877.

30. Ibid., October 18, 1879; *Dodge City Ford County Globe,* October 23, 1883.

31. *Dodge City Ford County Globe,* October 23, 1883; *Dodge City Times,* January 18, 1879, June 11, 1885.

32. *Dodge City Ford County Globe,* October 23, 1883; *Proceedings of the Convention of the Western Cattle Growers' Association,* p. 19; Robert K. De Arment, *Bat Masterson: The Man and the Legend,* pp. 134–37; *Dodge City Ford County Globe,* January 28, 1879.

33. Theodore F. Hobble, *This I Remember,* pp. 11–12.

34. Tocqueville, *Republic of the United States,* I: 301.


## Chapter 4: For the Defense: Harry E. Gryden

1. George N. Fenin and William K. Everson, *The Western: From Silents to the Seventies,* pp. 25–26.

2. United States Census of 1880, Dodge City and Ford County, Kansas; *Topeka Daily Commonwealth,* July 13, 1869; *Dodge City Democrat,* November 21, 1885; *Dodge City Globe Live Stock Journal,* September 2, 1884; *Dodge City Times,* September 4, 1884; *Dodge City Kansas Cowboy,* September 6, 1884; Ray Anthony, "H. E. Gryden," *Dodge City Daily Globe,* December 2, 1914; E. B. Long, *The Civil War Day by Day: An Almanac, 1861–1865,* pp. 579–80.

3. The *Kansas Cowboy* indicated that Gryden came to Dodge in 1871, but other accounts put his arrival somewhat later.

4. *Dodge City Ford County Globe,* June 17, 1879, May 25, 1880; *Dodge City Times,* May 29, 1880, June 16, 1881.

5. *Dodge City Ford County Globe,* September 2, 1878, August 1, 1882.

6. Ibid., January 29, March 4, 1879; *Dodge City Times,* Dec. 28, 1878.

7. *Dodge City Ford County Globe,* October 28, 1879.

8. *Dodge City Times,* October 27, November 10, 1877; C. Robert Haywood, "Comanche County Cowboy: A Case Study of a Kansas Rancher," *Kansas History* 4 (Autumn 1981): 189–90.

9. *Dodge City Times,* August 4, September 22, 1877, August 31, 1880; John J. Callison, *Bill Jones of Paradise Valley, Oklahoma,* pp. 47–49.

10. *Dodge City Ford County Globe,* May 25, 1880; *Dodge City Times,* January 19, June 22, 1878, May 29, August 28, 1880.

11. *Dodge City Times,* July 21, 1877; Wright, *Dodge City,* p. 183.

12. *Dodge City Times,* June 16, 1877.

13. *Dodge City Ford County Globe,* March 21, April 11, 1882; *Dodge City Times,* December 15, 1881, March 16, April 6, 1882; *Dodge City Democrat,* February 9, 1884.

14. *Dodge City Times,* March 24, 1877.

15. Ibid., January 28, 1879; Butler, *Daughters of Joy,* p. 115.

16. *Dodge City Times,* January 11, 1884; *Dodge City Democrat,* February 2, 1884.

17. Mary Sawyer vs. Nathan D. Sawyer.

18. *Kansas City Journal,* November 15, 1881, as quoted in Miller and Snell, *Great Gunfighters,* p. 290.

19. Ibid., pp. 178–84; Dora Hand vs. Theodore Hand; De Arment, *Bat Masterson,* pp. 116–25.

20. *Dodge City Times,* February 9, 16, 23, June 29, 1878; Geo. B. Cox and Albert H. Boyd vs. W. B. Masterson, R. M. Wright and James H. Kelley.

21. State of Kansas vs. Arista Webb; *Dodge City Ford County Globe,* January 1, 1878; *Dodge City Times,* January 17, 1880; *Topeka Daily Commonwealth,* May 23, 1885.

22. *Larned Daily Optic,* March 5, 1881.

23. *Dodge City Ford County Globe,* January 28, 1879; De Arment, *Bat Masterson,* pp. 135–37.

24. *Dodge City Ford County Globe,* October 2, 30, 1883, April 15, 1884.

25. *Dodge City Times,* September 1, 1877.

26. Program in possession of Joseph W. Snell, Topeka, Kansas; *Dodge City Times,* September 1, 1877; *Dodge City Ford County Globe,* September 30, 1879.

27. *Dodge City Ford County Globe,* December 7, 1880. The *Globe* also noted that Gryden's report of a sordid instance of incest in Ford County had appeared in the *Kansas City Times.* Ibid., July 1, 1880.

28. *Dodge City Times,* July 14, October 7, 1877, March 30, April 20, 1878; February 7, 1880.

29. Young, *Dodge City,* p. 116; *Dodge City Times,* August 7, 1880, May 19, 1877; *Dodge City Democrat,* July 12, 1884.

30. *Dodge City Kansas Cowboy,* September 6, 1884.

31. *Dodge City Times,* November 3, 1877.

32. *Spearville Enterprise,* June 29, 1878; *Spearville News,* October 12, 19, 1878; *Dodge City Ford County Globe,* October 15, 22, 1878.

33. De Arment, *Bat Masterson,* pp. 176-82; *Dodge City Ford County Globe,* September 10, 17, October 8, 1878.

34. *Dodge City Times,* August 31, 1878, April 10, May 29, July 31, August 28, 1880; *Dodge City Ford County Globe,* March 2, April 13, May 2, October 12, 1880.

35. *Dodge City Ford County Globe,* October 26, November 2, 1880.

36. Callison, *Bill Jones,* p. 186.

37. De Arment, *Bat Masterson,* pp. 206-209.

38. *Dodge City Times,* June 9, 1881.

39. Young, *Dodge City,* pp. 125-27.

40. Haywood, "Dodge City War," pp. 14-20.

41. De Arment, *Bat Masterson,* p. 256; *Topeka Daily Commonwealth,* May 20, 1883; *Dodge City Democrat,* May 31, 1884.

42. Harry Gryden to Governor G. W. Glick, June 4, 1883 (telegram); Miller and Snell, *Great Gunfighters,* pp. 408-409.

43. *Dodge City Ford County Globe,* July 31, 1883.

44. Ibid., August 14, 1883; *Dodge City Kansas Cowboy,* September 6, 1884; *Topeka Daily Commonwealth,* June 8, 1883.

45. Young, *Dodge City,* p. 131.

46. *Dodge City Times,* August 28, 1884; *Dodge City Ford County Globe,* September 2, 1884; *Dodge City Kansas Cowboy,* September 6, 1884.

47. *Dodge City Kansas Cowboy,* September 6, 1884.

48. *Dodge City Democrat,* November 21, 1885, September 6, 1884; *Dodge City Kansas Cowboy,* September 6, 1884.

## Chapter 5: For the Prosecution: Michael W. Sutton

1. The bare-bones description of his early life was furnished in a letter from Sutton to George Martin of Topeka; see also Andreas, *History of Kansas,* 2: 1561-62, and his obituary in the *Dodge City Daily Globe,* June 12, 1918; Capt. P. H. Coney, "The Story of Mike Sutton of Kansas," *Topeka Daily Capital,* July 14, 1918.

2. Ibid.

3. *Dodge City Daily Globe,* June 12, 1918.

4. McNeal, *When Kansas Was Young,* p. 110; *Dodge City Kansas Cowboy,* July 12, 1884, quoting the *Caldwell Journal:* "The only satisfaction we ever got out of the defeat," a fellow failure later admitted, "was that

the fellows who were elected ran the county into debt nearly $400,000 before they were forced to give up the game."

5. Muster and Description Rolls of the Fourteenth Heavy Artillery, New York; *Dodge City Times,* October 6, July 14, April 7, 28, February 24, 1877; *Dodge City Globe-Republican,* June 17, 1897.

6. *Dodge City Times,* August 31, 1878, November 3, 1877; *Medicine Lodge Barbour County Mail,* May 21, 1878; De Arment, *Bat Masterson,* p. 138; *Lakin Herald,* February 11, 1882.

7. *Dodge City Times,* November 3, 1879.

8. Young, *Dodge City,* quoting the *Dodge City Globe,* p. 118.

9. Wright, *Dodge City,* p. 306; De Arment, *Bat Masterson,* p. 60.

10. *Dodge City Ford County Globe,* June 8, 1880; *Lakin Herald,* February 12, 1882.

11. *Topeka Kansas State Journal,* May 18, 1883; *Dodge City Vox Populi,* November 1, 1884; telegram quoted in De Arment, *Bat Masterson,* pp. 274, 392.

12. Wright, *Dodge City,* p. 306; *Dodge City Times,* June 29, 1878.

13. Paul E. Wilson, "Reflections on Mike Sutton," *Journal of the Kansas Bar Association* 45 (Winter 1976): 277; *Dodge City Times,* March 22, October 4, 18, 1879.

14. *Dodge City Times,* October 4, 18, 1879; Andreas, *History of Kansas,* II, p. 1562; *Manhattan Nationalist,* July 2, 10, 1885; Miller and Snell, *Great Gunfighters,* pp. 303–305.

15. M. W. Sutton to Simeon Briggs Bradford, March 29, 1886.

16. *Topeka Commonwealth,* July 11, 1885; *Dodge City Ford County Globe,* March 25, 1884; Miller and Snell, *Great Gunfighters,* p. 430; *Dodge City Times,* December 17, 1885.

17. *Dodge City Times,* July 3, 17, August 14, 1880, October 6, 1880, February 9, 1882.

18. Ibid., October 10, 1880, December 17, 1885; Application for Pension or Compensation by Widow and/or Child of a Deceased Person, Form 534; Mrs. Merritt L. Beeson to Clifford Hope, May 8, 1947; Heinie Schmidt, "It's Worth Remembering," *Dodge City High Plains Journal,* August 10, 1950.

19. *Dodge City Ford County Globe,* February 28, 1882; *Dodge City Times,* March 2, 1882, February 19, 1885.

20. *Dodge City Ford County Globe,* June 18, 1878, February 13, 1883; *Dodge City Times,* March 28, 1878; Atchison, Topeka and Santa Fe Records, Court Dockets, 1874–1880, pp. 174, 183, 241, 244, 424, 442.

21. *Dodge City Times,* August 30, 1883; Haywood, "Dodge City War," pp. 14–20; Young, *Dodge City,* p. 131; *Dodge City Kansas Cowboy,* November 7, 1885.

22. *Dodge City Ford County Globe,* November 5, 12, August 27, 1878, February 1, 1879, February 8, 1881.

23. See, for example, ibid., January 29, 1881, August 1, 1882; *Dodge City Times,* January 29, 1881, March 22, 1883, October 9, 1884.

24. *Dodge City Times,* June 9, 1881; *Dodge City Ford County Globe,* October 30, 1883, February 12, 1884, June 12, 1883.

25. Sutton to Bradford, March 29, 1886.

26. *Dodge City Ford County Globe,* February 14, 1882.

27. Ramon S. Powers, "The Dull Knife Raid of 1878: A Study of the Frontier"; Ramon S. Powers, "The Kansas Indian Claims Commission of 1879," *Kansas History* (Autumn 1984): 199; Robert C. Carriker, *Fort Supply, Indian Territory: Frontier Outpost on the Plains,* pp. 116–28.

28. *Dodge City Times,* February 15, 1879; Todd D. Epp, "The State of Kansas v. Wild Hog, *Et. Al.,*" *Kansas History* 5 (Summer 1982): 141.

29. Wilson, "Reflections on Sutton," p. 277; *Dodge City Times,* October 18, 1879; State of Kansas vs. Wild Hog et al.

30. *Dodge City Times,* October 18, 1879; *Dodge City Ford County Globe,* July 1, 1879.

31. Epp, "Kansas v. Wild Hog," p. 146.

32. *Dodge City Times,* December 21, 1878, January 10, 17, 24, 1880; De Arment, *Bat Masterson,* p. 126; *Dodge City Ford County Globe,* September 9, 1879. The sentence was not carried out. Friends and family of Webb in Kentucky presented evidence of past "spells of insanity." Gryden was able to delay execution and had Webb transferred to the Kansas Insane Asylum. Finally, in 1885, a pardon was granted on the basis of insanity and with the provision that the prisoner would be removed to Virginia and never would be permitted to return within the borders of Kansas. *Dodge City Times,* February 28, 1880; *Topeka Daily Commonwealth,* May 23, 1885.

33. *Dodge City Times,* February 1, 1879, July 13, 1878.

34. State of Kansas vs. John Gill alias Concho; *Dodge City Ford County Globe,* November 23, 1880; Mari Sandoz, *The Cattlemen: From the Rio Grande Across the Far Marias,* p. 319; *Dodge City Ford County Globe,* January 25, 1881.

35. *Dodge City Times,* September 4, November 27, 1880, April 22, September 9, 1886; Harry E. Chrisman, *Lost Trails of the Cimarron,* pp. 107–108.

36. *Dodge City Ford County Globe,* March 16, 1880; De Arment, *Bat Masterson,* p. 96.

37. *Dodge City Times,* June 22, 1878; Miller and Snell, *Great Gunfighters,* pp. 209–22.

38. *Dodge City Ford County Globe,* January 11, 1879.

39. Ibid., June 19, 1883, February 5, 1885; State of Kansas vs. H. Gould alias Skunk Curley.

40. *Dodge City Ford County Globe,* November 23, 1880. The decision stood for six years until the legislature passed a law that the attorney gen-

eral interpreted as prohibiting sales "until three years after the organization of the county in which they lay." Jennie Small Owen and Kirk Mechem, *The Annals of Kansas, 1886–1925*, I, p. 6.

41. *Dodge City Times*, January 24, June 12, 1884. In re Hinkle; *Dodge
City Kansas Cowboy*, October 31, 1885; *Dodge City Democrat*, February 23, 1884.

42. *Dodge City Democrat*, March 8, 1884.

43. Galland had a long-standing feud with dance-hall operators that be-
gan in 1876 when he sued Alice Chambers, a dance-hall owner. Young,
*Dodge City*, p. 48; City of Dodge City vs. Alice Chambers; *Dodge City
Times*, April 3, March 27, 1884.

44. *Dodge City Democrat*, July 18, 1884; *Dodge City Live Stock Journal*,
July 22, August 5, 1884.

45. *Dodge City Times*, November 20, 1884, January 8, April 23, May
14, 28, June 11, 1885; *Dodge City Ford County Globe*, August 5, 1884;
*Dodge City Kansas Cowboy*, August 23, 1884; *Dodge City Democrat*,
May 30, 1885.

46. *Dodge City Times*, July 6, 1882, December 11, 1884, May 21,
1885; J. Evetts Haley, *Charles Goodnight: Cowman and Plainsman*,
pp. 316–17.

47. *Dodge City Times*, April 12, 1883; *Dodge City Globe Live Stock
Journal*, April 7, 1885; *Dodge City Times*, February 4, 1886.

48. *Dodge City Kansas Cowboy*, November 7, 1885.

49. The name *St. Michael of the Oily Tongue* took on added innuendo
when Sutton contributed money to place a bell in the new Catholic Church
tower, especially after it was consecrated in the name of the patron saint,
Saint Michael. Mike came in for considerable ribbing by his irreverent
friends, who knew he was not a Catholic. *Dodge City Ford County Globe*,
November 14, 1882.

50. Adams eventually settled for $1,750, of which $500 was paid in
cash and the balance in ten-year bonds. *Dodge City Kansas Cowboy*, August 30, 1884; *Dodge City Ford County Globe*, November 14, 1882, June
12, 19, 1883; *Dodge City Times*, May 31, 1883; *Dodge City Democrat*,
May 31, 1884.

51. Sutton to Martin, January 31, 1905; *Dodge City Daily Globe*,
June 12, 1918.

52. *Dodge City Sun*, May 4, 1886; *Dodge City Times*, August 27, April
30, 1885, December 18, 1884, February 24, 1887; Declaration of Invalid
Pension and Application for Pension or Compensation by Widow and/or
Child of a Deceased Person.

53. Wright, *Dodge City*, p. 307.

## Chapter 6: Mike's Boys

1. Colorado State Census, 1885, Gunnison County; *Dodge City Times,* April 28, June 2, 1877; *Dodge City Ford County Globe,* April 29, June 17, July 22, 1877; *Chase County Clippings,* p. 173.

2. *Dodge City Times,* June 2, 1877, April 6, 1878, July 19, 1879; City of Dodge City vs. Hattie Mauzy; John Blake vs. City of Dodge City; *Dodge City Ford County Globe,* January 29, 1878.

3. *Dodge City Ford County Globe,* January 28, 1879; *Dodge City Times,* April 13, 1878, January 17, February 28, 1880; *Topeka Daily Commonwealth,* May 23, 1885; State of Kansas vs. Arista Webb.

4. *Dodge City Times,* May 11, 1878, May 22, 1880.

5. Ibid., November 27, December 4, 1880, January 8, 1881; *Dodge City Ford County Globe,* June 22, November 11, 1880.

6. *Dodge City Ford County Globe,* November 13, 1881, May 23, 1882, August 1, October 16, November 20, 1883; *Dodge City Globe Live Stock Journal,* October 21, 1884; Colorado State Census, 1885, Gunnison County.

7. *Dodge City Globe-Republican,* February 11, 1909; Nellie Snyder Yost, *Medicine Lodge: The Story of a Kansas Frontier Town,* pp. 38–41.

8. *Medicine Lodge Barbour County Mail,* August 29, 1878; *Medicine Lodge Mail,* February 6, 1879; *Dodge City Journal,* September 23, 1948; Barber County Historical Committee, comp., *Chosen Land: A History of Barber County, Kansas,* p. 65; J. M. Adams vs. Jesse Evans and Charles D. Nelson; *Larned Chronoscope* quoted in the *Dodge City Ford County Globe,* April 4, 1882.

9. *Medicine Lodge Barbour County Mail,* May 21, 1878.

10. *Dodge City Times,* April 20, October 26, 1886; *Dodge City Ford County Globe,* October 3, 1882; *Medicine Lodge Index,* December 8, 1881, April 6, 20, 1882; W. A. Johnston to James T. Whitelaw, January 24, 1881; Heinie Schmidt, "The Big Bull Moose," *Dodge City Journal,* September 23, 1948.

11. Commissioners' Journal, A, p. 369; *Dodge City Ford County Globe,* October 3, August 1, 1882, January 2, 1883; *Dodge City Times,* December 14, 1882.

12. *Dodge City Times,* September 13, October 23, 1883, May 1, 1884; Kansas State Census, 1885, Dodge City; Maple Grove Burial Records.

13. *Dodge City Globe Live Stock Journal,* February 5, 1884.

14. *Topeka Daily Capital,* May 11, 1883; Geo. T. Hinkle et al. to G. W. Glick, May 15, 1883 (telegram); *Kansas City Times,* May 24, 1883; *Dodge City Times,* May 17, 1883.

15. *Dodge City Times,* April 7, 1883.

16. *Dodge City Ford County Globe,* August 30, 1883.

17. *Dodge City Kansas Cowboy,* July 12, 1884.

18. Stanley Vestal, *Queen of Cowtowns: Dodge City,* pp. 247–57; *Dodge City Times,* January 8, 1885; *Dodge City Globe Live Stock Journal,* August 5, 1884.

19. *Dodge City Times,* February 19, 1884.

20. Ibid., April 10, July 24, November 13, 1884; *Dodge City Kansas Cowboy,* December 5, 1885; *Dodge City Democrat,* August 16, 1884.

21. *Dodge City Ford County Globe,* May 15, 1883; *Dodge City Globe Live Stock Journal,* December 13, 1885; *Dodge City Times,* February 11, 1886; *Medicine Lodge Cresset,* December 17, 1885.

22. *Dodge City Globe Live Stock Journal,* March 9, 1886; *Dodge City Sun,* January 20, 1887.

23. *Dodge City Globe-Republican,* June 6, 1892, February 11, 1909; *Dodge City Kansas Journal,* February 12, 1909.

24. United States Census of 1880, Dodge City; Kansas State Census, 1885, Ford County; Andreas, *History of Kansas,* II, p. 1562; *Dodge City Ford County Globe,* June 2, 1883; *Dodge City Times,* December 21, 1882.

25. *Dodge City Times,* June 30, 1877, October 23, 1884.

26. Ibid., August 3, 1882. Chinese laundrymen had a difficult time in frontier Dodge. On two previous occasions Chinese had established laundries and were forced to leave town. Ibid., September 4, 1877; *Dodge City Ford County Globe,* October 26, 1880. Dodge's blatant racism is indicated by the announcement of Wenie's assistance, which appeared in the *Globe:* "Fred is chief mogol among the Chinese. He speaks their language fluently. But he can't go on their diet of rats, mice, and rice."

27. *Dodge City Times,* February 15, 23, March 22, April 5, October 18, 1883, May 28, October 1, 1885. *Dodge City Ford County Globe,* April 10, 1883, October 16, 1885.

28. Young, *Dodge City,* p. 128; Geo. T. Hinkle et al. to G. W. Glick; *Topeka Daily Capital,* May 18, 1883; *Dodge City Ford County Globe,* August 14, 1883; *Dodge City Times,* October 4, 1883.

29. *Dodge City Kansas Cowboy,* September 20, 1884; *Dodge City Ford County Globe,* April 10, 1883, June 17, 1884; *Dodge City Times,* August 28, September 18, 1884, April 23, 1885, March 18, 25, June 24, 1886.

30. *Dodge City Times,* March 18, July 29, 1886; *Dodge City Democrat,* December 16, 1886. The name of the Wenie and Bayer firm remained long after Fred left Dodge City. See description in *Dodge City Globe Live Stock Journal,* February 1, 1889.

31. *Hayes Kansas City Directory, 1905; Dodge City Daily Globe,* April 16, 1914; *Kansas City Star,* April 16, 1914.

32. *Dodge City Times,* March 4, 1886; *Dodge City Democrat,* April 24, 1886.

33. *Dodge City Times,* July 15, 1886; Tarbox vs. Sughrue; *Dodge City Globe Live Stock Journal,* August 17, 1886; *Dodge City Ford County Republican,* November 16, 1887, June 13, 1888.

34. *Dodge City Democrat,* October 1, 1884.

35. Ibid.; *Dodge City Times,* October 23, 30, 1884; *Dodge City Globe Live Stock Journal,* October 21, 1884.

36. *Dodge City Globe Live Stock Journal,* October 21, 1884.

37. *Dodge City Ford County Globe,* August 2, 1881, February 21, 1882, April 3, July 17, 1883; Wright, *Dodge City,* p. 229.

38. *Dodge City Globe Live Stock Journal,* October 21, 1884.

39. Wright, *Dodge City,* pp. 229–30.

40. *Dodge City Democrat,* March 8, 1884; *Dodge City Times,* May 31, August 30, 1883.

41. *Dodge City Times,* March 22, 1883.

42. Ibid.; *Dodge City Vox Populi,* November 1, 1884.

43. *Dodge City Ford County Globe,* February 21, 1882; *Dodge City Globe Live Stock Journal,* May 1, 1883; *Topeka Daily Capital,* May 18, 1883.

44. *Dodge City Times,* August 23, 1883.

45. Ibid., June 12, November 13, 1884, March 5, 1885, November 25, 1886, January 3, 1888; *Dodge City Ford County Republican,* November 2, 1887.

46. *Dodge City Globe-Republican,* November 17, 1898.

47. *Spearville Enterprise,* May 18, 1878.

48. Kansas State Census, 1885, Ford County; Andreas, *History of Kansas,* II, p. 1562; *Dodge City Times,* February 9, 1878.

49. *Spearville Enterprise,* August 17, 1878.

50. *Dodge City Times,* May 31, September 6, 1883, November 26, 1885.

51. Ibid., October 30, 1880, October 30, 1884, November 26, 1885; *Dodge City Ford County Globe,* November 2, 1880, August 1, 1882, February 5, 1885.

52. *Dodge City Vox Populi,* November 1, 1884; *Topeka Daily Capital,* July 2, 1885.

53. *Dodge City Ford County Globe,* February 5, 12, 1885; Tarbox vs. Sughrue.

54. *Dodge City Times,* March 26, 1885, April 23, 29, 1886; *Reports of Cases Argued and Determined in the Supreme Court of the State of Kansas,* Howard F. McCue, reporter, 140:lxxxiii.

## Chapter 7: The Last of the Gang Lawyers

1. *Dodge City Democrat,* October 30, 1886; Kansas State Census, 1885, Ford County; Charles A. Milton File; *Dodge City Kansas Journal,* September 22, 1915.

2. *Dodge City Ford County Globe,* December 4, 1883.

3. *Dodge City Democrat,* September 27, 1884; *Dodge City Times,* November 13, January 15, 1884; *Dodge City Kansas Cowboy,* November 8, 1884.

4. *Dodge City Times,* January 15, 1885.

5. *Dodge City Democrat,* November 15, 1884, April 17, 1886; State of Kansas vs. B. F. Daniels.

6. *Dodge City Democrat,* November 20, 1886; *Dodge City Times,* April 22, 1886. Daniels's later life was as exciting and trouble-laden as his time in Dodge. He rode with Theodore Roosevelt's Rough Riders in the Spanish-American War, was appointed United States marshal for Arizona by Roosevelt, was picked by the president to be one of Arizona's senators but failed to secure confirmation, and then was appointed warden of the penitentiary at Yuma. Heinie Schmidt, *Ashes of My Campfire,* pp. 51–53.

7. *Dodge City Kansas Cowboy,* June 27, July 4, 1885; *Topeka Commonwealth,* July 2, 4, 1885; *Dodge City Globe Live Stock Journal,* July 7, 1885; De Arment, *Bat Masterson,* pp. 280–83; Robert Smith Bader, *Prohibition in Kansas,* pp. 80–81; J. C. Strang to J. A. Martin, July 5, 1885.

8. *Dodge City Democrat,* March 13, 1886; *Dodge City Times,* November 11, 1886; M. W. Sutton to S. B. Bradford, March 10, 1886.

9. Tarbox vs. Sughrue.

10. Strang to Martin; *Dodge City Times,* April 1, 1886.

11. *Dodge City Democrat,* October 30, 1886.

12. Ibid., October 23, 1886.

13. *Dodge City Sun,* August 5, 1886; Edwin A. Austin, "The Supreme Court of the State of Kansas," *Collections of the Kansas State Historical Society* 13 (1915): pp. 100–101; *Dodge City Globe-Republican,* June 6, 1892; *Dodge City Kansas Journal,* September 22, 1915.

14. Andreas, *History of Kansas,* II, p. 1359; *Dodge City Sun,* October 28, 1886; United States Census of 1880, Dodge City; "Official Roster of Kansas, 1854–1925," p. 667.

15. *Chase County Clippings, 1876–1940,* pp. 127, 138, 151; *Cottonwood Falls Chase County Leader,* April 19, 1872, February 6, April 17, 1874; *Dodge City Times,* May 17, January 18, 25, February 15, April 26, May 17, 31, 1881; *Dodge City Ford County Globe,* March 11, 1874; United States Census of 1880, Cottonwood Falls; State of Kansas vs. E. P. Cochman.

16. *Garden City Irrigator,* July 10, 1884.

17. *Cottonwood Falls Chase County Leader,* December 5, 1878, April 3, June 5, 1879; *Dodge City Ford County Globe,* July 6, 1880.

18. *Dodge City Ford County Globe,* January 6, March 23, 1880, December 5, 12, 1882; *Dodge City Times,* May 7, 1885; *Dodge City Democrat,* February 9, 1884, March 15, 1885.

19. *Dodge City Democrat,* February 9, August 30, 1884, March 27, 1886, September 26, 1885; *Dodge City Ford County Globe,* May 31, 1881.

20. *Spearville News,* November 1, 8, 15, 1879; *Dodge City Times,* November 27, 1880.

21. *Dodge City Ford County Globe,* October 26, 1880, April 15, 1881; *Dodge City Times,* October 2, 1880.

22. *Dodge City Ford County Globe,* July 6, November 27, 1880, January 25, 1881; *Dodge City Times,* January 25, September 17, 1879, November 27, 1880, February 24, October 6, 1881.

23. *Dodge City Ford County Globe,* February 21, 1882.

24. *Dodge City Times,* April 29, March 2, 1882.

25. *Cottonwood Falls Chase County Leader,* April 17, 1883; State of Kansas vs. James Dempsy.

26. Dempster's name was spelled differently each time it was reported: Lemster, Dempsey, Dempsy, and Demser. *Cottonwood Falls Chase County Leader,* October 25, November 15, 1884; *Dodge City Globe Live Stock Journal,* October 7, 28, 1884; *Dodge City Times,* October 30, 1885.

27. *Dodge City Times,* November 13, 1884; *Dodge City Democrat,* August 30, 1884; *Dodge City Kansas Cowboy,* October 4, 1884.

28. *Dodge City Kansas Cowboy,* October 25, 1884; *Dodge City Times,* January 18, 1879, April 16, 1884, October 23, 1885; *Dodge City Democrat,* July 12, 1884.

29. *Dodge City Times,* April 16, 1885; *Dodge City Democrat,* July 18, 1885, quoted in Young, *Dodge City,* p. 138.

30. *Dodge City Times,* September 18, 1885. Editor Frost wrote of the transition with tongue in cheek: "The Long Branch Temperance Hall was opened up about a week ago as Messrs. [William H.] Harris & [Roy] Drake, Proprietors with such old-time lemonade and temperance drinks mixers as Edward Cooley and Moses Barber, who are both gentlemanly fellows and know how to entertain their numerous customers. The Long Branch has at all times been a popular resort, being a veritable art gallery as well as a billiard hall." *Dodge City Globe Live Stock Journal,* June 9, 1885.

31. *Dodge City Democrat,* March 27, April 10, October 23, November 13, 1886.

32. Ibid., March 27, 1886; *Dodge City Sun,* June 3, 1886.

33. *Dodge City Ford County Republican,* January 19, 1887; *Dodge City Globe Live Stock Journal,* January 3, 1888.

34. *Dodge City Kansas Journal*, June 29, 1916, April 24, 1934; *Dodge City Globe Live Stock Journal*, August 24, 1885. The name rarely was spelled the same way twice in newspapers and records, with variations from Findlay, Finley, and Findley to Finlay. *Dodge City Sun*, December 16, 1886.

35. *Dodge City Times*, April 1, 1886.

36. Commissioners' Journal Briefings, Ford County, November 8, 1884.

37. Records of the contested election, including the original poll book and tally sheet, the complete stenographer's recording of the initial hearing examination, and the records of the Kansas Supreme Court are found in Tarbox vs. Sughrue.

38. *Dodge City Globe Live Stock Journal*, November 23, 1886.

39. Robert R. Dykstra says that in the cattle towns of Dodge City, Wichita, and Caldwell, only cowboys and drovers were killed more frequently than lawmen: nine cowboys, nine drovers, and six lawmen. Dykstra, *Cattle Towns*, p. 146.

40. *Dodge City Kansas Journal*, June 29, 1916.

## Chapter 8: Editors and Real-Estate Men

1. *Coolidge Border Ruffian* quoted in *Dodge City Times*, May 15, 1886. The exaggeration of the *Border Ruffian*'s editor was not as wild as he no doubt intended. Early-day Kansas could boast of more newspapers than any other state. By 1889 there were 733 weekly papers and 48 dailies. Nyle H. Miller et al., *Kansas in Newspapers*, p. iii.

2. Kansas State Census, 1885, Dodge City; Andreas, *History of Kansas*, II, p. 1561; *Dodge City Times*, April 28, 1877, November 1, 1883.

3. J. B. Edwards to O. H. Simpson, November 18, 1925, as quoted in Young, *Dodge City*, p. 17; Andreas, *History of Kansas*, II, p. 1561.

4. *Dodge City Ford County Globe*, October 22, 1878, March 11, 1879.

5. *Dodge City Times*, June 9, 1877; De Arment, *Bat Masterson*, pp. 80–81.

6. *Dodge City Times*, December 6, 20, 1879, November 1, 1883; *Dodge City Ford County Globe*, December 2, 1879, Supplement, November 6, 1883.

7. *Dodge City Times*, June 7, 1877, April 20, 1878, October 14, 1876, January 11, 1879, October 2, 1880; *Dodge City Ford County Globe*, November 16, 1880, December 25, 1879, October 22, 1878; *Kansas State Gazetteer*, pp. 1878, 1882.

8. *Dodge City Times*, November 1, 1883.

9. *Dodge City Ford County Globe*, July 25, 1882; *Dodge City Globe Live Stock Journal*, July 15, 1884.

268                           NOTES TO PAGES 199–211

10. *Dodge City Ford County Globe,* September 24, 1878, July 25, 1882; Young, *Dodge City,* p. 165; *Dodge City Democrat,* November 28, 1885.

11. *Dodge City Ford County Globe,* February 24, 1880, October 10, 1882; *Dodge City Times,* October 12, 1882, October 30, 1884.

12. *Dodge City Ford County Globe,* February 14, 1882; *Dodge City Kansas Cowboy,* July 26, 1884.

13. *Dodge City Times,* May 29, June 5, 1880; *Dodge City Ford County Globe,* June 8, 1880; Haywood, "The Dodge City Census," pp. 96–98.

14. *Dodge City Globe Live Stock Journal,* November 7, 1884; *Dodge City Democrat,* July 31, 1886.

15. *Dodge City Ford County Globe,* February 14, 1879, August 18, 1885; Kansas State Census, 1885, Dodge City; *Dodge City Times,* March 4, 1886; *Dodge City Democrat,* March 20, 1886; *Dodge City Globe Live Stock Journal,* March 2, 1886.

16. *Dodge City Democrat,* November 15, 1889, June 13, 1902.

17. *Dodge City Times,* February 24, 1887; Young, *Dodge City,* p. 165.

18. *Dodge City Times,* March 9, 1878, May 29, 1800; *Dodge City Ford County Globe,* March 30, 1880; Aaron Frazier vs. Walter Shinn; Haywood, *Trails South,* p. 36; Haywood, "The Dodge City Census," pp. 96, 98; United States Census of 1880; *Kinsley Graphic,* November 29, 1879.

19. *Dodge City Ford County Globe,* February 14, 1882; *Dodge City Globe Live Stock Journal,* November 23, 1886; Galland vs. Shinn.

20. *Dodge City Ford County Globe,* July 12, September 1, November 13, 1881, April 10, 1883; *Dodge City Kansas Cowboy,* November 22, 1884.

21. *Dodge City Globe Live Stock Journal,* February 24, 1883, August 25, 1883; *Ford County, Kansas, Marriages, 19 February 1874 to 21 December 1886,* p. 54; *Dodge City Democrat,* March 20, 1886.

22. J. B. Bough, "Bricks, Top Hats, Guns Figure in Early History of Dodge Journalism," *Dodge City Daily Globe,* October 22, 1935.

23. *Dodge City Times,* October 14, 1876, June 30, 1877; Commissioners' Journal Briefings; *Dodge City Ford County Globe,* December 25, 1877.

24. *Dodge City Times,* June 30, August 11, 1877; Miller and Snell, *Great Gunfighters,* p. 184.

25. Wright, *Dodge City,* pp. 154–55; Morphy vs. Wright.

26. *Dodge City Ford County Globe,* September 17, 1878, February 2, 1878; De Arment, *Bat Masterson,* p. 87.

27. *Dodge City Ford County Globe,* September 24, 1878.

28. Ibid., August 27, February 1, 1879.

29. *Dodge City Daily Globe,* November 22, 1935.

30. Wright, *Dodge City,* p. 316; *Dodge City Times,* March 22, 1883, March 5, 1885.

31. Dykstra, *Cattle Towns,* p. 358; United States Census of 1880, Dodge City; Tarbox vs. Sughrue.

32. *Dodge City Ford County Globe,* June 29, 1880.

33. Ibid., January 6, February 10, March 30, 1880.

34. Ibid., October 19, 1886; *Dodge City Times,* July 16, 1885; *Kansas State Gazetteer,* p. 271; *Dodge City Globe-Republican,* various 1891 issues.

35. *Dodge City Ford County Globe,* December 21, 1883; March 21, 1882; *Dodge City Times,* December 25, 1880.

36. *Dodge City Times,* January 11, 1882; *Dodge City Ford County Globe,* July 10, October 9, 1883; *Dodge City Democrat,* February 16, 1884; *Sidney Advance,* October 3, 1882.

37. *Sidney Kansas Cowboy,* September 11, 1883; *Dodge City Democrat,* May 10, 1884.

38. *Sidney Kansas Cowboy,* November 3, 1883.

39. Ibid., December 8, 15, 1883, January 12, 1884.

40. *Dodge City Ford County Globe,* February 12, 1884.

41. *Dodge City Globe Live Stock Journal,* September 2, 1884; *Dodge City Times,* January 22, April 17, 1884; City of Dodge City vs. E. H. Borton.

42. *Dodge City Globe Live Stock Journal,* February 26, 1885.

43. Ibid., October 12, 19, 1886.

44. Ibid., November 9, 1886.

45. *Dodge City Republican,* June 13, 1888.

46. Kansas State Census, 1885, Dodge City: *Dodge City Democrat,* January 31, 1885.

47. *Dodge City Kansas Cowboy,* February 21, 1885.

48. See advertisement in ibid., May 23, 1885; Young, *Dodge City,* p. 69; Citizen of Dodge City to G. W. Glick, May 13, 1883 (telegram).

49. Bill Powell, "Trail City, Cattle Town," *Brand Book of the Denver Westerners* 20:87–92; *Dodge City Kansas Cowboy,* February 21, May 23, August 22, 1885; *Dodge City Times,* August 20, 1885; Chrisman, *Ladder of Rivers,* pp. 357–59.


## Chapter 9: Attorneys of Record


1. Commissioners' Journal Briefings; Criminal Appearance Docket A; *Dodge City Times,* June 30, 1877.

2. Criminal Appearance Docket A; *Dodge City Times,* June 7, 1877.

3. *Dodge City Ford County Globe,* March 18, 25, April 15, 1879; *Dodge City Times,* May 3, 1879.

4. *Dodge City Ford County Globe,* October 21, 1879; March 16, 30, 1880.

5. Ibid., March 11, January 7, 14, 1879; January 6, 1880.

6. Ibid., May 18, 1880; January 11, 1881.

7. Ex parte George M. [U.] Holcomb; the reasoning of the court fol-

lowed closely the brief presented by Sutton. *Topeka Commonwealth,* February 28, March 1, 1879; *Dodge City Times,* May 3, 24, March 8, 1879; *Dodge City Ford County Globe,* February 17, 25, 1879, October 2, 1883; *Cimarron New West,* June 1, 1879.

8. State of Kansas vs. George U. Holcomb and George Watkins; *Dodge City Times,* May 17, 1879.

9. United States Census of 1880, Dodge City and Ford County, Kansas; Hardesty vs. Lewis; *Dodge City Times,* May 3, June 28, September 16, 1879, April 10, October 2, 1880; *Dodge City Ford County Globe,* March 18, 1879, September 14, 1880.

10. United States Census of 1880, Hamilton County, Kansas; *Dodge City Times,* September 8, 1881; *Dodge City Daily Globe,* October 22, 1935; *Syracuse Journal,* March 8, 1908.

11. *Dodge City Times,* December 22, 1881.

12. Ibid.

13. Ibid., January 5, June 8, June 15, 1881; *Dodge City Ford County Globe,* February 14, June 13, 1882; State of Kansas vs. Edward F. Hardesty.

14. *Dodge City Ford County Globe,* June 26, 1883. A search of the *Denver Rocky Mountain News* and other Colorado sources failed to produce an obituary. Eleanor M. Gehres to C. Robert Haywood, August 15, 1985; *Dodge City Globe-Republican,* June 9, 1898; *Caldwell Commercial,* December 29, 1881.

15. Tarbox vs. Sughrue; *Dodge City Ford County Globe,* June 19, 1883; Commissioners' Journal Briefings, November 9, 1883; *Dodge City Times,* October 18, 1883. *Garden City Irrigator,* September 4, 1884.

16. Commissioners' Journal Briefings, March 3, May 20, 1884; *Dodge City Democrat,* May 24, 1884.

17. *Dodge City Globe Live Stock Journal,* September 22, 1885, August 17, 1886; Mormon Genealogical Files, Topeka, Kansas; Betty Braddock to C. Robert Haywood, October 17, 1985.

18. *Dodge City Democrat,* October 23, 1886; Commissioners' Journal Briefings.

19. Galland vs. Shinn and Galland vs. Masterson, et al.; Galland vs. Alice Chambers; *Cimarron Gray County Jacksonian,* August 28, September 3, 1886, September 30, 1887, May 11, 1888.

20. *Dodge City Globe Live Stock Journal,* August 24, September 7, 22, October 19, 1886; Sutton to Bradford, March 29, 1886; *Dodge City Globe-Republican,* May 13, 1891, May 13, 1892.

## Chapter 10: The Legacy

1. Ida Ellen Rath, *The Rath Trail*, pp. 192–94; Wright, *Dodge City*, pp. 325–26.
2. *Dodge City Times*, June 9, 1881.
3. Ibid., May 15, 1886.
4. *Dodge City Kansas Cowboy*, October 24, 1885. The mission of Prouty's paper was so diluted by the loss of the cattlemen's support that his was one of the few businesses that was not reestablished after the 1884 fires.
5. *Dodge City Times*, February 24, 1887, February 2, 1888; *Dodge City Globe Live Stock Journal*, May 15, 1885.
6. *Bloom Weekly Telegram*, April 5, 1888; Young, *Dodge City*, p. 138, quoting the *Topeka Capital*; *Dodge City Times*, March 3, 1887.
7. *Dodge City Times-Ensign*, August 11, 1898.
8. *Sixth Biennial Report of the Kansas State Board of Agriculture*, p. 225; *Eighth Report*, p. 76; *Fourteenth Report*, p. 804; *Dodge City Times*, February 27, 1891; Frank S. Sullivan, *A History of Meade County, Kansas*, pp. 104–11; Owen P. Wiggans, "A History of Dodge City, Kansas," p. 125.
9. Walter Prescott Webb, *The Great Plains*, pp. 497–98.
10. Oliver Wendell Holmes, *The Common Law*, p. 35.
11. *Atchison Daily Champion*, November 18, 1881.
12. Wright, *Dodge City*, p. 309.
13. Bander, *Mr. Dooley on Law*, p. 36.


## Appendix B: Doubtful Claimants to Cowtown Lawyer Status

1. *Dodge City Ford County Globe*, March 30, 1880, April 3, 1883, June 14, 1887; Andreas, *History of Kansas*, II, p. 1608.
2. Kansas State Census, 1885, Dodge City. Since Masterson also listed his place of birth as Canada in the census, perhaps the "attorney" listing was just another of the Masterson family's difficulties in keeping accurate account of their personal history. Bat was notorious for this weakness; he even listed himself as a farmer at one time.
3. *Wichita Eagle*, November 9, 1941; De Arment, *Bat Masterson*, pp. 10–14.
4. *Dodge City Ford County Globe*, November 9, 1886.
5. *Dodge City Sun*, March 10, 1887; Appointment Certificate, Masterson Collection; *Wichita Eagle*, November 9, 1941; Death Certificate No. 287-32293.
6. David Kay Strate, *Sentinel to the Cimarron: The Frontier Experience*

*of Fort Dodge, Kansas,* p. 71; Francis B. Heitman, *Historical Register and Dictionary of the United States Army,* p. 970; *Dodge City Times,* May 31, November 1, 1879, November 20, 1880; *Dodge City Globe-Republican,* January 13, 1898; "In the matter of W. S. Tremaine Esq. to be admitted to practice as an Attorney-at-law," Judge's Journal A; *Dodge City Ford County Globe,* January 22, 1878, March 9, April 13, September 21, 1880.

# Bibliography

## MANUSCRIPTS, DOCUMENTS, AND PAPERS

### Note on Documents

Normally the records of the courts would be considered a major source for any law-related study. However, the extant records of the Ford County district court are a frustrating and erratic body of materials. The documents apparently were not collected systematically in the first place, and those that were filed have had a hard life ever since. Today a case file may contain a single document or a hundred items providing a fairly complete record or no more than a summons or receipt. Mold also has taken a heavy toll, leaving many items so mutilated that they are of little value. In 1979, hundreds of items bearing valuable signatures of Dodge City lawmen were stolen. Fortunately, some documents were photocopied before the theft and some items were recovered by the FBI. Very recently, since the research on this book was completed, the staff of the Kansas State Historical Society (cited as KSHS herein) brought some order to the holdings that are still stored in the Ford County Courthouse. Even so, the collection remains a very flawed source of historical information.

Appearance Docket, Kansas Supreme Court. Vols. F, G, H, and I. Archives Department, KSHS.
Application for Pension or Compensation by Widow and/or Child of a Deceased Person, Form 534. Photocopy. M. W. Sutton File. Manuscript Department, KSHS.
Appointment Certificate. Masterson Collection. Manuscript Department, KSHS.
Atchison, Topeka and Santa Fe Records. Court Dockets, 1874–1880. Microfilm. Manuscript Department, KSHS.
*Biennial Reports of the Kansas State Board of Agriculture. Second* through *Fourteenth.* Topeka: Kansas Publishing House, 1881, 1887.
Colorado State Census, 1885.

Commissioners' Journal Briefings, Ford County. WPA Historical Records Survey, Vols. A and B. Archives Department, KSHS.

Death Certificate No. 287-32293. State Board of Health, Topeka.

Declaration for Invalid Pension. M. W. Sutton File. Manuscript Department, KSHS.

Department of Commerce and Labor Bureau of the Census. *Special Report: Marriage and Divorce, 1867–1906.* 2 vols. Washington: Government Printing Office, 1908.

Dodge City Police Court Dockets, 1885 through 1888. Ms. Box 377. Manuscript Department, KSHS.

Ford County Clippings. 4 vols. KSHS Library.

Ford County Coroner's Records. Boot Hill Museum Research Library, Dodge City, Kansas.

Ford County District Court Cases (KS), 1874–1910. Microfilm. Manuscript Department, KSHS:

1. Civil Appearance Docket A. Ms. Box 805.
2. Civil Cases, Nos. 0–229. Ms. Boxes 806, 807.
3. Civil Cases, unnumbered. Ms. Box 808.
4. Criminal Appearance Docket A. Ms. Box 808.
5. Criminal Cases, numbered and unnumbered. Ms. Boxes 808, 809.
6. Judge's Journal A, 1874–1882. Ms. Box 810.
7. Selected District Court Cases, Ms. Box 799.

*Ford County, Kansas, Marriages, 19 February to 21 December 1886.* Dodge City, Kansas: Kansas Genealogical Society, 1978.

General Statutes of Kansas, 1876, 1879.

Heitman, Francis B. *Historical Register and Dictionary of the United States Army.* Vol. I. Washington: Government Printing Office, 1903.

Hunnius, Carl Julius Adolph. "Survey of Staked Plains and Headwaters of Red River, April 25–June 30, 1876." Kansas Collection, Spencer Research Library, Lawrence.

Justice Docket, Dodge City, July 5, 1878, to October 5, 1882. Box 96. Photocopy. W. S. Campbell Collection. Division of Manuscripts, University of Oklahoma Library, Norman.

Kansas State Census, 1885, 1895, 1905.

Maple Grove Burial Records. Copy of City Hall Records. Kansas Heritage Center, Dodge City.

Masterson Collection. Manuscript Department, KSHS.

Charles A. Milton File. Boot Hill Museum Research Library, Dodge City, Kansas.

Mormon Genealogical Files, Topeka, Kansas.

Muster and Description Rolls of the Fourteenth Heavy Artillery, New York. Photocopy. Sutton File. Manuscript Department, KSHS.

*Proceedings of the Convention of the Western Kansas Cattle Growers' Association.* N.d., n.p.

*Reports of Cases Argued and Determined in the Supreme Court of the State of Kansas.* A. M. F. Randolph, reporter. Vol. 26. Topeka: Kansas Publishing House, 1887.

*Reports of Cases Argued and Determined in the Supreme Court of the State of Kansas.* Howard F. McCue, reporter. Vol. 140. Topeka: State Printing Plant, 1935.

*Roll of Attorneys of the State of Kansas.* Compiled by D. A. Valentine. Topeka: Kansas State Printing Plant, 1911, 1930.

Sedgwick County Grand Jury Records, 1887 and 1888. Archives Department, KSHS.

Session Laws of Kansas, 1868, 1875, 1876, 1881.

United States Census of 1880.

## CASES

(Cases listed in Ms. Boxes are microfilm copies located in the Ford County district-court cases, Manuscript Department KSHS)

J. M. Adams vs. Jesse Evans and Charles D. Nelson. Kansas Supreme Court Case No. 1016, Series II. Archives Department, KSHS.

Adams Express Company vs. David Rudabaugh. Judge's Journal A. Unnumbered. Ms. Box 799.

Beeman vs. Perea. Civil Cases. Case No. 168. Ms. Box 807.

John Blake vs. City of Dodge City. Selected District Court Cases. Unnumbered. Ms. Box 799.

Joseph Briggs vs. William Witkins. Civil Cases. Unnumbered. Ms. Box 808.

City of Dodge City vs. E. H. Borton. Criminal Appearance Docket A, Case No. 93. Ms. Box 808.

City of Dodge City vs. Alice Chambers. Selected District Court Cases. Unnumbered. Ms. Box 799.

City of Dodge City vs. Sallie Doke. Selected District Court Cases. Ms. Box 799.

City of Dodge City vs. Monroe Henderson. Selected District Court Cases. Ms. Box 799.

City of Dodge City vs. Hattie Mauzy. Justice Docket, Dodge City, July 5, 1878, to October 5, 1882. Box 96. Photocopy. W. S. Campbell Collection, Division of Manuscripts, University of Oklahoma Library, Norman.

City of Dodge City vs. Horace White. Justice Docket, Dodge City, July 5, 1878 to October 5, 1882. Ms. Box 96. Photocopy. W. S. Campbell Collection, Division of Manuscripts, University of Oklahoma Library, Norman.

Cook vs. Ford County Commissioners. Civil Appearance Docket A. Unnumbered. Ms. Box 805.

Geo. B. Cox and Albert H. Boyd vs. W. B. Masterson, R. Robert M. Wright and James H. Kelley. Selected District Court Cases. Ms. Box 799.

Ex parte George M. [U.] Holcomb. Kansas Supreme Court (21 Kans), pp. 453–64.

Aaron Frazier vs. Walter Shinn. Civil Cases. Unnumbered. Ms. Box 807.

Frost and Wood vs. Frazier. Civil Cases, Case No. 55. Ms. Box 806.

Galland vs. Alice Chambers. Selected District Court Cases. Unnumbered. Ms. Box 799.

Galland vs. Masterson et al. Civil Cases, Case No. 144. Ms. Box 807.

Galland vs. Shinn. Civil Cases, Case No. 143. Ms. Box 807.

Dora Hand vs. Theodore Hand. Selected District Court Cases. Unnumbered. Ms. Box 799 and Ms. Box 808.

Hardesty vs. Lewis. Civil Cases, Case No. 149. Ms. Box 807.

In re Hinkle. Kansas Supreme Court (31 Kans), pp. 712–15.

Mix vs. Hoover. Civil Cases, Case No. 79. Ms. Box 806.

Morphy vs. Wright. Civil Cases. Unnumbered. Ms. Box 808.

T. J. Philipin et al. vs. Thomas L. McCarty, County Superintendent, etc. Kansas Supreme Court (24 Kans), pp. 285–93.

Sawyer vs. Sawyer. Judge's Journal A, Case No. 246. Ms. Box 808.

Mary Sawyer vs. Nathan D. Sawyer. Civil Cases, Case No. 86, Ms. Box 806.

State of Kansas vs. Henry Borne alias Dutch Henry. Criminal Appearance Docket A, Case No. 34. Ms. Box 808.

State of Kansas vs. Joseph Briggs. Judge's Journal A. Unnumbered. Ms. Box 810.

State of Kansas vs. E. P. Cochman. Kansas Supreme Court Case No. 933, Series II. Archives Department, KSHS.

State of Kansas vs. B. F. Daniels. Criminal Appearance Docket A, Case Nos. 864, 887. Ms. Box 808.

State of Kansas vs. James Dempsy. Criminal Appearance Docket A, Case No. 654. Ms. Box 808.

State of Kansas vs. John Gill alias Concho. Judge's Journal A. Unnumbered. Ms. Box 810.

State of Kansas vs. H. Gould alias Skunk Curley. Criminal Appearance Docket A, Case No. 46. Ms. Box 808.

State of Kansas vs. Edward F. Hardesty. Judge's Journal A. Unnumbered. Ms. Box 810.

State of Kansas vs. George U. Holcomb and George Watkins. Criminal Appearance Docket A, Case No. 51. Ms. Box 810.

State of Kansas vs. Luke Short. Criminal Appearance Docket A, Case No. 521. Ms. Box 808.

State of Kansas vs. Arista Webb. Criminal Cases, Case No. 64, Ms. Box 809; Judge's Journal A, Case No. 279, Ms. Box 810.

State of Kansas vs. Wild Hog et al. Criminal Appearance Docket A, Case No. 56. Ms. Box 808.

Tarbox vs. Sughrue. Kansas Supreme Court Case No. 3940. Series II, Folder 3. Archives Department, KSHS.


## CORRESPONDENCE


Beeson, Mrs. Merritt L., to Clifford Hope, May 8, 1947. Photocopy. Mrs. Merritt Beeson File. Manuscript Department, KSHS.

Braddock, Betty, to C. Robert Haywood, October 17, 1985.

Citizen of Dodge City to G. W. Glick, May 13, 1883 (telegram). Records of the Governor's Office, G. W. Glick Correspondence Received. Archives Department, KSHS.

Gehres, Eleanor M., to C. Robert Haywood, August 15, 1985.

Gryden, Harry, to Governor G. W. Glick, June 4, 1883 (telegram). Records of the Governor's Office, Correspondence Files, Box 7. Archives Department, KSHS.

Hinkle, Geo. T., et al. to G. W. Glick, May 15, 1883 (telegram). Records of the Governor's Office, G. W. Glick Correspondence Received, Subject File, Dodge City War. Archives Department, KSHS.

Johnson, W. A., to Frank P. Kellogg, March 15, 1881. Attorney General Letterpress Book (Kansas), Vol. I, p. 91. Archives Department, KSHS.

Johnston, W. A., to James T. Whitelaw, January 24, 1881. Attorney General Letterpress Book (Kansas), Vol. II, p. 56. Archives Department, KSHS.

Strang, J. C., to J. A. Martin, July 5, 1885. Records of the Governor's Office, Correspondence (General). Archives Department, KSHS.

Sutton, M. W., to S. B. Bradford, March 3, March 10, March 25, 1886. Attorney General's Correspondence, Bradford File. Archives Department, KSHS.

Sutton, M. W., to Simon Briggs Bradford, March 29, 1886 (photocopy). M. W. Sutton File. Manuscript Department, KSHS.

Sutton, M. W., to George Martin, January 31, 1905 (photocopy). Mrs. Merritt Beeson File. Manuscript Department, KSHS.


## NEWSPAPERS


*Atchison Daily Champion*
*Bloom Weekly Telegram*
*Caldwell Commercial*
*Cimarron Gray County Jacksonian*
*Cimarron New West*

*Cottonwood Falls Chase County Leader*
*Dodge City Daily Globe*
*Dodge City Democrat*
*Dodge City Ford County Globe*
*Dodge City Globe Live Stock Journal*
*Dodge City Globe-Republican*
*Dodge City High Plains Journal*
*Dodge City Journal*
*Dodge City Kansas Cowboy*
*Dodge City Kansas Journal*
*Dodge City Messenger*
*Dodge City Sun*
*Dodge City Times*
*Dodge City Times-Ensign*
*Dodge City Vox Populi*
*Garden City Irrigator*
*Hays City Ellis County Star*
*Kansas City Journal*
*Kinsley Graphic*
*Lakin Herald*
*Larned Daily Optic*
*Manhattan Nationalist*
*Medicine Lodge Barbour County Mail*
*Medicine Lodge Cresset*
*Medicine Lodge Index*
*Medicine Lodge Mail*
*Sidney Advance*
*Sidney Kansas Cowboy*
*Spearville Enterprise*
*Spearville News*
*Syracuse Journal*
*Topeka Capital*
*Topeka Daily Commonwealth*
*Topeka Kansas State Journal*
*Wichita Eagle*
*Wilburn Argus*
MISSOURI
*Kansas City Star*
*Kansas City Times*

## THESES

Gribble, Gerald. "George M. Hoover, Dodge City Pioneer." M. A. thesis, University of Wichita, 1940.

Pendergast, Donald J. "A History and Reinterpretation of Dodge City, Kansas, 1872–1886." M. A. thesis, New Mexico Highlands University, 1964.

Powers, Ramon S. "The Dull Knife Raid of 1878: A Study of the Frontier." M. A. thesis, Fort Hays Kansas State College, 1963.

Wiggans, Owen D. "A History of Dodge City, Kansas." M. A. thesis, Colorado State College of Education, 1938.

## ARTICLES

Anthony, Ray. "H. E. Gryden," *Dodge City Daily Globe,* December 2, 1914.

Austin, Edwin A. "The Supreme Court of the State of Kansas." *Collections of the Kansas State Historical Society* 13 (1915): 95–125.

Bough, J. B. "Bricks, Top Hats, Guns Figure in Early History of Dodge Journalism," *Dodge City Daily Globe,* October 22, 1935.

Coney, Capt. P. H. "The Story of Mike Sutton of Kansas," *Topeka Daily Capital,* July 14, 1918.

Epp, Todd D. "The State of Kansas v. Wild Hog, *Et. Al.*" *Kansas History* 5 (Summer 1982): 139–46.

"From Mrs. Anthony's Diary," *Dodge City Globe-Republican,* June 30, 1898.

Haywood, C. Robert. "Comanche County Cowboy: A Case Study of a Kansas Rancher." *Kansas History* 4 (Autumn 1981): 166–90.

———. "Cowtown Courts: Dodge City Courts, 1876–1886." *Kansas History* 11 (Spring 1988): 22–34.

———. "The Dodge City Census of 1880: Historians' Tool or Stumbling Block?" *Kansas History* 8 (Summer 1985): 95–109.

———. "The Dodge City War." *Kansas Territorial* 3 (May–June 1983): 14–20.

Heller, Francis H. "Lawyers and Judges in Early Kansas: A Prospectus for Research." *Kansas Law Review* 22 (1974): 217–27.

"Interview of George M. Hoover," *Dodge City Democrat,* June 19, 1903.

Lewis, Philip H. "The Changing Practice of Law, 1882–1892." In Robert W. Richmond, ed., *Requisite Learning and Good Moral Character.* Topeka: Kansas Bar Association, 1982.

"Official Roster of Kansas, 1854–1925." *Collections of the Kansas State Historical Society, 1923–1925* 16 (1925): 658–45.

Powell, Bill. "Trail City, Cattle Town." *Brand Book of the Denver Westerners* 20 (1964): 87–92.

Powers, Ramon S. "The Kansas Indian Claims Commission of 1879." *Kansas History* 7 (Autumn 1984): 199–211.

Roberts, Gary L. "From Tin Star to Hanging Tree: The Short Career and Violent Times of Billy Brooks." *The Prairie Scout* 3 (1975): 1–86.

————. "Violence and the Frontier Tradition." In *Kansas and the West: Bicentennial Essays in Honor of Nyle H. Miller*. Topeka: H. M. Ives & Sons, 1976.

Schmidt, Heinie, "The Big Bull Moose," *Dodge City Journal*, September 23, 1948.

————. "It's Worth Remembering," *Dodge City High Plains Journal*, August 10, 1950.

————. "It's Worth Repeating: Clippings, 1947–1952." 2 vols. KSHS Library.

Wilson, Paul E. "Reflections on Mike Sutton." *Journal of the Kansas Bar Association* 45 (Winter 1976): 271–83.


## BOOKS


Andreas, A. T., ed. *History of the State of Kansas*. 2 vols. Chicago: A. T. Andreas, 1883.

Bader, Robert Smith. *Prohibition in Kansas*. Lawrence: University Press of Kansas, 1986.

Bander, Edward J. *Mr. Dooley on the Choice of Law*. Charlottesville, Va.: Michie Company, 1963.

Barber County History Committee, comp. *Chosen Land: A History of Barber County, Kansas*. Dallas: Taylor Publishing Co., 1980.

*Brand Book: Containing the Brands of Western Kansas Cattle Growers' Association Authorized by the Stockman's Convention Held at Dodge City, Kansas, April 2, 1884*. Kansas City: Isaac P. Moore, 1884.

Burch, C. S. *Hand-book of Ford County, Kansas*. Chicago: C. S. Burch Publishing, 1887.

Butler, Anne M. *Daughters of Joy, Sisters of Misery*. Urbana: University of Illinois Press, 1985.

Callison, John J. *Bill Jones of Paradise Valley, Oklahoma*. Chicago: M. A. Donahue, 1914.

Carriker, Robert C. *Fort Supply, Indian Territory: Frontier Outpost on the Plains*. Norman: University of Oklahoma Press, 1970.

*Chase County Clippings, 1876–1940*. KSHS Library.

Chrisman, Harry E. *Lost Trails of the Cimarron*. Denver: Swallow Press, 1961.

*Compiled Laws of Kansas, 1879*. St. Louis: W. J. Gilbert Publishers, 1879.

Dary, David A. *The Buffalo Book: The Saga of an American Symbol*. New York: Avon Books, 1975.

De Arment, Robert K. *Bat Masterson: The Man and the Legend*. Norman: University of Oklahoma Press, 1979.

Dykstra, Robert R. *The Cattle Towns*. New York: Atheneum, 1979.

Faulk, Odie B. *Dodge City: The Most Western Town of All.* New York: Oxford University Press, 1977.

Fenin, George N., and William K. Everson. *The Western: From Silents to the Seventies.* New York: Grossman Publishers, 1973.

Friedman, Lawrence M. *A History of American Law.* New York: Simon and Schuster, 1973.

Haley, J. Evetts. *Charles Goodnight: Cowman and Plainsman.* Norman: University of Oklahoma Press, 1936.

*Hayes Kansas City Directory, 1905.* N.p., 1905.

Haywood, C. Robert. *Trails South: The Wagon Road Economy in the Dodge City–Panhandle Region.* Norman: University of Oklahoma Press, 1986.

Herron, Jim. *Fifty Years on the Owl Hoot Trail.* Edited by Harry E. Chrisman. Chicago: Swallow Press, 1969.

Hobble, Theodore F. *This I Remember.* New York: Carlton Press, 1970.

Holmes, Oliver Wendell. *The Common Law.* Boston: Little, Brown, 1881.

*Kansas State Gazetteer and Business Directory, 1886–1887.* Vol. 5. Chicago: R. L. Polk & Co., 1886.

Larsen, Lawrence H. *The Urban West at the End of the Frontier.* Lawrence: Regents Press of Kansas, 1978.

Long, E. B. *The Civil War Day by Day: An Almanac, 1861–1865.* Garden City, N.Y.: Doubleday and Company, 1971.

McNeal, T. A. *When Kansas Was Young.* Topeka: Capper Publications, 1940.

Mayer, Frank H., and Charles B. Roth. *The Buffalo Harvest.* Denver: Sage Books, 1958.

Miller, Nyle H., and Joseph W. Snell. *Great Gunfighters of the Kansas Cowtowns, 1867–1886.* Lincoln: University of Nebraska Press, 1967.

Miller, Nyle H., Edgar Langsdorf, and Robert W. Richmond. *Kansas in Newspapers.* Topeka: Kansas State Historical Society, 1963.

Oliva, Leo E. *Fort Larned on the Santa Fe Trail.* Topeka: Kansas State Historical Society, 1982.

Owen, Jennie Small, and Kirk Mechem, eds. *The Annals of Kansas, 1886–1925.* 2 vols. Topeka: Kansas State Historical Society, 1954.

Prassel, Frank Richard. *The Western Peace Officer: A Legacy of Law and Order.* Norman: University of Oklahoma Press, 1972.

Rath, Ida Ellen. *The Rath Trail.* Wichita: McCormick-Armstrong, 1961.

Reid, John Phillip. *Law for the Elephant: Property and Social Behavior on the Overland Trail.* San Marino: Huntington Library, 1980.

Richmond, Robert W. *Kansas: A Land of Contrasts.* St. Louis: Forum Press, 1974.

————, ed. *Requisite Learning and Good Moral Character: A History of the Kansas Bench and Bar.* Topeka: Kansas Bar Association, 1982.

Sandoz, Mari. *The Cattlemen: From the Rio Grande Across the Far Marias.* New York: Hasting House, 1958.

Schmidt, Heinie. *Ashes of My Campfire.* Dodge City: Journal, Inc., 1952.

Shirley, Glenn. *Law West of Fort Smith.* Lincoln: University of Nebraska Press, 1957.

————. *Temple Houston: Lawyer with a Gun.* Norman: University of Oklahoma Press, 1980.

Skaggs, Jimmy M. *The Cattle-Trailing Industry Between Supply and Demand, 1866–1890.* Lawrence: University Press of Kansas, 1973.

Snell, Joseph W. *Painted Ladies of the Cowtown Frontier.* Vol. X. (December 1965) of *The Trail Guide,* published by the Kansas City Posse of The Westerners.

Strate, David K. *Sentinel to the Cimarron: The Frontier Experience of Fort Dodge, Kansas.* Dodge City: Cultural Heritage and Arts Center, 1970.

Sullivan, Frank S. *A History of Meade County, Kansas.* Topeka: Crane & Company, 1916.

Tocqueville, Alexis de. *The Republic of the United States of America and Its Political Institutions, Reviewed and Examined.* New York: A. S. Barnes & Co., 1867.

Trachtman, Paul. *The Gunfighters.* New York: Time-Life Books, 1974.

Vestal, Stanley. *Queen of Cowtowns: Dodge City.* Lincoln, University of Nebraska Press, 1952.

Webb, Walter Prescott. *The Great Plains.* New York: Grosset & Dunlap, 1931.

Wright, Robert M. *Dodge City: The Cowboy Capital and the Great Southwest.* Wichita: N.p., 1913.

Yost, Nellie Snyder. *Medicine Lodge: The Story of a Frontier Kansas Town.* Chicago: Swallow Press, 1970.

Young, Frederick R. *Dodge City: Up Through a Century in Story and Pictures.* Dodge City: Boot Hill Museum, 1972.

# Index